SURFARI

TIM BAKER

AUSTRALIA'S FAVOURITE SURF WRITER
ON THE ULTIMATE SURFING ROAD TRIP

SURFARI

TIM BAKER

EBURY
PRESS

An Ebury Press book
Published by Random House Australia Pty Ltd
Level 3, 100 Pacific Highway, North Sydney NSW 2060
www.randomhouse.com.au

First published by Ebury Press in 2011

Lyrics to 'I Lied About Being the Outdoor Type' by the Lemonheads reproduced by kind
permission of Universal Music Pty Ltd

Addresses for companies within the Random House Group can be found at
www.randomhouse.com.au/offices

National Library of Australia
Cataloguing-in-Publication Entry

Baker, Tim, 1965–.
Surfari/Tim Baker.

ISBN 978 1 86471 212 4 (pbk.)

Surfers – Australia – Biography.
Authors – Australia – Biography.
Surfing – Australia.

797.32092
Cover design by Adam Yazxhi/MAXCO
Map by Darian Causby/Highway 51 Design Works
Internal design and typesetting by Post Pre-Press Group, Australia
Printed in Australia by Griffin Press, an accredited ISO AS/NZS 14001:2004
Environmental Management System printer

To Mum and Dad, for taking me to the beach and teaching me a love of language. Here is the unexpected result.

In loving memory of my grandmother, Margaret H. Wilson, for caring enough to document our past.

CONTENTS

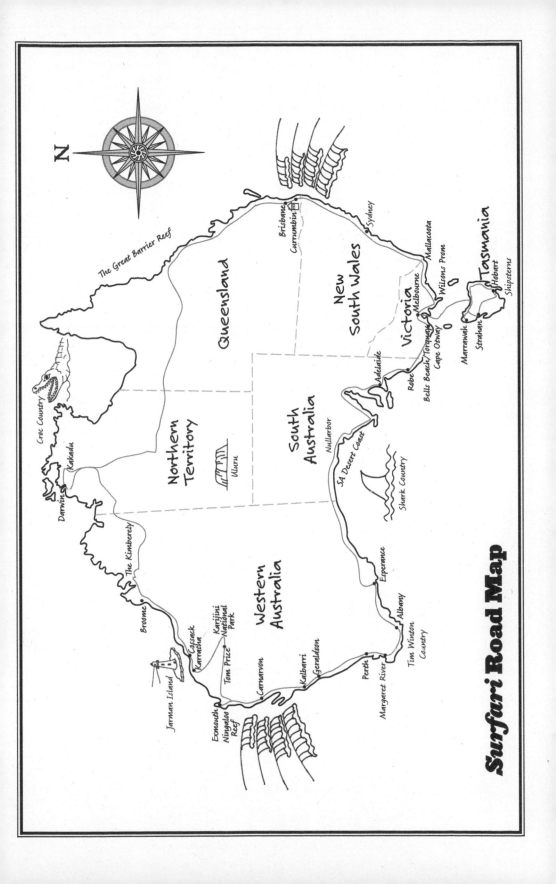

Surfari Road Map

INTRODUCTION

SURFARI HIGHWAY REVISITED

'Nature knows only one thing, and that's the present, present, present, like a big, huge, giant wave – colossal, bright and beautiful, full of life and death, climbing into the sky, standing in the seas.'

From *Seize the Day* by Saul Bellow

As a CALLOW, LANDLOCKED youth, I'd wander the bustling lanes of Camberwell's trash-and-treasure market, searching for glimmers of magic in my bland, middle-class, suburban existence. Bootleg cassettes of the Cure live. Legal herbal highs. An old pair of tartan stovepipes, a quarter-century before skinny jeans. A sighting of former Whitlam minister Jim Cairns, selling his scandalous memoirs from a folding bridge table.

My friends and I caught the train from Blackburn with a few bucks in our pockets and returned home laden with enough eclectic flotsam to terrify our parents. I argued I was saving them a fortune, outfitting myself in clothes and cultural accoutrements with my meagre pocket money each week.

Then, one Saturday, somewhere between purchasing a vintage Hawaiian shirt and a samosa, I stumbled upon an old, yellowing, dog-eared copy of *Surfari Highway*, written by one Ray Slattery. Somehow it caught my eye amid the mohair cardigans and greasy engine parts. Published in 1965, the year of my birth, it featured a quaint painted cover of two young, square-jawed gents in a tan convertible, longboards hanging out the back, speeding along a coastal road. A handful of surfers shared a delightful bowling left in the seascape background. As a newly surf-obsessed teen denied regular access to the coast, the image was irresistible.

I picked up the old paperback and started to read. It told the story of a pair of friends engaged in the great Australian surfing road trip, driving from town to town along the coast, discovering waves, romancing comely barmaids, playing impromptu guitar gigs in exchange for meals of unfeasibly large T-bone steaks at rough-and-ready country pubs. Inevitably, they'd fall foul of jealous, redneck locals and hightail it out of town in a screech of tyres, onwards to the next adventure. *Dukes of Hazzard* meets *Point Break*. I had discovered a road map to a different life than the one laid out for me in suburban Blackburn.

I threw down my $1.50 and was instantly transported. As I read, I vowed there and then that the minute I finished high school and obtained a driver's licence I would embark on just such a venture.

Somehow, in the ensuing years, the idea of the great surfing road trip receded as study and career opportunities beckoned. I became a journalist on a big-city newspaper, chasing ambulances and covering district cricket, was earmarked for the life of an Australian Rules football reporter, then landed a dream job on a surfing magazine. My surf lust was satiated . . . for a while. Eventually, I left the rigours of monthly magazine deadlines for the precarious path of the freelance writer. I married, had children, wrote books and squeezed in what fleeting surf sessions I could. Yet somewhere, all these years later, as middle age stole up on me, that teenage dream of the great Australian surfing road trip flickered back to life.

What fanned the flames of those teenage dreams I am still not quite sure. I am billing the journey that follows as a preemptive strike on my midlife crisis. I am forty-five. If I live to ninety, I'm halfway. If I work to seventy, I'm at half-time in my working life. Self-employed for the past fifteen years, no one was about to grant me long service leave, so I was going to have to grant it to myself. I wasn't sure how – I just knew something, somewhere, was going to have to shift.

It was the teeth grinding that first rang alarm bells. I'd wake in the morning with an aching jaw and sensitive molars. My dentist confirmed my suspicions and suggested sleeping with a mouth guard. Just what a receding, middle-aged married man – fending off a gut and accusations of snoring – needs to enhance his appeal in the bedroom. After ten years of marriage, my dear wife was only just beginning to accept my flannelette pyjamas. A mouth guard might render me a sexless codger. We couldn't have that – not just yet. Besides, I wanted to treat the root cause of the teeth grinding, not the symptom.

It wasn't supposed to be this way. I was the carefree surf writer guy, after all, who had forfeited serious career ambitions and material wealth for the footloose life of the freelance scribe – what the hell did I have to worry about? This wasn't rocket science. No lives depended on my scribblings.

My father had ground his teeth, I recalled, requiring the fitting of expensive caps. I remember my parents discussing it when I must have been six or seven; I was staggered at the costs involved, the thousands of dollars of long, painful dental work. At least he had good cause. Dad managed oil refineries when he was a lot younger than I am, and rose very close to the top of a large petroleum company. He had shit to deal with. This *was* rocket science.

As a kid, I remember pondering what sort of emotional condition could cause you to grind your teeth in your sleep. It was like you were trying to eat yourself in your dreams. Why would you want to eat yourself?

So, nearly forty years later, what is eating me? I think I am beginning to understand. Life is hard. Few of us are immune to feelings of being overwhelmed, dunked in relentless breakers, spluttering and gasping for air.

I've written thousands of words about the powerful, life-affirming lessons the ocean offers, how it teaches balance, timing, acceptance, humility, grace, slowly wearing away our rough edges. Yet I seemed to have forgotten my own teachings. It's probably not news for any family men out there, but it's easy to wake up one day and find yourself resembling a cliché, bowed down with work, mortgage, bills, familial responsibilities, the inevitable paunch, the expanding forehead, the myriad strains of supporting and raising a family, keeping a marriage together while gamely endeavouring to maintain body and soul.

I once wrote, in the afterword to an anthology of surf writing, 'If you are talking or writing about surfing more than you are surfing, maybe you should be doing more surfing.' In the subsequent few years, I'd got this equation so far out of balance as I took on one pressing book deadline after another that I felt in danger of becoming a laughable caricature: the surf writer who barely surfed, too busy chasing a paycheck to chase swells. And that seemed about as wretched a fate as I could imagine for myself.

What I needed was to immerse myself back into my subject, to indulge in a long, mad surf binge. How to achieve this in harmony with family life and financial commitments loomed as the most prominent challenge. Then I remembered the Great Surfing Road Trip dream.

I ran the scheme past my wife and she, to her undying credit, loved the idea. We sold it to our two kids on the strength of Alison Lester's delightful children's book *Are We There Yet?*, about a family road trip around Australia. Their little eyes lit up with wonder and delight.

Yet, even with familial blessing for my mad, indulgent scheme, there were several substantial impediments. By my calculations, we needed a book deal, a comfortable and reliable family SUV, a well-appointed caravan, someone to rent our house for the length of our trip in order to cover the mortgage, someone to pay a decent price for my wife's eight-year-old Forester with 130,000 k's on the clock, and the blessing of my new employers at *Surfing World* and Coastalwatch.com.

You see, this dash for freedom came only eight months after I had accepted regular paid employment from the country's finest and longest running surfing magazine and its most popular surfing website. Between them, they had made an honest man of me, providing the regular income I had long craved while allowing me to continue to work from home and write about the lifestyle I loved. It sounded like a dream arrangement and I had much to be grateful for. For the first time in a very long time, someone was paying me holiday pay, sick leave, superannuation. It was time to knuckle down and work hard, make a dent in the mortgage and start salting away super and school fees.

Just writing all that makes me shudder. We seem to need a lot these days just to get by, yet somewhere there needs to be room for adventure, dreams, a sense of one's spiritual well-being.

And so we are going.

The plan was simple but daring. Take off. Hit the open road. Take the family with me. Surf and write my way around Australia. Brilliant!

It always seemed a long shot, yet several of those large, implausible pieces of the puzzle seemed to fall into place with uncanny serendipity. Publishing deal? Check. Understanding employer providing a generous retainer while I travel the country? Check. A quick and painless sale of the Forester? Check.

Yet, even with a decent advance from my publisher and a half salary while on the road, I was going to need some benevolent lifestyle sponsors to pull this off. To wit, I put a proposal together, sent it off with copies of my previous books to Toyota's and Jayco's head offices, asking if they'd each loan me around $50,000 worth of their finest product for the best part of a year in exchange for the valuable media exposure my expedition would bring them. I'm not sure even I believed it. Remarkably, they both replied with a resounding and generous yes. One by one, the obstacles between us and our goal fell away until I had to eventually concede that we were actually going.

Now, I've read my share of New Age texts – I get the 'secret' of the Laws of Attraction – but this was all beginning to seem quite remarkable, like I was living out some far-fetched fantasy. When the brand-spanking-new V6, 3.5-litre Rav4 with twenty-eight kilometres on the clock turned up on the back of a big truck early one morning, it seemed like some great cosmic trick. Was it really this easy? Could I really manifest my most outlandish dreams just like that?

Well, no, apparently not.

Strangely, with our goal in sight and all impediments banished, I am gripped by a peculiar anxiety. I'm not sure I ever expected it all to work out. I have to admit, a few short weeks from departure, I am equal parts excitement and trepidation. The scale of the undertaking is only just beginning to sink in. Driving around Australia. It sounds so simple, rolls off the tongue, like, 'Going down the street,' or, 'Taking out the garbage.' Yet in the weeks leading up to our departure I read about a truck driver who died of dehydration after getting bogged on a remote outback road; an abalone diver torn to pieces by a pair of great white sharks at the ominously named Coffin Bay, South Australia; a group of campers air-lifted to hospital and a five-year-old boy fighting for his life after a gas bottle exploded at their east coast campground; a young female surfer raced to hospital after a potentially fatal jellyfish sting in Broome. Visitors to our fair shores often comment on the endless variety of potentially fatal mishaps awaiting the unwary, and I am beginning to see their point.

Then there is the weather. South-East Queensland and northern New South Wales are beset by floods that seem to spread like a contagion to parts of Victoria and Tasmania. Those few parts of the country not under water are suffering drought, bushfire and locust plagues. North Queensland is battening down the hatches for not one but *two* cyclones crossing the coast in quick succession. More cyclones are spinning off the coast of Western Australia. It is difficult to shake the feeling that the land is angry at us for generations of mistreatment. I wonder whether I should have been trying to procure a well-appointed ark rather than an automobile, however reliable.

Now, I don't want to try and overstate the element of adventure or danger here. Teenage girls sail solo around the world. Grey Nomads roll about our vast island home as if it were a gentile waltz around the dance floor. It's paved the whole way now. Mobile reception and a roadhouse are never too far away. And we are sticking to the coast, that delicious interplay of land and sea, never venturing into the lonely interior. We are, let's face it, lightweights. With our comfortable family SUV and all the creature comforts of the Jayco Expanda, I imagine we'll earn the scorn of hardcore tourers, with their massive diesel four-wheel drives, equipped with monstrous snorkels for raging river crossings, their compressors and heavy-duty winches, their jerry cans and extra spares and military strength, spartan camper trailers.

And I can live with that.

What I can't live with, what has prompted this whole wild scheme, is this nagging sense that, *this is it* – my life with no deviations, no risk, aspiring to nothing grander than smooth sailing, for the boat not to be rocked too much as we sail on toward the horizon.

I know plenty of older surfers who have sacrificed family relations and fled their responsibilities to pursue their obsession. I know plenty of others who have shelved their surfing pleasures altogether in the name of family commitments. But I don't want an either/or deal. Those older surfers who'd got the balance right, maintained both a happy home and the great wave-riding dance, are the ones who interest me. And as I contemplate guiding my own young children through the great maze of life, instilling a deep connection to the ocean and the natural world seems about as sound an approach as any. But let me be honest here: introducing them to the wonders of the wave-chasing lifestyle is a self-interested investment in my own surfing future. They will help keep me in the water, get me up for the early session when aching joints protest in years to come.

It's odd. Out of twenty-five years of interviewing surfers from all walks of life, strange and unexpected moments loom through the haze of recollections, perhaps because they chime with some longing in me.

Proud surfing patriarch Dorian 'Doc' Paskowitz, now ninety, once confided to me that he'd begun the world's first surf school simply so he could employ his kids as surf instructors and spend his days trading waves with them. He and his wife, Juliette, raised their nine children on the road, touring the California and Mexico coasts in a campervan, staging surf camps and lessons as they went.

The father of American pro longboarder Zack Howard once told me how he'd begun sailing so he could take his family surfing with him.

'When you're steering your yacht down fifty-foot waves with your family aboard, it's like having them all right there on your surfboard with you,' he gushed as we gazed out over Makaha Point, Hawaii, one dreamy afternoon.

Taking your family surfing – I like the sound of that. What I want is complete immersion. Some families go and live in the French countryside for a year, indulging in the delights of provincial cheese-making. I want to live at the beach for a year or, more accurately, many dozens of beaches, one after the other, in a great smorgasbord of wave-riding fun. I am aware of writing this in an attitude of naive idealism, untested by the harsh realities a year-long family road trip will inevitably bring. I am writing this introduction before we depart, with all that romanticism intact, so I can contrast its optimism and anticipation with the wisdom of experience that will hopefully emerge by journey's end. In this way, I hope to learn something about my country, family life and the delicate balancing act of personal needs versus larger commitments, and how I might intertwine them in the most enjoyable and healthy way for everyone.

The other thing I am looking for is simple inspiration. I have been a journalist my entire adult life, and at one stage travelled as much as I was at home. These days, I have put a bit of a lid on the far-ranging travels to exotic surf spots to be present and hands-on while the kids are little. Fortunately, I have found enough to write about in my home waters of the southern Gold Coast to keep the wolves from the door. I've had the rise of the famed Cooly Kids, the resurrection of Mark Occhilupo, and the wonders of the Superbank to document, as Coolangatta emerged as a world surfing centre. But this was beginning to feel like an increasingly difficult ruse to pull off. Even with half the country's pro surfers inhabiting the local waves, there are only so many ways of writing about a crowded day at Snapper Rocks before one's words resemble nor'-east windswept dribble.

I could relate to the homebound writer's predicament that John Steinbeck vividly articulated in his classic American road-trip narrative, *Travels with Charley*.

'I discovered I did not know my own country. I, an American writer, writing about America, was working from memory, and the memory is at best a faulty, warpy reservoir. I had not heard the speech of America, smelled the grass and trees and sewage, seen its hills and water, its color and quality of light. I knew the changes only from books and newspapers. But more than this, I had not felt the country for twenty-five years. In short, I was writing of something I did not know about, and it seems to me that in a so-called writer this is criminal.'

I was guilty of a similar crime. I, too, was writing from memory, if not complete ignorance. For years I'd trotted out tired clichés and stereotypes about the various subspecies of surfers to be found around our vast and varied coastline – hardy abalone divers in southern New South Wales, cray fishermen who chased crazy big waves in Tassie and Western Australia, feral cave-dwellers on the southern or western desert coasts. What on earth did I know about these people? Who were they? How had I acquired these impressions of them? From characters in a Tim Winton novel? I was passing on Chinese whispers about how I imagined the country and its people to be. I could endure the charade no more.

I was also chastened by Steinbeck's warning, that whatever idyllic scenarios I had dreamed up for our journey – camping in remote national parks, frolicking on deserted beaches, lazing in hammocks, gorging on the fruits of the sea – the reality would often be something else altogether.

'Once a journey is designed, equipped and put in process; a new factor enters and takes over,' wrote Steinbeck, before his own road trip around America. 'A trip, a safari, an exploration, is an entity, different from all other journeys. It has personality, temperament, individuality, uniqueness. A journey is a person in itself; no two are alike. And all plans, safeguards, policing and coercion are fruitless. We find after years of struggle that we do not take a trip; a trip takes us.'

Well, I am ready to be taken. As much as I will be writing about the country, I want the country to write upon me. As I age, the face staring back at me in the mirror grows more creased and haggard – the forehead spreads further north, the vanishing follicles seemingly migrating to odd, unexpected territories around the ears, out the nostrils, protruding crazily from the eyebrows. I am no longer a young man. I might never have been beautiful; perhaps now only the people who love me could find me attractive. Instead, I wish to appear interesting, for the lines etched on my face to convey stories, adventure, dreams realised, risks taken. If I cast about looking for role models for the road ahead, I am drawn more to the salty, sun-damaged old sea dogs who inhabit remote coastal zones around our country than the harried, be-suited CEOs or earnest politicians foisting their particular visions of progress and success upon us.

Where we live, a short hop from the Currumbin Wildlife Sanctuary, we often fall asleep to the sound of didgeridoo and Aboriginal singing, part of the 'nocturnal' activities at the popular tourist attraction. The sound is funnelled up a small valley towards our home, sitting high on a hill among the gum trees. It has always felt like a tree house. With the familiar drone of the didge and the haunting, unintelligible singing wafting through the treetops, it is tempting to mutter those most politically incorrect words: 'The natives are restless tonight.' Though it is not the natives who are restless. I know Indigenous elders who are deeply troubled by the young Aboriginal performers putting on a show for tourists ('the boys in the red nappies', as one matronly grandmother told me) – but I have to confess enjoying this peculiar feature of Currumbin life. I slowly dissolve into that delicious pre-sleep, semiconscious to the familiar, haunting rhythms of the faux-corroboree, feeling like the land is calling me. Often, it acts as a gentle lullaby, a comforting reassurance that this moment is one very small dot on an endless continuum. Other times, it awakens the yearning to roam, to follow that mournful drone out into the night, as if hypnotised, to feel the land, experience its condition, meet its people.

I have another, more personal reason for wanting to see some of the far reaches of our country. My great-grandfather, Harold Aubrey Hall, hailed from the north-west of WA, near Karratha, running cattle stations and serving as a lighthouse keeper on a small offshore island. My grandmother, Marnie to us, was a keen historian and had meticulously documented the lineage of the Halls back to Aubrey's grandfather. Henry Edward Hall left a comfortable existence in Shackerston Manor in Leicestershire, England, to bring his wife, Sarah, and five young children to this distant, unknown land. With a few scant provisions, livestock, seeds and farming equipment, they had sailed for months on the promise of a substantial landholding and the opportunity to pioneer an entirely new settlement.

Perhaps Aubrey's greatest legacy was a comprehensive dictionary of the local Indigenous language, that of the Ngalooma people. It was his life's work and he became renowned as the white cattleman fluent in the local tongue, and on friendly terms with the natives. His dictionary was rediscovered by academics in 1971 and published by the Australian Institute of Aboriginal Studies, Canberra.

Aubrey was reportedly a tough old bloke, famous for conducting dentistry on himself, pulling his own teeth with a pair of pliers when out on the station, or walking about for two weeks after a riding accident before being diagnosed with a broken leg. He rode horses well into his eighties. He only died in 1963, two years before my birth, so conceivably there are those in the north-west who still know him. To walk the land my great-grandfather worked, to see the lighthouse he manned, to meet those who speak the language he helped preserve – these things have become a powerful impetus for the journey into the remote north-west that I otherwise know almost nothing about. At the point where the surfing component of our journey comes to an end, I hope to discover something else about myself and my country.

And, so, after almost a decade dedicated to order, routine and the joy and revelation of parenthood, we are striking out. I want my son and daughter to experience what American writer Lenore Skenazy terms 'free-range' childhoods – outdoors, amongst nature, grazing knees and climbing trees and chasing crabs. To be honest, I want a free-range adulthood. I want my marriage to be strong and loving and robust, bonded by shared adventures and rich memories. I want to be healthy and vital as far into my life as possible.

As you read this, I will have some idea how this grand scheme has panned out, what trials and rewards it has delivered. We will be safely back at home, resuming our old lives by then, but forever altered, I imagine. Already, I sense changes taking place just in the planning and anticipation – the old life slipping away, something new and unknown arising. So, wish us well, as we strap on the boards, fill the jerry cans, pore over the road atlas and head off. The trip is taking us, the country is writing upon us, the sea and land are calling.

1

BE PREPARED

IT'S THE DAY BEFORE my forty-sixth birthday, the surf is perfect, and an excited senior citizen is forcibly fitting a small plastic device, a bit like a hearing aid, behind my ear.

'Go on, nod forward, as if you're falling asleep,' Ken instructs eagerly, stepping back to better appreciate the impending spectacle.

He is so adamant I dare not disobey. Instantly, the plastic device starts vibrating furiously and I raise my head with a start. Ken laughs and claps his hands with delight. 'There's another kind that makes a beeping noise,' he informs me, in case that suits my fancy more. With the aid of one of these gadgets, Ken assures me, it is almost impossible to fall asleep behind the wheel.

Ken has a veritable arsenal of these devices, all aimed at taking the danger and discomfort out of the Great Caravanning Experience. He reminds me of James Bond's offsider Q, the mad scientist who outfits the spy with hi-tech contraptions at the beginning of every movie.

I already knew I was a newbie, ignorant and unprepared for the challenges that lay ahead, but I hadn't realised quite how much knowledge – and how many accessories – I had yet to acquire.

Ken and I, our wives and another charming couple are all students at a caravan and trailer towing workshop at the RACQ's driver training facility in lovely Eight Mile Plains on the southern outskirts of Brisbane.

Having never towed so much as a trailer in my life, I had decided I needed some professional tuition before I hitched up a caravan to the family car and drove 25,000 kilometres around the country. So I booked my wife and me into this course. It seemed like the sensible, responsible thing to do – until I saw the surf forecast.

As we drove north on the Gold Coast Highway over Currumbin Bridge, I watched long, exquisite waves peel away across the creek mouth sandbar, a solid four to six feet and groomed to perfection by a gentle sou'-west wind. Well, this elaborate plan to manufacture more surf time for myself is going well, I mused as I steeled my focus to the one-hour drive north up the Pacific Highway, my every instinct protesting.

The safety of my family has to come first, I reasoned, hands gripping the wheel with white-knuckled resolve. Heading north from the Gold Coast, we sped through ugly industrial enclaves, past the corkscrew roller-coaster rides and water slides of the dreaded theme parks, glimpsing new Legoland housing

estates that rise abruptly out of the monotonous stands of eucalypt, leaving the real surfer's paradise farther behind.

In the midst of this no-man's-land, halfway between the
Gold Coast and Brisbane, an unintentionally ironic billboard
announces, 'If you lived in Forest Lakes you'd be home right
now.' My face involuntarily contorted into a reasonable facsimile of *The Scream* at the very thought. It was all counterintuitive,
the soulless landscape mocking my naive, idealistic plans for a
circumnavigational surf binge of Australia.

Soon enough, Kirst and I dutifully took our places in the
workshop classroom with our fellow students, friendly senior citizens who seemed inordinately delighted to make our
acquaintance.

Ken's soon-revealed enthusiasm for small, vibrating, battery-
operated apparatus could qualify him for a career in the adult
industry. In fact, I am beginning to suspect all is not as it seems
among these bright-eyed Grey Nomads on their carefree jaunts
about the country. They appear almost too spritely for their years,
too keen to make our acquaintance, the gleam in their eyes a bit
too bright. Is it my surf-deprived imagination, or are they eyeing
us with salacious intent, thrilled by these fresh-faced novices, not
yet too far removed from their prime. Disoriented and anxious
this far inland, I begin to conjure chilling visions of a depraved
swingers' circuit among the retiree caravanning community,
gathered in circles in their camp chairs, enjoying their regular
'fivesies' ritual of drinks and nibbles, tossing their keys to the van
park toilet block into a salad bowl to see who will be showering
with whom that evening. There is something a little suspect, I
worry, about all those couples' names painted on the backs of
their vans, together with their favoured CB radio frequencies,
like artistically rendered toilet graffiti promising a good time –
'Tom and Barb, UHF 18 and 40, Adventure before Dementia'.

It stands to reason, after all. If these are the Baby Boomer retirees, the Great Demographic Hump we keep hearing about, do the maths and you soon realise these same staid grandparents were probably flower children of the Revolution back in the 60s, with their penchants for free love, skinny dipping and cheesecloth. If I was concerned about my midlife rumblings, the Nomads at least make me feel young again.

Thankfully our tutors, Brian and Peter, are professional enough to keep proceedings on track. We are drilled on road rules, dazzled by interactive PowerPoint quiz questions, warned of the myriad dangers this unwieldly counterweight attached to the back of our vehicle poses to the unwary. This theory is all fine and good, but it is the practical component we have come for.

We have yet to take delivery of our new Rav4 or Jayco Expanda, so we've booked the RACQ's own humble Holden Commodore station wagon and a large box trailer, which will have to serve as proxy for our van. Feelings of inadequacy again swell. Our fellow students have arrived with their shiny new rigs, luxurious four-wheel drives attached to top-of-the-line caravans with optional everything. Ken is rolling in a $100,000 Lexus four-wheel drive and a van so imposing and opulent I wonder how he is game to risk it out on the open road. The coupling between his car and van is festooned with more wires and cables than a Telstra exchange. He has a satellite dish for phone, internet and TV reception, video cameras mounted on the back of his van that beam his rear view onto a heads-up display on his dash, and Lord knows what else. The car and van fully loaded weigh well over 3 tonne each, the entire rig pushing 6.5 tonne and guzzling 25 litres per 100 km/h, he reports proudly. It seems a bit like carting U2's concert infrastructure around the country for kicks. Roy and Idie are hardly less modestly equipped, and the two couples are able to converse quite happily in a language I barely understand. With close to a quarter of a million dollars in retirement funds laid down on their rigs, this is a serious lifestyle investment. We are dilettantes, imposters, mere hobbyists among serious, long-term tourers who have irreversibly crossed the threshold from suburbia to the open road. For them, there is no turning back.

The practical component of the workshop is no less daunting. We are taught to find the 'jackknife' point of our rigs and not go beyond it, and thus the mysteries of reversing a caravan are revealed to us. Sophisticated mathematical formulae seem to guarantee a swift and hassle-free reverse park between two witches hats – at least when practised in the spacious dimensions of the RACQ car park. How that translates to the rather less generous confines of the typical van park remains to be seen.

Yet, for all the complex equations and techniques we learn, my mate Eric, over a few beers the night before, gave me the best bit of advice about reversing a van: 'If you see the van in your left mirror, turn left. If you see it in your right mirror, turn right.' I try it, and it works beautifully.

MECHANICS AND TECHNOLOGY

I have a theory: if you ever find yourself lost in the Australian bush, simply announce loudly and generally that you are planning a road trip around the country. Inevitably, a complete stranger will wander out of the undergrowth and offer you copious amounts of expert advice. I never knew so many people had completed the 'Big Lap', until I decided I was going to do it, and then the flow of information quickly swelled into an overwhelming torrent. They say, when the student is ready, the master appears. I must really be ready.

Our neighbours have just sold their house and we've been waiting to see who will move in. One day, about a month before our departure, a large LandCruiser drives up the street towing a dusty, road-worn camper trailer, rusted jerry cans affixed to every available surface. It turns out our new neighbours, Michael and Michelle, have just returned from their own circumnavigation of the country, though they'd reached Denmark, in southern WA, and ended up living there for three years. After all this time on the road – homeschooling, living the dream, drifting like gypsies – they are looking forward to putting down roots, enrolling the kids in school and settling into a regular routine, like a mirror image of ourselves. Michael has taken time out from his career designing computer software to get out of the rat-race, to be present and involved while the kids are young. He is now contemplating kickstarting his career again, but he reckons the world has shifted while he's been out adventuring. Apps for iPhones were barely a twinkle in Steve Jobs's eye three years ago. Now, the Apple website proudly boasts that the ten billionth iPhone app is about to be downloaded, and the Western World's best and brightest minds are engaged in a feverish arms race to come up with the next Angry Birds.

Their nine-year-old daughter, Maddie, is the same age as our Vivi, and they eagerly exchange tips for their new respective realities, neatly swapping roles and becoming instant best friends. An enormous cargo container is delivered to their house a few days later, packed with their worldly possessions, and they are literally unpacking boxes and setting up house as we swipe those same boxes and pack our old lives into storage. They donate their dog-eared old copy of *Camps Australia Wide, Volume Three*, the veritable bible of the serious cross-country tourer, with comprehensive national roadmaps and guides to every campground in the country. Though a few years out of date, it comes annotated with their own notes on favourite camping grounds and a scrawled recipe for damper.

Other friends of friends seem to appear out of the woodwork, full of wise counsel and earnest advice on what safety equipment to take. Most of these characters are such self-reliant, knowledgeable, multi-skilled outdoorsmen as to make me feel totally inadequate. I've had notions of getting fit, doing a basic mechanics course, getting my first-aid certificate, shaping my own surfboard to take on the trip. I'll research every highway, roadhouse and campground in the country. I'll learn to fish. None of it happens. As it is, I am buried in yet another book deadline right up until Christmas, and by the time the plastic pine tree is packed away our departure date is almost upon us. I imagine clambering into our vehicle on day one of our journey and feebly asking my wife, 'Okay, where to, love?'

I make attempts at preparation. I join online forums on caravanning websites and am quickly mired in a world of tow ball weights and stabiliser bars, compressors, jerry cans and safety chains, sat phones, generators and GPS coordinates.

Strangely, I have given most of my time and attention to our IT needs on the road. A confirmed Luddite, I have held off owning a mobile phone all these years but realise I will soon have to relent. After a decade of resistance, I go straight to the top shelf and procure an iPhone 4, and within days I am smitten. How have I managed without this wondrous device in my life? The world of apps is a revelation. Of course, I'd heard people talk about them, but I figured they were all inane games for adolescents or bored office workers, trivial gimmicks to amuse fellow drinkers in pubs. The reality is so much more impressive: weather, surf forecasts, maps, the nearest petrol stations, guitar tuners, FatBooth, Fart Piano . . . Finally, I feel the miraculous future depicted in *The Jetsons* is upon us. I have a remote control to the world at my fingertips.

I've always been dismissive of the world of social media and have token Twitter and Facebook accounts that I barely use. My good friend Rob, who runs a smart and edgy web design and branding studio, R&B, convinces me of the vital role social media can play in my expedition, updating an army of followers about our journey and thus cultivating a readership for this book even as I write it. He sets his staff of hip young creatives to work designing a comprehensive strategy for me, and within days I have been transformed – Eliza Doolittle style – from frumpy obscurity to the leading edge of the social media revolution. Before I know it, I am the proud owner of a fleet of accounts specifically set up for the *Surfari* mission. And not just with the ubiquitous Twitter, Facebook and YouTube, but with other mysterious services I can only vaguely grasp the function of: Flickr, Tumblr, Hootsuite, Gowalla, TubeMogul. (I liked the sound of that last one.) It is . . . astounding.

'Just play around with them and see how you go,' my efficient social media consultant Bree advises me. Soon after, I find myself at the local library with my five-year-old son, Alex, toying with my iPhone and trying to make sense of this strange new virtual reality, the baffling array of usernames and passwords I have acquired. I log in to my Gowalla account to see what it does. Do I want to 'check in', it asks me? Well, sure, why not? It is only later I discover that I have just announced to the world, via my suite of social media channels, that I am at the Pines Shopping Centre, a sorry circumstance that I usually try to keep secret from even my closest friends.

Undeterred, I take to this brave new world with alarming gusto, while my wife and close friends observe this midlife metamorphosis with concern. Am I secretly chatting with would-be Russian brides as I pore over my touchscreen? A group intervention is almost deemed necessary. My dear friend Andy is brave enough to inform me I have perhaps gone too far the day I take a photo of my new pair of Birkenstock sandals and tweet to my twelve followers how much my feet love them.

Apple shares soar as our departure date draws closer. As well as my phone, I have procured a new MacBook Pro upon which to write my masterpiece and pilot my new social media empire. And we have buckled to the seductive powers of computer entertainment for our children, buying them an iPod Touch each for Christmas, armed with enough games, music, audio-books and movies to keep them sedated through the long drives ahead.

I am just congratulating myself on all the technological fire-power we have assembled for our trip, how well prepared I am for any eventuality, when it dawns on me that, even though there appears to be an iPhone app for just about everything, there probably isn't one that can get you out of a bog, or fix a burst radiator hose, or carry out some rudimentary bush first aid in case of an emergency. In the virtual world of online amuse-ments and media, I am thoroughly sorted. In the real world of potential mishaps and misadventure, I remain hopelessly ill prepared.

And so, only a week out from departure, I take myself off to my local ARB four-wheel drive accessory retailer, hitting up a friend of a friend for yet another spurious media discount. The young salesperson Jason is friendly and knowledgeable, and draws up a comprehensive shopping list of everything I need, several things I've never heard of, and a few more items the functions of which remain unclear to this day. There is the compressor, the snatch strap and dampener, the puncture repair kit, a basic tool kit, the CB radio (who knew they still existed in the age of the internet?). Then Jason gets out his calculator, sharpens his pencil, factors in a generous media discount, and comes up with a grand total a little over $3000. I've already spent most of our pre-trip preparatory budget on ensuring Steve Jobs a comfortable retirement, so I have little left in the kitty for such extravagance. Like a treasurer at budget time, I get out the razor and slash the shopping list. I draw the line at the MaxTrax: large rectangular sheets of tough, textured plastic covered in protruding nobs and ridges that are allegedly designed to free you from the most intractable bog. They will have to go. So too will the CB radio, sadly. And the basket roof rack and the jerry cans.

I get the total down to a little over $700, roughly one sixth of what I had spent on Apple products, a feat even Wayne Swan would be proud of – and probably a neat reflection of our current government's enthusiasm for hi-tech infrastructure, like the National Broadband Network, over nuts-and-bolts services. The real world might go to hell in a hand basket, but at least we'll be able to stream live porn and download the latest update of Angry Birds from anywhere in the country.

Perhaps this belated, enthusiastic embrace of techno gadgetry is my own way of avoiding real-world horrors. Once you start talking to people about the realities of the Great Australian Road Trip, two broad subcategories of advisers reveal themselves. One group is full of practical, useful tips about the endless and dizzying variety of tools, safety gear and skills required to navigate the country. This is alarming enough. The other group just wants to scare the crap out of you with horror stories: flipped caravans, crocodile attacks, potentially fatal bites and stings, and horrific skin conditions contracted from van park shower cubicles.

I've always been amused by those thin-skinned tourists who come to Australia filled with terror at the many varieties of lethal wildlife our fine country is home to, the array of grisly fates that can be met with here – sharks, jellyfish, red-back spiders, blue-ringed octopus, backpacker murderers, outback crazies, bushfires, cyclones – but I am beginning to come around to their way of thinking. The daily news has become a rollcall of the unkind ends we might meet out there on the road. My sense of foreboding climaxes with the story of the Gold Coast couple who had just collected their $86,000 dream caravan . . . and promptly flipped it at high speed on the M1 a couple of kilometres from the van dealership. Online news items show the demolished van on its side on the highway, or being winched onto the back of a large tow truck. In the photos, a small group of people stand by watching the wretched scene, one man holding his face in his hands, clearly inconsolable. It is unclear if this is the driver or the caravan salesman.

I quickly grow overwhelmed with a mounting sense of ignorance and anxiety. I toss and turn at night, dreaming up all the foreboding circumstances I am unready and unqualified to deal with, agonising over the many dire dangers I am about to subject myself and my family to.

An old Lemonheads song springs into my head as I lay sleepless one night, 'I Lied About Being the Outdoor Type', which contains those immortal couplets:

I can't go away with you on a rock-climbing weekend;
what if something's on TV and it's never shown again?

It's just as well I'm not invited, I'm afraid of heights;
I lied about being the outdoor type.

To whom can I turn for guidance in my hour of need? Of course, my wise Oracle, the author of *Surfari Highway*, Ray Slattery, who has inspired this whole ill-conceived adventure. I need reassurance that the simple, uncomplicated Australian coastal existence he depicted so evocatively can still be found, that all it requires is the will and a sense of adventure. Jonnie Grant and Rick Miller never agonised over their choice of safety equipment or where mobile phone signals would fade out. And so I google Ray Slattery to find out more about my wise literary guru . . . and quickly wish I hadn't.

It turns out Mr Slattery is quite the cult figure in pulp fiction circles, a prolific author who wrote dozens and dozens of novels for Horwitz Publishing in the 60s and early 70s, pumping out one a month for the grand sum of $250 to $300 each, some under his name, others under noms de plume like John Slater, Frank O'Hara, Karen Miller, James Bent, Frank F. Gunn, Terry West or Roger Hunt. The reason for his coyness soon becomes clear. *Surfari Highway* and its sequel, *Wildwater*, are mere fleeting diversions from Slattery's stock-in-trade, a niche literary genre that can best be described as Nazi Bondage, or War Prison Sex Slavery. The titles alone probably reveal enough of their story lines: *The Horror Camp, Beast Woman of Buchenwald, Sin Camp, Women of Auschwitz, Terror of the Swastika, War Lord's Women, Valley of Slaves, Jungle Captive, Samurai Slave, The Sadist's Slave.* The cover blurb of *Buchenwald Hell* declares, 'She was forced to submit. The beautiful French model was subjected to pain and degradation at the hands of her female guards until the notorious Ilse Koch forced her to make a decision – further sadistic rape and torture or Prisoner of Love.'

Lurid cover art inevitably depicts a near-naked, buxom prisoner cowering in terror at the feet of a scowling Nazi commandant or Japanese soldier. There is neither encouragement nor reassurance to be found in these books. I begin to question the wisdom of taking my family on a wholesome cross-country vacation on the inspiration of a man who appears to take great pleasure in the torture of innocent women. I like to think the *Surfari Highway* series came towards the end of Slattery's career, when he had been through some sort of ocean-inspired, midlife epiphany of his own. Though Slattery's penchant for gratuitous violence arises again in *Wildwater*. 'The waves peaked like WoW and the fights got fiercer on the second leg of Rick and Jonnie's surfari shindig,' the cover blurb trumpets. This is not the kind of surfari I'm after.

But, ultimately, regardless of dubious literary mentors, racy Grey Nomads, horror news stories, extreme weather events or conflicting advice, I have to concede one thing – I am on my own. Out there, on the road, I will have to rely on my own judgement, my own paltry survival and mechanical skills. It is a disturbing realisation, especially as the country suffers one natural calamity after another.

With floods closing the Pacific Highway just near our favourite coastal retreat of Yamba, even the delivery of our car and caravan are looking doubtful. A week out from our departure date we have neither of the two principle components for our trip. We have already committed to a date to move out of our home to make way for our delightful new tenants and so find ourselves literally homeless, of no fixed address, with the flood waters rising to the north, south and west, cyclones bearing down on Far North Queensland, drought and bushfire ravaging the west.

We prop at my gracious father-in-law's place, one of the few original old beach houses left on the Gold Coast foreshore, in a holding pattern – our world packed up in bags and boxes, my competency as skipper of this particular ship looking suspect and friends who have already bade us half a dozen farewells beginning to wonder if we will ever leave.

And, in truth, so am I.

2

A BEGINNING IS A DELICATE TIME

FAR FROM CURING MY teeth-grinding, the approach of our departure date just seems to aggravate my condition. I lie awake during the night, my heading spinning with countless real and imagined issues still to be resolved, terrifying fates I am about to subject my family to, a sudden, deep affection for the life, region and community we are leaving behind.

There are many moments when it seems easier to call the whole hare-brained scheme off. Except that I have already banked and spent a third of my book advance; we have signed a lease to rent our house out for the next eight months; and I have a brand-new Toyota Rav4 and a Jayco Expanda being trucked up from Sydney and Melbourne respectively.

Early 2011 is an interesting time to be embarking on the great round-Australia road trip. I mean, I love a sunburnt country, its droughts and flooding rains, as much as the next jingoistic patriot, but in my paranoid state of insomnia it seems the country is exhibiting its ruthless muscle purely to intimidate me, to test my resolve.

Each day, I check the state of the Pacific Highway on the RTA website, confer with my people at Toyota and Jayco about the options and likely delivery dates and report back to my family. It's as if I have them assembled in the departure lounge to take off on the dream holiday only to have our flights constantly delayed.

Just as the floods abate and highways reopen, Cyclone Yasi bares down on Far North Queensland and it looks like we will at least have the mother of all tailwinds while our northern neighbours bunker down for a long night of destruction. My petty anxieties suddenly pale in comparison.

Finally, one sunny morning in late January, I get a call on my new iPhone from a charming truck driver named Bob to say he is five minutes away – he has a car to deliver. Alex and I wait outside, waving frantically as he pulls into my father-in-law's street. Most boys like big trucks, but even big boys like big trucks when they are carrying a new car being delivered to their door free of charge, on extended loan. My man at Toyota, Nic, has commented casually in a recent email that he is fairly sure he can secure a fuel card for our trip. He says it so flippantly, as if he's talking about throwing in a free steering-wheel cover. I dare not believe it. *Fairly sure?* What does that mean? And does a fuel card actually do what it sounds like, that is, qualify the bearer to free fuel? It seems preposterous.

But when our charming truck driver pulls up out the front of our temporary home in Tugun, unchains the Rav, expertly reverses it down the ramp and hands over the keys, there in the centre console between the two front seats is the small plastic card. I am left standing there holding the keys in one hand, fuel card in the other, as the truck pulls away, looking at Alex with an expression of stunned disbelief. The 'Starcard' is decorated with both the Caltex and Toyota logos, and the word 'Marketing' is hand written on the back in black texta. I turn the prized thing over in my hand, trembling ever so slightly. Alex is more transfixed by the spectacle of the receding truck. I am still almost too nervous to believe in the magical properties this object possesses lest it break the spell. Perhaps they have me confused with someone else. I can imagine the Toyota marketing meeting where they discussed my proposal.

'We're loaning a Rav4 to Tim Somebody – you know, the surf writer guy.'

'Who? *Tim Winton*? The Miles Franklin winner? I loved *Breath*.'

'You're kidding me – Tim Winton is going to drive a Rav4 around the country and blog for us free of charge? Good God, get the man a fuel card!'

What will happen when they realise their mistake? I conjure up a frightening scene, wherever it is bound to transpire – at the Ceduna or Eucla or Karratha Roadhouse – when I have my privileges revoked, my Starcard seized and confiscated, and am presented with a bill for all the complimentary fuel I have extorted up to that point. Will my own *Surfari Highway* end in some tiny outback jailhouse?

I still have a few days to kill before the Jayco is due to arrive. I use up a quarter of a tank driving around close to home, running errands, and decide to test the Starcard. I'm decidedly nervous as I fill the tank and head for the cashier. According to my instructions from Nic, I have only to saunter to the service station counter, present my Starcard, swipe it, punch in the odometer reading when prompted, and press OK. Just like that. I follow the instructions to the letter, tap in a ludicrous '116 km' for the odometer reading while eyeing the security camera in the corner anxiously. I offer a thin-lipped smile at the cashier and wait for sirens to sound and lights to flash. Instead, she smiles back and hands me a receipt. Just like that. It is only twenty bucks, but I scoot out of there like Ronald Biggs, adrenalin surging through my system. I've gotten away with it.

Over the next few days I keep up regular communications with my people at Jayco HQ and their Tweed Heads dealership about the arrival of our Expanda. There seems to be some uncertainty about the due date of our van, or whether, in fact, it has left the Melbourne factory at all, due to the flooded highways to the north. I report the latest grim news back to the family. In the meantime, I am feverishly racing around taking care of last-minute details, each one seeming to expand into a complex puzzle all of its own. Bike racks, extension mirrors, sway bars – each accessory, no matter how trifling, comes in a bewildering array of styles and brands that only suit certain configurations of vans and vehicles. Each retail experience in the booming auto accessory industry introduces me to another dogmatic expert ready to pour scorn upon my inadequate preparations. Surely there is a TAFE course for all this. The Visa card takes a beating as I vainly attempt to purchase peace of mind.

Finally, we get news that the Expanda is due to arrive at Tweed Heads, but it will take another day for them to do all the necessary checks and give us a thorough induction in the operation of our new mobile home. We call in at the appointed time and set eyes on her for the first time and, if it isn't love at first sight, it is at the very least an exceedingly warm affection. In fact, our family has already composed a jingle in its honour. Cue the big-band show tune and men in top hats and canes:

It's the Expanda;
there's nothing grander.
What's good for the goose,
is good for the gander.
It's the Expanda;
it's big enough for a panda.
It even comes with its own,
roll out verandah . . .

From there our rhymes begin to scrape the bottom of the barrel:

I don't want to hear any slander;
all the other caravans are so much blander.
It's as beautiful as a flowering jacaranda;
it can't float or fly, 'cause it's an overlander.

Hours of fun for the whole family, really. The YouTube clip will have gone viral by now.

A lovely man named Cedric takes us through our induction, explaining everything in easy, step-by-step instructions, from folding out the bed ends to firing up the hot water service to running the fridge on gas, battery or main power. There's a lot to take in. We've been given our choice of optional extras and have gone for the solar panel, roll-out barbecue and external hot-and-cold shower, though we've drawn the line at the onboard toilet. At some point those things have to be emptied out.

And, with that, we hitch up the Expanda to the back of the Rav, screw up the safety chains, heave the sway bars into position and we are ready to go. Just like that. It's hard to imagine as I make my way down Machinery Drive, through the dense, grimy, industrial environs of South Tweed Heads, that I will soon be steering this rig through some of the most picturesque coastal scenery our country has to offer. Only one more obstacle stands between us and our departure.

My father-in-law Ken's place is idyllic in many respects, with its beachfront position, gracious hosts, bottomless esky and gourmet catering. One feature that fills me with dread, though, is its driveway – a long, narrow artery lined with a high concrete wall that runs from the main street to the rear of their battleaxe block. For nights I lie awake, worrying how I will negotiate the driveway with the van in tow, running over the options in my head: Reverse in to load up so we can drive out forwards? Drive in forwards and reverse out into a busy road? The driveway looms in my late night anxiety as a veritable Everest – the ultimate challenge at my very first hurdle. Despite my credible efforts at the towing workshop, a couple of witches hats in a large car park is a very different thing to a long, thin driveway. I imagine myself ping-ponging off the sides of the driveway walls like an errant bowling ball, trashing the Expanda before we've even left.

Why not simply park on the street and lug our accumulated possessions the fifty metres down the driveway, you ask? A neighbour had recently parked his brand-new ute on the street overnight and woke to find it without wheels and up on blocks. I will subject our new pride and joy to no such risk.

Ken's next-door neighbour Karl, a solidly built, fifty-something fellow, has been sizing up our dilemma from the steps of his second-floor apartment, contemplating the complex geometry of the scenario. With his snow-white hair, goatee and glasses, he resembles Colonel Sanders and seems a similarly jovial, accommodating chap. And, best of all, he has a solution.

'Drive it in forwards,' he tells me assuredly. 'Unhitch it and we'll swing the van around.' Then I can simply reverse the car out on its own, reverse it back in, hitch up and drive the van out. Brilliant. A simple solution to a dilemma I have agonised over for days. I could kiss him. Buoyed by Karl's wisdom, I quickly adopt the goal of navigating our way around the country without ever having to reverse the van. Karl carefully oversees the operation, having taken on the responsibility for our safe departure, and I follow his instructions studiously.

The blessing of our delayed departure is that we've had a week to observe and contemplate all the stuff we are planning on taking, to consider the amount of space it takes up and compare it to the storage available in the Expanda. Some last-minute culling is called for. One of the wives at the towing workshop had advised us to be strict in our wardrobe allocations. 'You don't need all those clothes out on the road,' she urged, which only heightened my suspicions about the unnatural, or rather naturist, lifestyles of the caravanning community.

Our Tugun layover has also provided a useful transition period between our old lives and our new ones, a kind of antechamber where we begin to adjust to our homeless state before we hit the road. After the mad scramble of packing up the family home for eight months' absence, it is actually a strange kind of relief to have the enforced stillness of this limbo.

I am awake before dawn, watching the slow creep of grey spread over a drizzling Gold Coast morning. We've had the big official send-off party, with dancing and merriment, several impromptu drop-ins and heartfelt farewells from close friends, and now our actual departure is an oddly sombre, low-key affair. There's no brass band, no crowds of well-wishers, no crepe banner for us to drive through as our mate Al had threatened. The van is hitched up, packed and ready to go. The kids are bleary-eyed and quietly picking up on the unspoken anxieties of their parents. Familiar, comforting soft toys are stuffed in place like decoys in the back seat. A light breakfast is eaten and snacks packed.

And then, with a minimum of fanfare, and a grand total of

about half an hour's towing experience under my belt, we inch out that long, thin driveway. The Expanda swings into line behind the Rav just as Karl has calculated, and we slowly edge out into the big, wide world and a new life. The driveway suddenly seems to me a kind of birth canal. The security of our old lives, the 'placenta' of home which has fed and nourished us as we've grown together as a young family, is being left behind, our umbilical cord cut, and we will now have to make our way independently in the outside world, removed from the comforting womb of familiarity. There is, mercifully, no whale music or screaming.

The drive south from the Gold Coast down the Pacific Highway is a familiar one, the beginning of many a family holiday and quick surf mission, but it comes with a jolt of realisation that there will be no return trip this time, no retracing of our steps, no calling into a favourite store or café, or side trip down a quiet beach road. We will be returning home from the polar opposite direction, having circumnavigated the country, covering some 25,000 km, over the best part of a year.

Just calculating the length of the Australian coast has proven a puzzle for generations of academics. The *Year Book of Australia* (1978) gives the distance as 36,735 km, while the *Australian Encyclopedia* gives it as 19,658 km. Who's right? Well, both apparently. It all depends by which increments you are measuring, and, thus, how many of the innumerable twists and turns, nooks and crannies of the coastline you take in. According to the *Australian Geographer* (1979), if you measure it in 1 mm increments, the length is 132,000 km. I decide against attempting that. Presumably, if you measured it in large enough increments it would become progressively shorter until it was no distance at all. All I needed was a 10,000 km ruler and we'd be home by now.

ACCIDENTAL HAIKU IN ANGOURIE

Our late departure does mean a rush trip through from the Gold Coast to Sydney to make a family wedding, where Vivi is to be a flower girl. We've done the old Goldy to Sydney run plenty of times – know it well and will do it plenty more in the future – so it's no great shame. Still, I find it hard to go past the Yamba turn-off south of Ballina in New South Wales, the scene of many fond family holidays.

On our last visit, nine months prior to this trip, we enjoyed perhaps the quintessential East Coast beach experience. Holidaying at the little seaside hamlet of Angourie, we'd been enjoying a glorious autumn day on the beach, pushing the kids into waves, when a little dinghy cruised into the bay. A wizened old sea dog jumped out and guided his craft through the gentle shore break towards the boat trailer he'd left parked on the beach, attached to a rusted four-wheel drive. It was none other than local surf legend Dave 'Baddy' Treloar, star of the seminal 70s surf flick *Morning of the Earth*. The film's creator, Albe Falzon, had always credited Baddy with the great wisdom and intuition to know that their 70s North-Coast experience during the filming of *Morning of the Earth* was as idyllic as the surfing lifestyle could be, a golden moment in time, and so Baddy had never left. While many of his contemporaries ventured to the four corners of the surfable world in search of kicks and fortunes by various, dubious means, Baddy simply stayed put. To this day, you can find him doing exactly what he was doing back in 1972 – surfing the local point, catching fish, shaping the odd board.

I'd met Baddy a few times over the years and trotted over to help him bring his boat in. Baddy had a reputation for some stern localism in the line-up, but I've always found him a perfectly amiable bloke, keen for a chat, with a remarkable recall of every swell, every subtle shift in mood of the ocean and elements, stretching back for decades. We got the boat into the shallows and I held it while he reversed his boat trailer into place with his old LandCruiser and winched it aboard.

'How'd you go?' I asked. Baddy survives by his fishing, sells his catch to local restaurants and always saves a couple for the town doctor, his own form of health insurance by barter. He opened the big blue esky in the bow of the tinny and held aloft a few good-sized mackerel. A couple were ear-marked for a regular restaurateur client and another for the good doctor, but he had a couple to spare.

'Can I buy one?' I asked. He held up a spotted mackerel as long as my arm and said it was ours for $25. I had the cash on me, handed it over and ran up the beach to our rented holiday apartment, wrapped the fish in newspaper and shoved it in the fridge. And so we dined on fresh mackerel, direct from the Pacific Ocean and caught by a surf icon, for the next two days, carving off thick steaks and preparing them by various simple combinations of lemon, salt, pepper, tamari and sesame oil. The rest of my time was divided between lazy sessions with a hand-ful of locals out at the Point, family mornings on the kiddy beach, long siestas, the obligatory counter tea at the pub – Australian beach holidays don't get much better.

In the local corner store, Baddy had scrawled an inscription on a *Morning of the Earth* poster that summed up that 70s North-Coast lifestyle: 'No legropes, singlefins, swordfish diet.' Baddy had captured perfectly a simpler time in six words, a kind of accidental haiku. In the subsequent decades, increasing numbers of city dwellers have headed here searching for the same utopia Baddy had recognised early on.

After years of working and hustling in the cities, forging careers and starting families, many had come to see, just like Albe, that Baddy had got something profoundly right when he settled here. They bought up holiday apartments and built increasingly opulent beach houses, pushing up local real estate prices. The second generation of local surfers, the children of the *Morning of the Earth* crew who'd got in early were clearly uncomfortable with the growing popularity of their surf sanctuary, and tensions sometimes rose out at the Point. It was here that Baddy's fellow local surf legend Nat Young had been viciously beaten a decade earlier in an infamous surf rage incident.

The resentment of the local crew to the influx of city dwellers was summed up in a bit of graffiti in the toilets at the Point:

Bald men,
bad genes,
old kooks,
if you moved here
in the last 10 years.

Accidental haiku seemed to be popular in Angourie. Indeed, I'd often thought the long-time locals looked like they were in the process of evolving a super race of impossibly beautiful, fit, tanned, young amphibians. The balding, pale, pot-bellied accountants and lawyers who were moving in like the dreaded cane toads were clearly in danger of weakening the gene pool.

In other ways, this little coastal community is a model of highly evolved environmental consciousness. A dedicated Coastcare group had successfully eradicated the dreaded bitou bush, once used to stabilise sand dunes, from the Angourie foreshore and replanted it with native species. It must be one of the few strips of coast in the country where a photo from today shows it in better shape than in the 70s. Dedicated cane toad drives help keep the accursed northern invader at bay, dispatching them ruthlessly with golf clubs and cricket bats, or popping them in plastic bags to be frozen alive. Strategies to reduce the impact of sea changers have not yet become so drastic.

A SHORT AND SORRY HISTORY OF BITOU BUSH

Some things we simply take for granted as we travel the Australian coast, because they are so ubiquitous. Take bitou bush. This waxy, green-leafed shrub is so dominant along many stretches of the east coast that we almost don't notice it, as all-pervading as the sand dunes it infests. Yet, it is an alien invader, another in a long line of disastrous introduced species that have wrought havoc on native species.

It is believed bitou bush was first introduced to Australia near Newcastle in 1908, its seeds deposited from the ballast of ships from South Africa along the banks of the Hunter River. Between 1946 and 1968 it was planted extensively along the New South Wales coast by Soil Conservation Services of NSW to stabilise dunes after sand mining. However, like many introduced species, it quickly proved problematic, out-competing indigenous plant species for sun, water and nutrients, forming impenetrable tracts where little else can grow. It now infests some 36,000 hectares along 900 kilometres of the New South Wales Coast, and is considered dominant in pure stands along some 220 kilometres. It is rated the worst plant pest on the Australian coast and leads to serious declines in biodiversity.

Strong efforts are now being made to eradicate bitou bush, with varying results. Determined community efforts through volunteer groups like Dunecare and Landcare have had some success in reducing or even eradicating the pest in areas like Angourie, in northern New South Wales, and Crowdy Bay National Park.

Quite incredibly, plans to control bitou bush appear to hinge on yet another introduced species. Bitou's natural enemies include the bitou tip moth, the bitou seed fly and the bitou leaf roller moth. The last of these was released at Broadwater, New South Wales, in 2002 in a trial to see if it could succeed in decimating the bitou bush. The theory is that the moth

40

will simply eat every last scrap of bitou and then, when it has destroyed its own food source, simply die out. It remains to be seen whether it works, or creates yet more unforeseen problems, like the dreaded cane toad introduced to eat the dung beetle. The whole merry-go-round reminds me of the song 'There Was an Old Lady Who Swallowed a Fly'.

FIRST NIGHT ON THE ROAD

Sadly, we have no time for Angourie on this journey. We drive on with mixed emotions, speeding south with only a couple of days to make Sydney. I don't think we've ever driven beyond Yamba with the kids before and they are unaccustomed to the prolonged stint in the car, but the iPods work their magic and there are relatively few complaints. Four hours seems about their limit, though, and Kirst and I begin tossing around possible camp sites for the night. We eventually settle on the sleepy little coastal town of Urunga and its charming foreshore van park. It is $32 a night for a patch of grass with water and power, free wi-fi, toilets, showers and games room.

The manager directs us to a spot by the estuary that is almost devoid of neighbours. 'You'll get a nice cooling breeze down there,' he assures us warmly. The nor'-easter is blowing a gale, as if the tail of Cyclone Yasi is reaching this far south. It occurs to me that perhaps we are stuck down here so our kids don't disturb the genteel repose of the Grey Nomads who seem to favour this place, with their top-of-the-line Jayco Sterlings, their TV antennas and air-conditioning units. Still, it is a beautiful spot by a stunning waterway with nothing but green hills rolling off to the west. We have few complaints. North Queensland is expecting 300 km/h winds and seven-metre storm surges tonight, so Urunga is looking pretty good.

I embark on what will soon become a familiar routine:

unhitching the van, heaving off the sway bars, unscrewing the safety chains, securing the jockey wheel in place, putting down the stabiliser legs and attempting to level the van. It's a relatively quick set-up, and I try not to look like too much of a novice. Mercifully, we've been able to drive into our camp site forwards, and my no-reversing goal remains intact.

As I go about my tasks I can hear my daughter's voice, but I can't see her. I walk around the back of the car and there she is, hunched in a ball, towel over her head, gently sobbing.

'What's wrong?' I ask, giving her a hug.

'I want to go home,' she bawls.

Homesickness has already set in after just 350 kilometres and four hours. Alex is watching on, trying to imitate his sister's distress, but his heart isn't in it. I gently go through a long list of all the fun things we have to look forward to in the weeks ahead: being a flower girl in Sydney; seeing her grandma, uncle, aunts and the cousins in Melbourne; another wedding in Tassie, where she has another flower girl gig; more grandparents in WA.

'Do you really want to miss out on all that?' I ask. She ponders this, shakes her head, brightens a little, then Mum walks around the corner and she bungs it on again for another round of gentle consolations.

Vivi has begun her own blog of the trip, and shortly before our departure she wrote, 'It's a little hard to keep up with everything that's going on around me.' I realise the kids have no real idea what's in store, even less than Kirst and me, and that must be unnerving. Their entire lives have been played out in our home, apart from a few brief excursions, and 'driving round Australia' is as vague and unknown a description of what lies ahead as 'flying to the moon'. Before we left I'd joked with Kirst that if things went badly we could just drive to Crescent Head and back and tell them that was Australia.

We resolve to consult the kids more often on our travel plans and head out to the local Chinese restaurant for dinner to celebrate our first night on the road. Tomorrow is Chinese New Year, and the teenage waitress tells us her family is planning a celebratory feast. We enjoy a feast of our own: barbecued duck, tofu and vegies, special fried rice. Hundreds of lorikeets are suddenly audible every time the restaurant door opens, squawking madly in the Norfolk Island pines. I wonder what it is like to be a Chinese teenager in a little Australian coastal town, what sort of welcome they'd get in the line-up if they chose to paddle out. How multicultural is our Anglocentric surf culture, really? Of all the time I've spent in the surf, I can't recall seeing a Chinese Australian. All those Southern Cross, Aussie pride and postcode tattoos, the New Yobbo Patriotism worn in the form of Australian flag board shorts, beach towels and bandanas must be a little off-putting to migrant Australia. Or is surfing just not in their cultural expression?

I'm curious to see how localism will rear its head throughout this trip; territorial surf communities in far-flung places are often wary of outsiders and contemptuous of a surf media that threatens to expose their little slices of heaven. It strikes me as a similar attitude pandered too so shamelessly by our politicians in their scare-mongering over refugees: fear the intruder lest our paradise and coveted lifestyle become swamped by a tide of newcomers. In the meantime, we squander that paradise through our own fears.

GOOD MORNING, URUNGA

I wake up on our first morning on the road and step outside the van to be greeted by the most perfect dawn: the tide rushing out through the estuary, the sun creeping over the horizon, a magnificent timber boardwalk stretching out over the sparkling water to the ocean headland. Alex is quick to jump on his scooter and go exploring, and I struggle to keep up.

Noticeboards explain the variety of native wildlife teeming on land and water, the rare seabirds that nest here, the marine species thriving in these sparkling waterways. The place is a stunning interface of verdant forest and pristine coast.

An elderly woman strides past on her morning walk. 'How do you like Urunga?' she beams proudly. 'Beautiful, in't it?'

I have to agree.

An old timber building in the main street declares itself grandly as the 'Urunga Arts and Literary Society', founded in 1896. Might Urunga have been an enclave of bohemian hipsters way back then, a kind of nineteenth-century Bondi? The Boardwalk Café boasts itself as 'Urunga's favourite café', though it appears to have no competition for the title. A grand old pub offers panoramic views of the estuary and ocean. We are almost sorry to leave.

As we cruise out of the van park an elderly man waves us down, gesturing frantically. We pull over and discover we've forgotten to fold away the pull-out metal step of our van. Spot the novices.

A few hours' drive later and we're cruising through the stunning Myall Lakes district, looking for our second camp site of the trip. Kirst is lobbying for the rustic charms of a good old national park campground. The kids are more keen on the mod cons of the commercial van park. I spy a turn-off to Seal Rocks and the name resonates with some vague memory of a local surf spot that might be offshore in this howling nor'-easter. In a sudden, reflexive action, I take the exit – not a recommended manoeuvre when towing a seven-metre long van. The sign says it is only eleven kilometres, so it seems a gamble worth taking. The rest of the family aren't so sure. The afternoon is getting on and everyone is keen to stop, especially once the bitumen gives way to a heavily pot-holed dirt road.

It is our first time on an unsealed road, and our rig rattles and shakes its way down the bumpy drive to an uncertain end. Dark looks are gathering. You cross a definite line once you leave the security of the sealed road. The smooth ride and the sense of a civilised and ordered world suddenly gives way to a mounting feeling of remoteness as the forest encroaches. There will be no power here, no potable water, only basic pit toilets but, hopefully, a surfable wave. This tension between modern comforts and the most desirable surfing coast is likely to be a recurring theme of our trip – a tug of war between the domestic and the wild, where my family will be most safe and comfortable and where my surfing ambitions might be fulfilled.

Towards the end of the dirt road, as the forest thins and the coast comes back into view, we pass a modern, well-appointed van park. Vivi's mood brightens, but only briefly. We've also spotted the turn-off to the national park campground, and it's a few more kilometres down a rapidly deteriorating road that seems to take an eternity to navigate. The afternoon shadows grow longer, and we finally emerge into the most delightful bush campground nestled in a paperbark forest in a hollow behind steep sand dunes. It is heaven, and eighty per cent empty. The dirt driveways and camp sites are largely undefined; rough tracks crisscross the forest floor as dappled light dances through the canopy. It's a kind of free-range camping park devoid of neat, numbered rows and favoured by young European backpackers and groups of surfers in tents. We feel conspicuous with our modern van but find a cosy spot among the trees to set up camp.

Mum and Dad are delighted, the kids less so. 'I want to go back to civilisation,' moans Vivi.

The apparently simple process of setting up the van can be a great relationship tester. Kirst and I have been through the whirlwind Jayco induction process together, yet we recall certain aspects of our van's operation differently. I've become a bit cocky about our arsenal of modern equipment, but that cockiness quickly evaporates when I turn on the external tap to wash

Alex's feet and the torrent of water quickly slows to a trickle and then stops altogether. Have I filled the water tank? Do I need to switch the water pump on? I am clueless and grow testy when Kirst questions me on the particulars of our van's water system.

I'd been reluctant to fill our eighty-litre tank to capacity because of the extra weight, but I won't make that mistake again. As a Western, urbanised human, I take abundant drinking water for granted but quickly come to appreciate its primary importance when it is in short supply. Our camp site has just one tap with potable water, and it is a long walk to carry every available receptacle to stock up.

But there are a few little waves to be had – clean peelers in the protected northerly corner, flanked by a mighty headland and steep sand dunes. I'd almost forgotten about the surfing component to our trip, the purpose behind those finned, fibreglass objects strapped to the roof, with my focus squarely on ferrying my family down the east coast safely and coming to grips with the dizzying technology of the Expanda. After the sweaty exertions of the set-up on a hot afternoon, the kids are keen for the beach and Kirst encourages me to go for a paddle, God bless her. I know the swell is small and the wind nor'-east – if there is a wave to be had on this coast today, it will be here. I take the kids to the beach to cool off, a board under arm, leaving Kirst to finish the home-making in peace with an undertaking to tag-team the kids in a half-hour so I can have a surf.

It is a hot march up steep dunes and then a mad rush down through the bitou bush to leap into the ocean. We are instantly transported from the blazing afternoon heat by a bracing, icy chill. The water is cold for these climes, positively freezing to us Queenslanders, the result of upwelling – cold, deep-ocean water brought to the surface by the howling northerlies. I have my own emotional upwelling going on, subterranean feelings pushing to the surface as the winds of change blow away the veneer of our familiar world.

The kids and I swim happily, and I watch a handful of surfers enjoy the small, zippering peaks until Kirst appears over the dunes like the French Foreign Legion, liberating me to go ride some waves. This sometimes all seems like a mad, self-indulgent folly for a family man. How will I ever make it up to her? If she announces she wants to do the whole *Eat, Pray, Love* thing and go and find herself at an ashram in India, in the rice paddies of Bali or through cooking classes in Tuscany (with the family in tow, of course), there is no way I can deny her now. We will mutually support each other's dream. Feeling like a pact has been made, I jog up the beach to grab my board and consider where to paddle out.

There are small waves struggling against the stiff offshore, and a few game souls scratch into the fast, windswept peaks. This first surf is one to be cherished, despite the indifferent conditions – the culmination of months of planning and organisation, the final realisation of a distant teenage dream. I've done it. It seemed like a far-fetched notion as a kid in surfless, suburban Blackburn, to somehow fashion a lifestyle engineered around riding waves. It has been the elusive goal of generations of surfers all over the world for hundreds of years, from the ancient Hawaiians who were eventually badgered out of the surf by Bible-thumping missionaries, to the first pro surfers dreaming up the unlikely scam of travelling the world disguised as an organised sport.

And yet, here I am, on this vast stretch of beach with my family, a quiver of boards, a reliable SUV and a comfortable mobile home. With my laptop, mobile broadband and iPhone, I am open for business, living the dream. I remain as incredulous as anyone.

Yet, just as I'm marvelling at my good fortune, half a dozen blokes with boards appear over the dunes en masse, and my odds out in the inconsistent peaks suddenly look unappealing. Don't they know they are spoiling my moment? I've been spying an occasional right peak down the beach, but it looks quite lonely down there in the fading afternoon light. The odds seem unfavourable in a different kind of way – the probability of becoming a meal for a large marine creature. I figure I'll take my chances and trot down the beach, determined that this first session will at least be an adventure.

The occasional sets are flayed by a stiff offshore. Visibility is poor with the sea spray and the line-up shifty. I turn and paddle for a wave with one distinct thought: *this is the first wave of the trip.* I claw my way into it desperately, blindly, and leap to my feet, trimming unsteadily toward shore, weaving gingerly through the looping sections. The surf works its instant, magical therapy. The long drive and road fatigue are washed off in a moment. I find another, longer, bigger set and race through a couple of fast high-line drives, and try to clout the end section, falling off in a graceless, high-speed collision with the close-out. Yet, I am giddy with excitement in two-foot waves – a forty-six-year-old man playing in the ocean like a kid on a slippery dip.

Out the back I am all alone – the other surfers a good 200 metres to the north – when I suddenly start and freeze. A fin, coming straight towards me. I've never been particularly paranoid of sharks, can usually identify dolphins when I see them, but I find it impossible to distinguish this fin front-on. The next moment, another fin breaks the surface in that playful, rolling arc, and I know I am safe. Dolphins, more than a few in number, casually cruise through the swells as a set approaches. I turn and paddle, my heart relieved of its momentary terror. I can already feel my old life slipping away as the dolphins race me along the watery blue wall.

When I come in I bump into a lovely man from Amsterdam, who can't quite believe his good fortune at discovering this idyllic coastal campground few Australians even know of. He wants to share his excitement with someone: 'We just met another couple yesterday, and now we're hanging out and they said, "You have to come to this place we know."' He gestures at the beauty all around us, as if they've gained entry to an exclusive club.

That evening a fellow camper walks by our Expanda, regarding it admiringly as I grill polenta for dinner on our external barbecue under the roll-out awning. 'Been putting up your tent?' he quips, as if gently admonishing me for the opulence of our set-up. I almost feel guilty, for about three seconds, until I walk inside and fetch an ice-cold beer from our gas-powered fridge and sit down at our comfortable dining suite to enjoy dinner by solar-powered light with my family, before retiring to our comfortable fold-out sleeping quarters.

In the van parks we have one of the more modest abodes. In the campgrounds we are the ones basking in relative luxury. We exist between these two worlds, not entirely belonging to either, yet it's a space I am already beginning to feel comfortable in.

Almost everyone in the camp seems to light a fire on dusk, grab beers and sit around talking story and laughing. It is easy here to believe Homo sapiens is a highly evolved species who has perfectly adapted to its environment in such a way as to maximise its own happiness.

Steve, the camp manager, is a classic, jovial, baby boomer/ sea changer who's given up a car dealership to run this operation. 'We're still recovering from Christmas,' he reckons, when they had 400 people in the camp. Even this coming weekend they have 250 booked. We run into an old mate from home, Noel, who spends six weeks here every year and has logged up to five months at a stretch, fishing and surfing and generally chilling to a level most of us would find hard to fathom. He's a keen fisho, full of knowledge that my wife, determined to learn to fish over the course of our trip, is eager to soak up. She probes him with questions.

'I use old knife handles as lures. Learnt that from the local fishos. They know stuff you wouldn't believe,' Noel confides in hushed tones.

Our trip seems to have started well, yet new challenges lurk around every corner. We are packing up the next day when we fail to observe proper procedure for rolling up our awning and manage to get it thoroughly jammed. Neither Kirst nor I can recall the instructions we were given for operating the awning and have clearly, comprehensively buggered it up. One side has retracted faster than the other; the frame has become twisted and the sliding arms are hopelessly stuck. A sympathetic fellow camper tries to help to no avail. The kids are becoming distraught. Today is supposed to be an easy three-hour drive into Sydney, but we spend two hours struggling with the awning, and we can't exactly drive to Sydney with the thing hanging off the side.

I ask Steve the camp manager if he has any experience in such matters, and he shrugs apologetically. 'You've got the wrong bloke – I'm no kind of a handyman,' he confesses, which I imagine might be a bit of a drawback in his line of work. He offers us a can of WD-40 and trundles down half an hour later on his quad bike to see how we are getting on, just as we've doused the thing in the spray and managed to wrestle it into a closed position, lashed with a bit of rope. But it is truly stuffed. Vivi, eager for the big smoke and the excitement of wedding preparations, is inconsolable.

I just want to get to Sydney and deal with the thing later. Kirst, in her infinite wisdom, insists we find the nearest Jayco dealership and deal with it now. She gets on the iPhone, talks to Mathew at Jayco's Hexham branch in West Newcastle, and so we make an unscheduled detour to this heavy industrial zone, weaving through semitrailers and negotiating perplexing off ramps. But Mathew is a saint and quickly, expertly fixes the awning, giving us a lesson in its proper operation. He refuses all payment and sends us on our way within half an hour.

'Just get a few good waves for me,' he urges. I suddenly have developed a new respect for my wife's superior judgement. Kirst is an acupuncturist by trade, has worked in health resorts much of her adult life and has seen her share of spurious, self-appointed New Age gurus. 'People like Mathew are the real Zen Masters,' she observes wisely. She is right. Stuck out here in a hot, charmless industrial zone, Mathew sends people off on their dream holidays all day long, dealing with the hassles and grievances that inevitably arise with grace, patience and humour. It is a gift few of us could match.

We hit Sydney just in time for the Friday-afternoon school run and inch our way towards the Northern Beaches through a gridlocked North Shore. It takes an hour to get from Hornsby to Palm Beach, and the luxury of a shared Pittwater holiday rental with the in-laws for the wedding weekend. Our flower girl makes a quick recovery and happily immerses herself in the pre-wedding hubbub, relieved to see the end of the whirlwind first leg of our journey.

THE PIPE MASTER RIDES AGAIN

We dine with friends in Newport: Kirst's good mate Mary, who shares her birth date, and Mary's beau, Tom – Tom Carroll, that is, the two-time world surfing champion and big-wave charger who is showing no signs of slowing down as he approaches fifty. Their romance has blossomed through a shared love of long-distance ocean paddling. Mary recently tackled the dreaded Molokai Challenge, the world's most gruelling paddleboard race, over fifty kilometres of open ocean between the Hawaiian Islands of Molokai and Oahu.

I sometimes congratulate myself on the lengths I have gone in order to maintain the surfing lifestyle, but Tom makes me feel like a lightweight. He has had three trips to Hawaii this northern hemisphere winter, reacquainted himself with the giant waves of Waimea Bay after breaking his ankle there last year and surfed Pipeline again for the first time in seven years. A three-time Pipe Master, Tom set the performance benchmark at Pipe in the late 80s and early 90s with his celebrated 'snap' under the lip in 1991, sealing his position at the top of the Pipe totem pole. Rediscovering the intensity of the wave and the crowd there, long after his competitive peak, has been an illuminating experience, he reckons.

'You've got to be really decisive and really confident and really quick, or the crowd just feeds on you,' he explains over dinner. I am happy to take his word for it. I would be as likely to paddle out on a big, crowded day at Pipeline as go over Niagara Falls in a barrel.

Ten-time world champ Kelly Slater had dragged Tom out to some crazy, secret spot in huge surf, and he engaged in a spot of Outer Reef tow-surfing for good measure. At an age when many men's greatest physical exertion is their golf swing, Tom continues to push the limits. He is planning to undergo a titanium knee replacement so he can keep doing what he does, even as his body wears out and he is shooting a new season of *Storm Surfers*, a cable TV show he stars in alongside his old sparring partner and fellow maniac, Ross Clarke-Jones. He tells me of recently surfing the wildest surf he's ever seen – raw, mountainous seas in open ocean off the north-west coast of Tasmania. Our bold expedition around the Australian coastline suddenly seems a fairly sedate affair, and yet Tom is envious of us – he's always wanted to do the great round-Australia thing – and wonders whether we might rendezvous somewhere further south in the weeks ahead. His energy and undimmed enthusiasm for the surfing life in all its rich variety is infectious and inspiring.

There is much about modern surf culture that appalls and disheartens me – the relentless commercialism; the aggro young bucks butting heads and beating chests; the misogyny; the often narrow, Anglo monoculture in the water; the slavish fashion consciousness — but folks like Tom reassure me that wave-riding remains a fundamentally noble pursuit.

THE WEDDING FURNACE

Extreme weather events seem to be a feature of our journey. The wedding transpires on the hottest day in Sydney for fifty years, and our flower girl almost wilts, suffering heat stroke in the relentless afternoon sun at Palm Beach. The bride and groom, another surf-obsessed Tom and the lovely Claire, look radiant despite the scorching heat and guests melting around them. The nuptial celebrations stretch long into the night, over-looking the stunning beauty of Pittwater. It is hard to credit that this largely pristine environment exists on the outskirts of Australia's largest city.

After a few short days in the big smoke, we are ready to plunge further south. We have a month scheduled for the Sydney-to-Melbourne coastal leg, four weeks to cover a dis-tance only a little longer than the one we have just driven in three days.

This south-east corner of the country still holds a few surfing secrets and, with abundant time to explore, I can hardly wait.

3

AT THE FEET OF THE MASTER

I HAVE SET OUT on this journey with one very specific fantasy in mind – and it has nothing to do with the Grey Nomad Swingers' Circuit. Instead, it involves an idyllic coastal camping ground, a quality surf break at the end of a bush track, some convivial fellow campers, playmates for the kids, and a contented wife reclining in a hammock reading a good book. And ample, unhurried, guilt-free surf time for my good self. If I achieve this only a handful of times on our journey, I figure I will be doing well. And the NSW South Coast is somewhere I have pegged as a likely setting for my fantasy.

To improve my odds of finding my surfing Shangri-la I have adopted a guru of sorts, a man who knows more about Australian beaches than anyone, chiefly because he has set foot on every one of them – all 12,500. His name is Professor Andy Short, and after a lifetime in academia at the top of his chosen field in marine science, he has recently retired to his very own idyllic South-Coast retreat. Even in retirement, Prof Short can find himself summoned to Sydney at a moment's notice by the NSW Planning Minister to consult on coastal management policy, jumping on a light plane at the tiny local airstrip and winging his way to speak his rare brand of common sense to the pollies and bureaucrats.

I've known of Prof Short and his impressive life's work for years. He is a co-founder and driving force behind the National Surfing Reserves movement, a remarkable volunteer effort to recognise Australia's great surf spots and enshrine them as places of special recreational, environmental and even spiritual significance. Somehow, he and his partner in this ambitious endeavour, Brad Farmer, have been able to negotiate the complex maze of government bureaucracies, community sensitivities and legal hurdles to successfully have a dozen or more Australian beaches declared National Surfing Reserves. The movement has now gone global, with Malibu and Santa Cruz in California, Manly in Sydney, and Ericeira in Portugal formally recognised as World Surfing Reserves, with more locations to follow.

And so our South-Coast run has become a kind of pilgrimage, an opportunity for me to go and sit at the feet of the master. I contacted Andy before we left and he warmly invited us to come and visit him at his property. We could stay in his 'shed', he assured us, and he'd pull out his maps and notes and share his accumulated wisdom. But we have several hundred kilometres of the NSW coastline to negotiate before enjoying the benefit of that wisdom, with only my own vague recollections from a few brief trips south twenty years ago to guide me.

I experience relief and a great soaring in my heart as we exit Sydney's confounding maze of tunnels, tollways and traffic jams. The onset of the verdant, rolling hills, the exquisite conga line of coastal villages and picturesque beaches encourages belief in a benevolent creator. The sheer spectacle of the Grand Pacific Drive (surely named after its Victorian cousin, the Great Ocean Road) suggests that benevolence can even exist within the Department of Transport and Main Roads. And the stunning Sea Cliff Bridge, surely designed and built to excite the creators of automobile commercials, takes coastal motoring to new levels of sexiness – even if you are taking that sweeping bend over the ocean with a one-and-a-half-tonne caravan behind you.

The whole giddy experience is only tainted by the intrusive dictates of our sat-nav, a technological advance that cares nothing for romance or beauty. I've never driven a car with satellite navigation before and, despite its undoubted convenience, the vocal overlays do take some getting used to. We dub our navigator 'Satnita' to make her spooky omniscience seem more human. It's a bit like having a second wife – a particularly cold, officious, monotone, know-it-all second wife who makes her disembodied proclamations from somewhere within the dashboard, whether they are needed or not.

We have falling-outs, too. Satnita is only interested in the pragmatic approach – there is no concession given to the most scenic route to a destination, only the most direct. If I ignore her dictates and take some recommended tourist route, she icily reconfigures her directions before resuming her duties.

Still, nothing can spoil my mood as we rise and fall, twist and turn through one coastal village after another, round a bend to be greeted by yet another panoramic coastal vista. These unfashionable seaside towns live in the considerable shadow of their larger, industrialised neighbour, Wollongong, and so have never attained the desirability of, say, Noosa Heads or Pearl Beach. Yet for me, the rather drably titled towns of Austinmer, Coledale and Thirroul possess more unaffected charm than many of their more glamorous rivals to the north. Old Art Deco pubs, timber cottages, semi-derelict warehouses, classic beach-front surf clubs, all nestled around cosy bays and beaches – all the area needs is an influx of sea changers and celebrity chefs ready to open eateries and art co-ops and galleries. With some snappy marketing, it'll become the next Sydneysider holiday hot spot. But I'm sure the locals prefer their coast just the way it's always been.

THE BATTLE OF SANDON POINT

Nowhere are the issues of coastal development and the whole sea-change phenomenon brought into sharper focus than at Sandon Point, near the once-sleepy South Coast village of Thirroul. Here, the developer, Stocklands, has built a large, master-planned residential estate despite determined local community opposition for over a decade. The Sandon Point Aboriginal Tent Embassy has kept up a constant vigil at the site for ten years, claiming Indigenous heritage and environ-mental issues have been ignored. The conflicts between local sensitivities and the aspirations of newcomers to the area are graphically illustrated in the contrasting websites of the earnest Save Sandon Point community group, and Stockland's glossy representation of the development. The discovery of Aboriginal burial sites, concerns over flooding issues and traffic problems have all failed to halt the project, though it has been down-scaled substantially. Meanwhile, the developer's website boasts how its design will 'enhance and compliment Thirroul's exist-ing vibrant town centre' and extols its 'seamless integration with the local community'. Feelings are clearly running high in Thirroul. The Aboriginal Tent Embassy and a community picket line have been hit by arson attacks.

Interestingly, the real estate marketing makes no mention of the adjacent famed point break of Sandon Point, even though its proximity to a world-class wave would normally be a selling point. Could it be because when you google 'Sandon Point' it brings up a litany of protests and controversies surrounding the development? Instead, it goes by the innocuous name of 'McCauley's Beach', a search term that brings up only the developer's own promotional material, including a slick 'community website', which purports to keep the community up to date with all aspects of the development, including a detailed page devoted to 'Indigenous consultation'.

All this reflects a drama being played out round Australia's coastline, as city dwellers flee the congestion and social ills of urban life in search of the ideal coastal community, yet risk bringing many of those same ills with them in the process. This 'suburbanisation of Coastal Australia' is now a hot topic for demographers, academics, urban planners and government departments as they struggle to plan for this large-scale coastal migration. The Australian Bureau of Statistics projects that from 2002 to 2022 populations will increase in key coastal centres like Victoria's Surf Coast by as much as 71 per cent. In Margaret River, WA, the increase is an estimated 64 per cent, and in Maroochydore, Qld, it's 58 per cent.

The *State of the Environment Report* (2006) prepared by the federal Department of Environment and Heritage points out:

'Although sand mining along the eastern Australian coast was a major source of conflict between conservation and mining groups from the mid-1960s through to the mid-1990s, the main pressure on coastal locations in the twenty-first century is arising from both residential development, tourism pressure and the synergistic interaction between these two pressures . . .

Ironically, tourists or individuals fleeing "overdevelopment" can in fact lead to the next "discovery" and initiate the next phase of development . . .

'People are continuing to move to the coast to live, and the cumulative impacts of this trend are now apparent in some coastal areas. If this trend continues, we risk further damaging the natural and cultural values and characteristics of the coastal environments that historically have made coastal living so attractive.'

The free-and-easy, open Australian coast enjoyed by Jonnie Grant and Rick Miller in the original *Surfari Highway* is not to be taken for granted.

These issues are brought into sharp relief for us as we head south from Wollongong, trying to find a camp site for the night. Parts of NSW's South Coast are close to becoming one long suburban ribbon – Wollongong and its surrounds have almost become an outer suburb of Sydney – and there are only small pockets of the wilderness I had been so eagerly anticipating. We eventually settle on Killalea State Forest, on the outskirts of Shell Harbour, just south of the Gong. This sounds like an idyllic camping spot, close to two quality surf breaks and enshrined as one of Prof Short's National Surfing Reserves. Yet, as we follow Satnita's curt directions off the Princes Highway and make our way through the dense new housing estate, we begin to have our doubts. Can a state forest and a National Surfing Reserve really reside somewhere within this lobster pot of bland, tightly packed McMansions? We are almost ready to turn around and assume Satnita has lost her way, if not her mind, when we come upon the entrance to the state forest, the houses literally crammed right up to the fence line.

While the campground itself is pleasant enough, and in close proximity to two choice surf breaks, the looming presence of a dense suburbia and the sound of careering trucks along the adjacent highway does somewhat dilute the wilderness camping experience. This bit of coast was once the chosen retreat of champion surfer Mark Occhilupo as he attempted to recover from a bout of depression that had left him overweight and reclusive in his childhood home at Kurnell, in Sydney's south, in the early 90s. Back then, it was somewhere he could find refuge and surf away from prying eyes as he attempted to rekindle his surfing career and personal mojo. This South Coast surf sanctuary helped Occy resurrect his illustrious surfing career, culminating in him winning the world title in 1999. These days, he'd have had trouble finding his way to the beach, and when he did he'd discover a tight pack of new 'locals' clogging the line-up.

I'm reminded of the animated kids film *Over the Hedge,* in which a group of forest animals awaken from their winter hibernation and are horrified to discover a vast housing estate where their forest used to be, bounded by an apparently endless, towering hedge to keep them out. Could Australia's surfers wake up one day and find themselves feeling like those forest creatures, desperately trying to find a green corridor to the beach through a maze of human habitation? Australians have always considered free and open access to the coast as a birthright, unlike the US and many European countries where private beaches and entire residential enclaves monopolising the foreshore are commonplace. It is an ideal that will be sorely tested in the years ahead.

I also recall a family holiday to Italy a couple of years ago, to visit my mother-in-law. It was the first time in my life I'd been told a beach was 'full' in any language, a concept completely alien to me – and it happened twice. In the first instance, we had strolled into a charming cove by the ocean on the Tuscan coast and selected two vacant sun lounges that were arranged in neat rows along the narrow strip of beach. A courteous attendant informed us that, not only were the lounges taken, but the entire beach was booked out – we would have to go elsewhere to swim and sun ourselves. On another occasion, we were stopped on the approach to a popular beach and told it was not possible to drive any further as all parking within a ten-minutes' drive of the coast was full. Our only option was to park there and wait for a bus. If you couldn't park within a ten-minutes' drive of the beach, I wondered how you'd go finding a spare patch of sand or ocean. We turned around and went elsewhere. It was a shock to realise that exclusive access to the coast could be attained through dumb luck or privilege.

But for now our little coastal perch in the Killalea State Forest is ours for forty dollars a night, which is fairly steep as camp sites go, with no on-site power or water. But with light fading and suburbia's incandescent glow all around, we aren't about to quibble. We are all a bit ratty by the end of our first day back on the road after our Sydney layover, still coming to terms with the rigmarole of uncoupling the van and setting up camp. Moods are brittle.

There is a number to call to contact the park management, but we select an empty site and set up our van before the light fades. 'You're not in site fifty-three are you?' a terse female voice asks when I eventually ring. 'I have someone coming in to site fifty-three tonight.' I walk towards the site marker, trying to discern the number, praying it isn't fifty-three, but of course it is. Actually, we're on a small flat area behind what appears to be site fifty-three, I explain.

'Ah yes, fifty-three-A,' she declares, knowingly. 'Well, the man has a boat and he might want to use that space.'

My heart sinks. I'm not about to move, and fortunately the mysterious boatman never shows up, though I have palpitations each time I hear a car for the rest of the evening. This isn't quite the remote beach experience I have been imagining. It's too late for a surf by the time we've pitched camp, but I have a look anyway, as a rising south swell sweeps into a gorgeous crescent bay in the golden light of sunset. I resolve to get up for the early and investigate.

Dawn reveals a tight local crew gathering in the car park, who paddle out and dominate the punchy, shifting beach-break peaks. I feel conspicuous as an outsider and park in the second tier, not wanting to presume to take a front-row spot. But this only serves to give me an elevated position where I feel on show, and I sense unfriendly eyes following me as I retrieve a board off the roof and suit up.

It is four to five feet with plenty of push, and the locals are good, solid surfers but friendly enough. I exchange nods and small pleasantries, and find a few stray peaks. It feels good to get in the water, for the family road trip to once again become a surf trip. I'm a bit stiff from the driving and camping, but the muscles soon warm up. This is only my second surf of the trip, and I am beginning to understand how challenging it will be scheduling surf time. It is a sobering realisation – it was actually easier to go for a surf at home. I hold that confronting thought at bay and savour the moment.

I notice a fleet of new arrivals pull in, including a minibus and trailer, unpacking a flotilla of longboards, bridge tables, folding chairs, sun shelters and assorted club contest infrastructure. It is a weekday, so I can't imagine it's the local boardriders club. I note the crew cuts, the tattoos, the muscled physiques and naval stickers on the cars and trailer – it's a Navy surf contest setting up. The times have a-changed. The real estate developers and the armed forces have found Occ's old secret spot.

The local crew appear unfazed by the intrusion, but it is going to get brutal out there with a longboard contest underway so I cut my losses, finding a long right to take me in. It will have to be enough until we head further south, settle into one of those remote national park camping grounds and get down to business. The forecast is indifferent – this little southerly pulse and then not much else in sight – but I try to remain buoyant. My time will come.

KILL THE PIGS

Back on the road, my next herculean test soon reveals itself. I am going to have to learn to tolerate the sound of Angry Birds as I drive. The wisdom of the iPod Touch purchase is beginning to look suspect. Our children's favoured diversion, this hugely popular app has brought up over 100 million downloads, a figure growing by 1.2 million a day. At that rate, within a year, if Angry Birds players formed a nation only China and India would be more populous. For the handful of people unfamiliar with this astounding pop-culture phenomenon, this game may appear trivial and nonsensical upon first viewing. I scoffed, too, when I first encountered it – until I found myself eagerly taking part. Now the children have become thoroughly smitten, and so I drive on to the sounds of projectile birds whistling through the air, the crash of timber, stone and glass towers and the mortal groans of expiring pigs. If you are one of those curmudgeonly spoilsports who questions the worth of the skills such games develop, just remember this: when we find ourselves at war with a tribe of militant pigs, barricaded inside precarious towers, with only exploding birds and a slingshot to defend ourselves, you'll be grateful for those of us who have prepared for battle.

WELCOME TO BOODEREE

I am about to have my own opportunity to shape impressionable young minds on our next stop as we head towards the scenic environs of Jervis Bay. Here, I am booked in to address the students of Vincentia Public School on the peculiar existence of the freelance surf writer. It strikes me as another odd turnaround in the perception of surf culture by our public institutions. Once a surf writer would have been shooed away from the company of school children like a peddler of narcotics. Surfing was a road to delinquency, drugs and the ruination of all future prospects for gainful employment. And writers weren't much better. Combine the two and you had a character of Timothy Leary-esque moral danger. Yet, these days, I am welcomed as an unlikely source of motivation to encourage school children to embrace the quaint ol' pastimes of reading and writing. As our educators become gripped by panic over literacy levels in our younger generations, anything that holds the promise of cultivating an enthusiasm for written language is worth a shot – even the dubious literary merits of surfing biographies. And, so, I've been asked to come and speak to the children of Vincentia about my previous books on the lives of surf champions Rabbit Bartholomew, Mark Occhilupo and Mick Fanning. The fact that none of these characters showed great enthusiasm for formal education, that they often eschewed class time in favour of wave-chasing, didn't seem a deterrent.

And so we head for the stunning Booderee National Park on the shores of Jervis Bay to set up camp for the night, within striking distance of my speaking engagement the next morning. Now this is a camp site more to my liking. You will sometimes hear the views expressed that our coastline is in danger of being locked up by national parks and native-title claims, that special interest groups are trying to deny average Australians free and open access to their own land – the right to ride trail bikes or graze cattle or shoot animals or cut down any trees they take a dislike to. This is, of course, utter nonsense. If our coast is to be 'locked up' in any sense, I'd rather it was in the name of preventing destructive activities and preserving native habitat and returning some places of special Indigenous significance to their traditional owners. Booderee National Park is a wonderful case in point.

The land was handed back to the Wreck Bay Aboriginal Community in 1995, changing its name from Jervis Bay National Park back to its original, Booderee. Jervis Bay was named by

Lieutenant Richard Bowen in 1791 after British Admiral John Jervis, 1st Earl of St Vincent. The town of Vincentia was also named after the Earl, despite the fact that he never set foot on Australian soil. Why we are still stuck with placenames given arbitrarily by British sailors to please their military masters or aristocratic financiers back home is an odd quirk of history. Booderee means 'Bay of Plenty' in the Indigenous Dhurga language of the region, an altogether more appropriate name by any measure.

We pull into the Booderee visitors' centre mid-afternoon and are booked into a camp site by a friendly and efficient young Indigenous woman. It is a busy afternoon and she deals with a couple of French tourists and a Canadian before me, swiftly and cheerily, in between taking calls from various aunts and uncles. The fact that I find this a somewhat novel experience says much about the way we are used to the portrayal of Indigenous Australians. I consider myself one of the converted when it comes to the grand theme of 'reconciliation', yet it strikes me that this simple encounter – handing over a small amount of money to an Indigenous community to camp for the night in a pristine beach setting – is a significant one. It provides a heartening model of how traditional ownership can provide an economic base and employment opportunities for Indigenous communities, and how past crimes of dispossession can be redressed. We are bombarded with images and stories of dysfunction, petrol-sniffing youths, abuse and neglect. It seems that focusing a little light on those communities that function well in a caretaker's role might bring us closer to real reconciliation. Yet there are no television crews lining up in Booderee to document the healthy, functioning Aboriginal community here as they enjoy an uninterrupted relationship with their traditional lands – surfing, fishing, caretaking the land and educating visitors on their culture. It is a story you will never see on *Today Tonight*.

Booderee is home to the only Aboriginal-owned botanic

gardens in Australia. The eighty-hectare Booderee Botanic Gardens showcase local Aboriginal use of native plants and the coastal flora of south-eastern Australia, where visitors can learn about bush tucker and the medicinal properties of plants. The Aboriginal community is based at nearby Wreck Bay, also well-known to surfers as home to a particularly notable wave, variously known as Aussie Pipe, South Coast Pipe, Summercloud Bay, Wreck Bay or, simply, Pipe, for its similarity to Hawaii's famed Pipeline. It was the scene of Australia's first Indigenous surfing contest in 1993, and a proud lineage of local Indigenous surfers have dominated the line-up for years – Ray Ardler, Nick Carter, Steve and Jeff Williams. And it is where some of the South Coast's great goofy-footers refined their act – Terry Richardson, Mark Occhilupo and Robbie Page.

Wreck Bay was originally named for the frequency with which ships came to grief on its reefs, leading one reader of *The Sydney Morning Herald*, in December 1886, to implore masters to 'see what can be done to render a voyage less like a scheme for manufacturing widows and orphans than it is now'.

Wreck Bay presents its own challenges for the visiting surfer. It requires a very precise and infrequent combination of wind and swell direction to work. It's a long walk in and its remote bush car park is notorious for break-ins. I've been advised to take all valuables out of my car and leave it unlocked to avoid having windows broken or locks forced. While this keeps numbers down in the water, it makes life difficult for the long-distance traveller. With an enormous amount of valuable gear stuffed in the car, and arriving at our camp site late in the afternoon, I am faced with an increasingly frequent dilemma: the conflict between responsible family commitments and selfish surfing urges. With Wreck Bay very possibly firing, I can deposit my family at the camp site, empty the car, leave Kirst to set up camp unaided and then hightail it straight to Pipe and possibly get a quick surf in before dark. Thus, my family and vehicle will be left to uncertain fates. I decide to do the responsible thing and stay to set up camp. In every way, it is the right and easier option, but it still gnaws at me.

The campground is gorgeous, nestled among eucalypt forest teeming with wildlife. Each site is separated by vegetation to give privacy but offers the mod cons of hot showers, electric barbecues, picnic tables and shelters. It is a little tight manoeuvring a van through the forest setting, and I struggle to reverse the Expanda into our allotted spot. A neighbouring vacant site looks a little easier, so I decide to give that a go but still have trouble. This is my first time reversing into a tight camp spot, and I am failing dismally. A kindly, older gent, Col, takes pity on me and explains that there is a site recently vacated by a friend of theirs who had to go home sick, with easy access for a van. Col warns us that our allotted site is adjacent to a group of young campers who were a little noisy last night; we might find the spot next to them more peaceful. Is this the Grey Nomad Swingers' Circuit recruiting new members? He looks harmless enough and I am quickly growing frustrated trying to reverse the van, so I accept his kind offer. Soon we're ensconced in a cosy camp site next to a charming retiree couple who have adopted our children like surrogate grandparents, offering to cook them sausages for tea. Most Grey Nomads have grandkids somewhere whom they are missing desperately, and kindness, attention and food is the holy trinity of grandparenting. It seems I've been too harsh on our seniors. 'He reminds me of my grandson,' Col's wife, Joan, beams, moving in on Alex with a look common to smitten grandmas the world over. Alex relishes the attention and is soon under their spell at the very mention of the word 'sausage'.

We unload the kids' bikes and they are away, free-ranging through the park in a manner that would make Lenore Skenazy cheer with glee. If they aren't playing up to the cooing of the retirees, they are amusing the rowdy youths at the other end of the campground, and having no less success in exercising their charms. Now *this* is what I'd hoped for. Here, we can be hands-off parents, enjoying time to ourselves while increasing our children's socialisation skills.

A short walk through the bush, across a small creek and past lolling kangaroos is a beach with allegedly the whitest sand in Australia – though I'm unsure how that claim might be tested. Inside the bay the water is calm and perfect for the kids, and I give myself over to the children's delight in this vast, natural playground. There are few joys to rival watching your children at play outside, splashing in the water, clambering over rocks, investigating rock pools, marvelling at the teeming wildlife.

In the morning I head off to Vincentia Public School for my speaking gig, just like any other working dad. It is an easy ten-minute commute through the eucalypt forest from our campground into the local village. The school has put up a little welcome sign for me, and the kids swarm, firing questions and smart remarks as I arrive. This visiting author/speaking business is still pretty new to me, but it will help pay the bills while we are on the road. I like the idea of encouraging youngsters to enjoy reading and writing, to embrace the power of story. I give them a brief précis of each of my books – Rabbit's far-fetched teenage daydreams of a pro surfing tour, Occy's remarkable resurrection from being a couch-bound recluse, Fanning's determined rise above adversity. The binding theme is the power of dreams, and how others' stories can inspire and help us believe that our own dreams are attainable. My current circumstances, for example, travelling the country with my family funded by the specialist vocation of surf writing, would have once seemed entirely preposterous to me back in suburban Blackburn.

At the end I invite questions and there are the inevitable ones: 'Have you met Kelly Slater?', 'What's the biggest wave you've ever ridden?' A rosy-cheeked girl down the front is waving her hand frantically, so I give her the nod. She beams up at me. 'Will you ever give up on your dreams?' she asks. She's so sweet and bright-eyed and innocent; she can't be taking the piss. I tell her, no, I think not. I suddenly feel a weight of obligation fall upon me, as if I have just made a lifelong pact not to take a well-paid job as a media advisor or advertising copywriter. It is an oddly heartwarming moment.

I wave goodbye to the children of Vincentia Public School and return to camp, committed to moving on far too soon. We have a date further south with Prof Short before he disappears on his next jaunt to the city to sort out the state government's coastal management policies, and it is a window I can't afford to miss.

The hurried pace, though, is beginning to take its toll on the children. Vivi, after all the excitement of the Sydney wedding, is developing a severe case of homesickness. I normally wouldn't be a huge fan of the overly quaint tourist town of Berry, with its trinkets, gourmet delis and over-priced collectables catering to busloads of retirees on day trips from nearby bowls clubs. But as a pit stop on a grey, wet day with testy kids, it hits the mark. My cynicism is washed away by the effect the local clock shop, Cuckoo Corner, has on our girl. One look at the crowded shopfront of twee timepieces and Vivi has disappeared inside, transfixed by the swinging pendulums of fake pine cones, the music boxes, the little wooden birds and elves and god-only-knows-what-else that ticks and chirps and chimes on the shop's walls. The kindly shopkeeper indulges her fascination without pressuring us to make a purchase. As Vivi gently cranks the tiny handle of a miniature music box and softly sings along to the delicate strains of 'You Are My Sunshine', some clouds shift and her mood brightens. 'You make me happy, when skies are grey,' she sings softly as the shopkeeper compliments her on her voice. 'You'll never know, dear, how much I love you. Please don't take my sunshine away.' It feels like a gentle turning point in her whole attitude towards our journey.

LIFE'S A BEACH

I don't mean to idealise anyone's circumstances, but on my list of 'surfers who got it right', those individuals who've achieved a high degree of work/life/surf/family balance, Professor Short rates highly.

For one, both his wife and his daughter have been students of his. To raise a child to adulthood and have them still be prepared to sit in a classroom and listen to what you have to say strikes me as quite an achievement.

Andy and his wife, Julia, have only recently retired here from Narrabeen, on Sydney's Northern Beaches. The coastal forest setting was jointly chosen so he can indulge his love of surfing while she can have her horses. Here, they can ride through the forest to the beach, as fine a recipe for marital harmony as I have come across.

We arrive late one afternoon to their sprawling property, and I'm wondering how comfortable we'll be in their 'shed'. On the outskirts, a converted freight container has been fitted with a makeshift verandah. Is this the shed? A fine new homestead-style dwelling is the centrepiece of seventeen acres of eucalypt forest, a model of sustainable design, with banks of solar panels, rainwater tanks, a dam and a solar-heated water system that is circulated through the house as a form of heating in winter. The trees cleared for building the house have been neatly chopped and stacked as several years' supply of firewood.

The shed turns out to be an enormous steel hangar fitted out as a comfortable guesthouse with loft-style bedrooms upstairs and a fully equipped kitchen, bathroom and lounge downstairs, along with a ping-pong table, rows of Driza-bone jackets hanging on hooks, old surfboards and all the accumulated flotsam from decades of travelling the Australian coast. A mounted Australian map on one wall is covered in different coloured pins to indicate all the locations Prof Short has visited, and they form a virtually continuous border around the entire length of the coast. It's as if we have arrived at some themed tourism museum honouring the great Australian coastal road trip, or a specialised training facility for precisely the type of journey we are undertaking.

The Shorts prove gracious hosts, Andy barbecuing for us on the verandah while I quiz him on his academic career and the inevitable questions about his favourite beaches in the country. He promises to break out his maps and photo albums after dinner, and I feel like I've stumbled upon buried treasure. Andy is a goldmine of fascinating statistics: the average length of beaches in Australia is 1.2 kilometres. There are only three beaches in Australia over 200-kilometres long – the modestly titled Eighty Mile Beach in Western Australia, Ninety Mile Beach in Victoria and the Coorong in South Australia. The beach with the greatest wave energy in the country is Strahan, on Tasmania's rugged west coast, with an average daily wave height of three metres and a highest recorded wave height of eighteen metres.

Andy studied geography at Sydney University before discovering he could combine his academic career and recreation. 'When I realised you could study beaches it was even better, because I was very heavily into surfing then.' He subsequently completed an honours year on beaches and won a fellowship to continue his studies anywhere in the world.

'Everyone else before me who had received this fellowship had gone to Oxford or Cambridge, and of course I decided to go to Hawaii.' He laughs.

He studied Maili Beach on Oahu's infamous and underprivileged Westside, notable because it receives both north swells in winter and south swells in summer. 'So from winter to summer the sand would move from one end of the beach to the other. I was studying the impact of seasonal variation of north and south swell on the beach,' he explains. 'That's a nice break – it's like a low-key Margaret River down the southern end, a nice left and a shorter right, but not as big. Makaha was just up the road, a lovely spot.'

It was the late 60s and Andy experienced none of the hostile localism that the Westside has become notorious for since. 'There weren't many people around. I never had any trouble with the locals. Those were the early days, the 60s – Peter Drouyn was going over there, Midget was still surfing there. Rabbit and them hadn't arrived yet. On the North Shore I used to surf Laniakea, Haleiwa, all that. I was never into the big stuff. I went out at Sunset once and got cleaned up. I used to surf Waikiki a lot, down the Queens end. At a good size it's a beautiful wave out there. Ala Wai Canal is a good wave. It was good, a good time,' he says with obvious fondness. He stayed in Hawaii for three years before moving to the US mainland to complete his doctorate.

The research project that came to define his career began in the mid 80s when Surf Life Saving NSW approached him to create a database of every beach in the state. 'I started looking at all the New South Wales beaches. They thought there were around 180. It turned out to be 755.'

It took three years and numerous field trips by land and sea to finish the NSW project. 'The whole thing evolved – the methodology, the best way to approach it. In those days, no one had ever done it before. I had to develop the whole methodology.'

As idyllic as it sounds, the project was not without its hazards. 'We did one boat trip from Mallacoota up to Kiama. We were going to go to Sydney but we hit these horrific nor'-easterlies and gave up at Kiama. I got hit by the propeller at Tura Point, and the next day I had to go into Tathra to get stitches in my heel.' Their boat flipped in heavy seas at Narooma, but Andy escaped with nothing worse than grazes and a lost pair of Ray-Bans.

In 1990, Surf Life Saving Australia asked him to make the study national, and I get the distinct impression by this point that Prof Short didn't require too much convincing to continue his survey. 'That provided the catalyst. I had a reason to do it, a research project around it,' he says keenly. Some might have been daunted by the prospect of surveying 20,000 kilometres of often remote coastline, but not Andy. 'You've just got to keep at it . . . I started doing state by state, basically. I'd done a lot of work in South Australia already. The first state I finished was Victoria. I did a lot of that by boat, all the Great Ocean Road, the Twelve Apostles by boat, all around Wilsons Promontory by boat. I did Queensland – we went by boat from Burnett Heads to Cook-town, and then from Cooktown round to Karumba, Borroloola to Darwin, and then Wyndham to Broome all by boat, just two of us. They were really good trips.'

I need to type the names into Google Maps to find half these places and appreciate that there were vast ocean voyages between some of those most remote points in Australia. The final pieces of the puzzle were put in place during an epic family road trip, towing a caravan around the country in 1991. They covered around 35,000 kilometres in eight months, Julia doing most of the driving while Andy consulted maps and a compass, taking notes in the passenger seat, long before GPS and iPhones were standard equipment. They suffered just one flat tyre and one flat battery the entire journey.

Did he discover many waves? 'Not many, because you're only at these beaches one day. I found some across the southern coast, but I wouldn't know what their names were. Over at Cactus, South Australia, I think I found some of the ones that they surf now – west of Cactus, a bunch of breaks over there. You've got to know where to go; you've got to know the ter-rain. There are all these tracks going everywhere.'

I tell him of my coastal campground fantasy – the mental image I have of a beachside camp site in an unspoilt setting, where the wife and kids are happy and I can surf out the front to my heart's content. Are there many of those locales?

'No, not many,' he says bluntly.

He cites the well-known desert campgrounds of southern and western Australia as some of the best family-friendly surfing locations, and I am left wondering if I've been too optimistic about this trip and my prospects for unrestricted surf time. But I am also beginning to understand that a trip like this is about much more than chasing waves.

The Shorts' youngest daughter, Pip, was five when they did the trip. She has recently finished her own studies in marine science and is visiting her parents during our brief stay, working out whether to take a job waitressing at the local restaurant while she plots her next career move. 'I still mention that trip in every job interview I go for, what a formative experience it was,' Pip tells us.

It suddenly dawns on me: it is almost exactly twenty years since they embarked on their trip. Our youngest is five. I begin to understand why they are so helpful and hospitable.

Andy is full of wise words and advice, not all of it geographical. 'Try and feed the children in the car so when you stop they can just exercise,' he suggests.

Andy is due off at 6.30 the following morning to fly to Sydney for a meeting with the state minister, so I try not to keep him up too late, hurriedly poring over his maps and scribbling down recommendations. He shares a lifetime's experience exploring the Australian coast in one evening, and I couldn't feel more grateful.

I ask if he ever has trouble getting taken seriously in the scientific community, if there is any stigma around beaches as a legitimate field of study.

'Everyone wants to live on the coast,' he replies. 'They want to build there, and they need to know about it. People just envy you. The number of times they say, even in the media, "the man with the best job in the world . . ."'

Before we're done we get on to the thorny subject of climate change, what he makes of the science and how Australia's surfing coast might fair. His views on the topic are some of the most even-handed and sensible I have heard.

'The climate is changing; there's no doubt about that. What is less predictable is how fast it's changing and what the impact will be of those changes. The temperature is rising both in the atmosphere and the ocean. All the climate boundaries are going to shift pole-wards, so northern Australia is going to get more tropical stuff coming down from the north, like we have had this season. More rain from the north in summer, less rain in the south in winter, because those southerlies will be pushed further south. That's changing already. The ice is melting; the sea level's rising. It's all happening.'

It all sounds fairly alarming, until Andy strikes a reassuring note of simple wisdom. 'The thing is, we have the luxury of knowing it's happening and planning for it, if we want to plan. If we want to,' he repeats, seriously. 'We can choose to plan ahead in coastal management, flood-plain management, agriculture, if we want. Some countries will, some won't, but it's not a bad thing. Climates change all the time, but it's just at a faster rate than it has been in the past. But we have time on our side to plan and mitigate the impacts.'

Purely out of self-interest, I ask whether a surfer in his thirties or forties, who could live for another fifty or so years, might notice significant changes to their local surf spots in their lifetime.

'Probably not, no. In a lifetime you might see a bit of a change. It will be in sea level for the surf spots. It will be more like high tide. Places like North Narrabeen, that's good – Northy breaks better on a high tide than a low tide. Some breaks are going to start petering out; some other new breaks will get better. It's going to be a trade-off.'

And with that, it's time for bed. Dragging a retired man out of his South Coast retreat for a day of earnest conference in the city seems a tough call. I hope the politicians are paying attention.

The next morning, Julia and Pip take up the hospitality where Andy left off. Leading Vivi on one of their horses and installing Alex and me on their quad bike, they take us on a delightful trek through the forest to a deserted beach. The horses roll on the sand and splash in the shore break while we soak up the kind of coastal solitude we've been craving. The swell is tiny but it hardly matters. We're finally encountering the great, unspoilt Australian coast – and I couldn't wish for more.

But with a date with friends at a van park in Tathra, it is again time to move on too soon. I am learning an important lesson in road trip scheduling. This early stage has become filled with fixed appointments and, while they are all welcome and pleasurable on their own, the combined effect has made our journey less spontaneous, more structured, than I'd imagined. Even so, as we plunge further into what I consider the Far South Coast, my mood lifts. There seems to be another stunning coastal vista around every bend, another magnificent spotted gum forest, yet more quaint villages, tantalising glimpses of ocean and beach, stunning rivers and estuaries, ramshackle old farm houses and sheds. I drive on, mesmerised, blissfully ignorant of the tests Tathra will soon throw up.

WAKE IN FRIGHT

Reg and Amanda are dear friends who live in the Alpine village of Thredbo, and so we've arranged to rendezvous at their closest coastal escape. Their kids, Arkie and Joey, are similar ages to ours, and in every way they are ideal holiday companions. They've booked a cabin at the Tathra Family Holiday Park on the beachfront, and we have a site for the Expanda nearby. Our host is none other than former Ol' 55 frontman, veteran rocker Frankie J. Holden, prominently advertised as the park proprietor, though he fails to make an appearance during our stay. He packs the vans in tight, though, and it's not cheap at fifty dollars a night – the place is almost full, so he must be doing all right.

One old-timer knows why it's so busy here: 'All the weather up in Queensland has got people spooked, so they're all heading south instead of north,' he reckons.

Within minutes of setting up, a man carrying a foam box full of ice and oysters walks by our site, selling the fresh local shellfish for ten dollars a dozen. Soon we are happily installed on Reg and Amanda's cabin deck, scoffing oysters and sipping cold Coopers Sparkling Ale.

The surf is small, but the weather fine, so we swim, push the kids into waves on their softboards and beachcomb. It is a perfect weekend until dusk on Saturday, when a menacing presence cruises into the van park like a circling shark. The maroon Falcon has trouble written all over it, and the van park residents hold their breath as they wait to see where the vehicle, and the finger of fate, will come to rest. Our boy, Alex, has been making a song and dance at bedtime, and we seem to have developed a bit of an exclusion zone around us in the otherwise crowded park. I fear it will prove our undoing as the dreaded Falcon pulls in behind our van, a metre from where our children will be sleeping, and its five occupants spill out, each swilling warm stubbies of Melbourne Bitter. Three young men and two largish women immediately set about arguing and fumbling over the complex business of erecting their tent, almost coming to blows. Our hearts sink.

The two older men look like cartoon thugs straight off a wanted poster – one thick-set with close-cropped red hair, square jaw and permanent scowl, the other hollow-cheeked with a scraggly beard and trucker's hat pulled low over his shifty eyes. They pull a large slab of roo meat from an esky and begin carving rough chunks off it to barbecue. I start thinking about that classic Australian novel and movie *Wake in Fright*, in which an ill-fated teacher attempting to escape a tiny redneck town inadvertently falls in with a gang of crazed, drunken roo shooters.

I try not to pre-judge our new neighbours, but the hallmarks of boganism are on full display. We hit the local pub for dinner, and after a disappointing meal we return to a quiet camp site. Our neighbours are gathered about the communal barbecue area, happily grilling their roo steaks and sculling their warm beer, and so we retire, hopeful that the evening will pass without incident.

Those hopes are dashed around 1 am as the stillness of the van park is shattered by blood-curdling screams and vicious threats. With our fold-out bed ends, the kerfuffle in the adjacent tent sounds like it is happening right there in our van. It's a terrifying way to be woken up. Vivi is having a sleepover at the cabin with Arkie, and the boys are bunking in with us. Mercifully, they sleep through the whole drama. Kirst and I are not so fortunate.

I venture outside and ask them to keep it down, and one of the women stumbling about in the dark assures me they will. A short time later, hostilities resume. It goes on like this all night, like a delicate Middle East ceasefire – an uneasy calm shattered by a sudden outburst of aggression, then retaliation, more threats, then a fragile peace. At one stage, by 5 am, not having slept a wink, I have the number of the local police station punched into my phone and am ready to report a domestic violence incident when calm seems to be restored. By this stage, they have been drinking for at least twelve hours and any efforts to intervene seem certain to end in a dust-up. Another outbreak of threats and abuse ring out – someone is vowing to cut another's throat, someone else is going to kick their boyfriend's head in. I've had enough and stumble out to the office, ring an after-hours bell and wake the manager. It is not Frankie J. Holden but a remarkably composed woman who hears out my complaints and vows to send her husband down. I'm not sure it is a wise move to wake up the entire park with the commotion that will surely result, and so we agree to deal with it in the cold light of a new day. When I return to our site all seems calm again.

Kirst takes the boys to the cabin when they awake to spare them any unpleasantness. And then, remarkably, one by one, the bogans emerge over the next couple of hours as if all is right in the world. One goes fishing. Another showers. The management arrive in their golf buggy and give them their marching orders. They are polite and agreeable, the red-headed thug laying all the blame on his girlfriend, who he explains 'is a bit crazy'. The other campers stifle cheers as the maroon Falcon finally cruises out of the park.

I find myself inordinately rattled by this isolated incident, and it throws a profound funk over my mood. I'm disappointed that the magic spell of friendly strangers and idyllic settings has been broken. They say you can't pick your neighbours, and that applies especially in the concentrated confines of a van park.

A NEW MASTER APPEARS

My faith in humanity is restored by a charming old bloke who looks like he's put down roots at the Tathra Family Van Park. He has a little hand-painted sign out the front of his van that reads 'Fishing rods and reels repaired (sometimes)' with either an 'open' or 'closed' sign pinned to the larger sign with a clothes peg. The sign is decorated with sweet little drawings of a crab, a shark, a half parrot/half fish creature labelled a 'parrotfish' and a stick figure fisherman. Kirst is keen to take up fishing and a friend has kindly donated an old surf rod and reel for this purpose, so I am dispatched to make this kindly old gent's acquaintance, check our rod and reel in for a service and acquire some of his wisdom.

I wait until the open sign is pegged up and knock on his van. He shakes my hand firmly and introduces himself as Doug McKenzie. I explain our pitiful situation: as complete novices, we haven't a clue how to operate our old surf rod. He takes a look at it and seems quite pleased with its old-school reel but scratches his head at the prospect of training me up from scratch. 'Geez, where do we start?' he mutters.

He decides he'll grease the reel, then shows me the basics of its operation, and tells me to come back the next day. When I do, he has prepared several intricate loops of fishing line, called 'ends', upon which to attach hooks and sinkers in a carefully balanced arrangement. He shows me his collection of 'poppers', small colourful lures decorated with feathers, and he recommends we acquire a few of our own.

I ask him how much I owe him, and he assures me it is a complimentary service. I protest, arguing that a man has to earn a living, which sends him into a hearty chuckle. 'I don't do this to make a living, I do it to help people out,' he says.

This simple statement stops me in my tracks, being the antithesis of what I've come to expect from the prevailing culture. My wife bakes him a batch of pikelets as a thank you and Vivi delivers them. I call on him later as he is stuffing some into his mouth with delight. There is something about this small exchange that feels enormously uplifting, like an antivenin to the 'Night of the Bogans'.

Suddenly, it seems everyone in the van park is being inordinately nice to us, as if they witnessed the night's horrors and are directing their sympathies our way, a kind of *esprit de corps* and recognition that, at such close quarters, we all better get along.

There are other small details of van park life that I find variously charming and challenging. There's no room for pretence – you see old ladies waddling to the communal bathrooms in dressing gowns and slippers in the morning, glimpse their voluminous underwear hanging on the communal clothes line, hear your neighbours' arguments, their coughing fits and farts. The children have their own unique perspective on the fine details of this lifestyle. I escort Alex to the bathroom one day and, as he's washing his hands, he comments thoughtfully, 'Don't you reckon a lot of caravan parks have pink soap? Pink soap is pretty popular.' And he is dead right.

DON'T SLAM CARAVAN DOORS

Another day, and the van is starting to feel a bit small. The kids squabble over lunch and I start to lose my cool. Viv snatches some prized morsel off her mother's plate, Kirst quips, 'That's the sort of thing your father would do,' and I take extravagant offence, storming out of the van and slamming the door to register my ill-temper. This proves to be a poor idea: the door swings closed with such force that it pushes past the door frame and wedges itself shut so firmly that it cannot be budged. I'm intent on stomping off to the beach like a petulant child until someone comes looking for me, when I hear the children's screams from the van and realise I have trapped my entire family inside. I turn on my heels and start trying to prise the door open, my silly flash of anger now thoroughly backfiring as the children howl their distress at their incarceration. When I finally get the door open, I realise I am going to be in the penalty box for a while for this one.

Valentine's Day is almost upon us and, though retail options are limited in Tathra, I find a little beach-themed gift shop with blue-and-white striped everything, lots of shells and driftwood and washed-out watercolour seascapes. After much perusing, I settle on a gift box of scented soaps and some little envelopes of petals and potpourri that you slip in drawers and cupboards to make them smell nice. It's the sort of thing I might have bought Mum for Mother's Day at the school fete when I was a boy, but I figure it's the perfect gift for life on the road in a van, a little hint of womanly luxury. I complement it with the one witty card I can find among all the naff, florid greeting cards.

It is a simple cartoon of a male peacock with its plumage on full display, spectacular feathers spread out high and wide before an unimpressed peahen. The peacock is saying, 'What do you mean, no?'

The nice old gent in the shop, a classic sea changer – supporting his own wife's dream of the pretty seaside gift shop and café, I'd wager – wraps up the lot and ties it with silver ribbon. Unable to delay my redemption a moment longer, I promptly present it to Kirst as she watches our boy charge the local skate park on his scooter over the road. We are not usually big on the crass commercialism of Valentine's Day, but I'm a desperate man. I watch her open the card and read it, a smile spreading across her formerly stern features. She is suitably touched and I sense my door-slamming episode is, for the moment, forgiven. Vivi is also impressed by my choice of gift, but not so impressed by the need to get back in the car and resume our road trip.

'Can we put one in the car with us?' she asks of the scented envelopes.

'Why?' I ask, puzzled.

'Because the car smells of boredom,' she grizzles. At such times I have to remind myself that she will, like Prof Short's daughter, Pip, thank her father for this one day.

It gradually dawns on me, though, over the next several days as we head south from Tathra, that Kirst's little fragrant parcel travels back in the van. Conversely, when we are occupying the van, the parcel seems to have been mysteriously transferred to the car. Eventually, I query this curious phenomenon, and Kirst confesses that the synthetic perfumes of the soaps and the envelopes are too much for her. She is touched by the thought, but they are making her feel nauseous. Eventually, we have to throw them out. I feel as if I have given her an old fish carcass.

SAD NEWS FROM HOME

As we head out of Tathra we receive the shocking news that a house has burnt down in our street back home. Our elderly neighbour, Norm, was killed in the blaze but somehow his invalid wife, Gwen, was rescued. The entire street was awoken by the blaze in the middle of the night and tried to come to their aid, but the house was engulfed before they could get Norm out. No one yet knows how it started. We receive emotional texts and messages from our other neighbours. The couple has no children and few close relatives. I've never so much as laid eyes on Gwen in twenty years of living a few doors away. It strikes me as remarkable that I have grown closer to some of our camp neighbours within the space of a few days than I did with this old couple in two decades. I cannot begin to imagine what it must be like for that poor old lady, already suffering ill-health, to wake up in a hospital bed, her whole world – her life partner, her home – gone in an instant. It contrasts so sharply with our own happy circumstances that I feel momentarily guilty.

How is it that we can live side by side with people in the suburbs for years without knowing them? We live close enough to annoy each other with petty disputes over noise, parties, trees, leaves and parking, but at a distance where we can avoid any real intimacy or sense of shared community. In the close quarters of van parks and campgrounds, at least we can't ignore each other and are forced to revisit a dormant state of tribalism or village life, seated in fivesies circles or round camp fires. The desire to help, the offers of advice and assistance, the sharing of knowledge of the road ahead or the loan of equipment, is another heartening feature of park life.

We vow to get to know our neighbours better when we get home.

THE ROAD TO KNACKLEHHO

We have plunged deep into the South Coast now, further than I have ever gone before. The Sydney crew rarely venture south of Ulladulla. Beyond Moruya is too far for weekends. Now we are almost closer to Melbourne than Sydney. I've had a little camp-ground recommended to me by three independent sources, and I feel as if it is calling me. It's not exactly a secret spot but sensitive enough that I don't want to use its real name. In my blog I refer to it by the fictitious name of Knacklehho, and locate it only as 'somewhere in the south-east corner of the country'. Even this is enough to attract a string of hostile emails from aggrieved, alleged locals, one threatening to break my legs if I am unwise enough to pay another visit. I am shocked, to be honest. This place seems far enough away from major population centres for crowds not to be a worry. In fact, my biggest problem surfing here is finding someone to share the waves with, to lessen my growing shark paranoia. Bounded by national parks, I wonder who qualifies as a genuine local here anyway, apart from the long-dispersed Indigenous population.

But I have other things troubling me as we dive deeper into the South Coast. One thing I've been looking forward to about this trip is spending more time with my kids. Dropping them at school and kindy in recent times, I'd been beset by some powerful pangs, as if there was something fundamentally unnatural about jettisoning them for most of the day to have relative strangers look after them. I missed them and wanted to make the most of these early years when they still liked hanging out with their dad. There was, of course, the small matter of my work to be tackled, a living to be earnt, but the idea of having copious amounts of unstructured time just to hang out and be together thrilled me. Until I experienced the reality: being with your children all day is exhausting. What's more, they don't necessarily *want* to spend their every waking moment cradled in the bosom of the family unit, either. The first thing they do when we pull into a new campground is turn on their 'kid radar', scanning the surroundings for anyone within a few years of their own age. Once they locate someone, they latch on instantly, become immediate best friends, get on their bikes and disappear.

Don't get me wrong; we are what I'd call a happy family. We love each other – delight in each other's company most of the time – but forced into the close confines of an extended road trip and a caravan, we all start craving our own personal space. This manifests in some spectacular meltdowns from the kids when they feel they aren't getting this space, or that their social options are too limited. It also plays out in some rather appalling episodes of ill-temper from their father.

I have to confess I'd grown accustomed to my quiet office retreat. On the road, forced into day-long child management, my teeth grinding hits new peaks. I can rationalise it as the stress of trying to work out of a caravan, with no quiet space to do my thing and no structured work parameters to quarantine my time away from the family. It is hard. My wife is accustomed to the ebb and flow of long, uninterrupted days with the kids, the way their behavior is influenced by sleep, diet, their level of comfort with their surroundings. To me, the days are an unfathomable rolling brawl of more or less constant, outrageous demands from the children, relentless complaints when they don't get their way, increasingly loud harassment for me to accede to their wishes, and an inevitable dummy spit from one or more parties when it all becomes too much.

Things come to a head at Merimbula Woolworths as we cruise the aisles, stocking up for our first protracted journey into a national park camping ground. While Kirst darts about with stunning efficiency, collecting the makings of enough healthy, palatable meals to sustain a family of four for the best part of a week, I push the trolley and weather continuous heckling from the children to include more sugar, salt and fat-based products in our diet.

By the time the shopping is done my head is ready to explode. We decide to treat ourselves to lunch at a little Asian noodle café before we plunge into the Spartan deprivations of bush camping. A plate of pad thai is a welcome indulgence in an otherwise trying day, and I want only to enjoy my meal in peace. Alex, however, decides he will spend his time harassing me for a turn on my iPhone to play the dreaded Angry Birds. Foolishly, I agree, trying to buy myself some peace on the strict condition that he does nothing else with it. During an earlier session, he nearly wiped my entire photo gallery and lost half my apps while randomly hitting buttons. But he can't help himself. Even with the phone in his grasp he keeps peppering me with questions and demands, wanting to buy new games or demanding to know what other apps are for. I give him a couple of warnings, but when the harassment continues I . . . just . . . snap.

Wild-eyed and hyperventilating, I snatch Alex up and carry him, screaming, to the car, where I strap him into his booster seat and proceed to hurl my accumulated grievances at him: he is ruining our holiday; he must learn to do as I say; I won't stand for it.

I'm not proud of the tirade. My child is bawling, gasping for air, complaining that he feels sick. I suddenly realise how terrifying I must appear to this small boy, but my anger is still not spent. I try to moderate my tone. I tell him that when we get to our camp site he and I are going for a long walk to have a big talk. This idea seems to completely terrify him. I leave him strapped in his seat with the windows down, straight out the front of the café, while I return to finish my lunch, but I can taste only my own guilt and anger. This is not how I'd imagined things.

⌒

Calm seems to be restored as we continue south and descend further into increasingly thick eucalypt forest. We find our turn-off and head towards the coast. This road doesn't even appear on Satnita's little screen and our car appears as a small red triangle forging its way through a dense patch of green. I like the image. Our mobile phone signal disappears. We are, officially, off grid. It is a long, winding, bumpy drive and the kids are growing restless again. At such times, it is easy to become sceptical about what waits at the end of the road.

It is a Monday morning, so we are hoping any weekend crowds will have moved on. You can't book sites here; it's simply a matter of turning up and hoping for the best. We pass a couple of cars on the way out and they wave cheerily, even though the Jayco barely leaves room for them to pass. Few vans venture into these places; the Grey Nomads generally stick to the van parks and sealed roads, but this is what we've come for. Sunlight dances through the canopy of stringy bark. We have slowed to forty and our rig feels like a big old ship swaying amid choppy seas, bouncing between potholes.

I start to imagine that we'll have the place to ourselves, roam this pristine coast nude for a week like latter-day hippies. It's a good half an hour before we finally pull into the most perfect bush camping ground, but I'm surprised to find about a dozen groups taking up most of the camp sites, nestled between twisted banksias and towering gums. This is the hard-core tent-and-trailer crowd, and we feel conspicuous with our modern van.

The camp site is teeming with wildlife. Roos lounge on grassy patches. Birdsong rings out through the trees. A large goanna trundles off towards the bush as we pull in. I stop and urge the kids to look before he disappears. We wind down the windows and marvel at the lizard's slow, regal gate, as if it's straight out of a May Gibbs book. There are gasps of appreciation from the back seat. This is more like it.

We cruise a lap, looking for a spot to accommodate us, and eventually pull over and park. I've already learnt prospective camp sites are best surveyed on foot. There are no obvious spaces that will fit the van, many of the sites are for tents only, with parking a short distance away. And all the spots with vehicle access seem to be taken. It is nearly 4 pm and we are late arrivals, pushing our luck to still find room at the inn. Within minutes, we have met a friendly woman who informs us that she has been coming here for thirty years, establishing her primacy in the subtle campground hierarchy.

There is one empty site in prime position, with plenty of room for the van and a fire already made up in the fireplace, with newspaper and twigs neatly organised. It is marked 'Camp Host Site'. I assume it is for the ranger when he comes by. We ask the woman and she says it is only used during Christmas, Easter and school holidays. We can have it, she insists, and we don't need any convincing. I get myself in a now customary jam trying to reverse into the plum spot on the site, pinning the van up against a fence on the other side of the dirt road. In the end, I have to unhitch the van, put on the jockey wheel and ask Kirst to help me push it back into position. I bluntly recruit a passer-by, a foreign man with bald head and spectacles. He seems a bit surprised at being so hurriedly recruited to our van-positioning exercise.

We quickly set up camp while the kids go off to make

friends. It doesn't take long. Alex is racing round the camp site on his bike with a gang of mates within minutes. Vivi and some girls amuse themselves with a collection of small plastic farm animals – no batteries or screens involved. We meet parents, uniformly friendly country folk dining on freshly caught fish. I know we are near the Victorian border when one of them says 'grouse', and he is being completely sincere.

Alex and I go for a walk to check out the beach, while Kirst transforms the van's interior into a comfy home. We head down a bush track towards the ocean, and Alex asks me if I am going to yell at him again. While I have been swept up in the delight of our new surroundings, I realise he is still feeling some trepidation. I try and reassure him that I'm not going to yell at him anymore, as long as he listens to me when I talk calmly.

'Do we have to go for a big walk?' he asks, anxiously.

Not now, I tell him. We end up having a lovely time at the beach – swimming, laughing, beachcombing – and the earlier unpleasantness seems forgotten. In a quiet moment, I tell him I'm sorry for yelling at him and pick him up to give him a cuddle, but he doesn't want to talk about it, wriggles free and runs off along the beach. There's very little swell, but I barely care, feeling only relief that we have made it to the kind of coastal sanctuary I have been craving, perhaps just in the nick of time for the restoration of family harmony. There is a hint of a wave at the southern end of this small cove, a rocky point with tiny crumbling whitewater barely capping on the reef. If I can have all this, *and* surf, I will have found my Shangri-la.

We return to camp and it's Kirst's turn for a beach walk. Inside the van, everything is miraculously in its place, the kids' beds made up, complete with stuffed toys carefully placed beside their sleeping bags. I crack a beer and get the guitar out for the first time, settle into my camp chair and begin the process of decompression. At last, everyone's needs are being met. I sip my stubbie and strum my guitar contentedly.

Our closest neighbours are a top-notch lot – Dave and Don and their families are from Marysville, south-east of Melbourne, an area decimated by the Black Saturday bushfires of 2009 that claimed forty-five lives out of a population of 500 and destroyed ninety per cent of the town's buildings. Like good country folk, they don't play up the horror of those awful events, offer only that they were lucky to get through it with loved ones and property unscathed. They are keen fishermen, equipped with numerous rods, kayaks and a small collapsible dinghy. Each day, the two men disappear before dawn or head off on dusk, and more often than not return with a brace of fish. Don is also a keen nature photographer.

Vivi decides to make a fairy shrine out of found objects, complete with a little hammock that she hand-sews, topping it off with a canopy of interwoven herringbone fern and a string of little flags. We light a fire, prepare a simple meal and get the kids to bed early. My naive plan is that I will write at night, when they are asleep, but without power here my laptop is running on battery, and so I have to write in short, sharp, concentrated bursts, carefully rationing the battery power, hoping it outlasts my inspiration. By day, we loll about the camp while the kids play and get into an easy rhythm.

CARAVANNING AS A PATH TO MINDFULNESS

I take the longboard for a paddle in ludicrous one-foot close-outs, and I don't mind a bit. Surfing and the family road trip, I'm learning, are both exercises in the gentle art of being present. The practical necessities of transporting, feeding, clothing and providing shelter for a family of four on the road for eight months is a kind of Zen art requiring constant awareness – caravanning as a path to mindfulness. Everything needs to be done with awareness – where you put things so you can find them again; how you use space in the van; the ritual of hitching and unhitching; driving long, unfamiliar roads while towing a large weight. Some days, all of this can feel like a daunting exercise, an onerous responsibility, like you're the captain of a ship bobbing according to the whims of the ocean.

The prize, however, is great – entry into a parallel universe in which all the old rules and assumptions fly out the window. It is the other Australia, beyond mortgage stress, traffic gridlock, terrorist threats, consumer madness, shock jocks, tabloid television, politicians' cynical sound bites, where all the crap and static of the modern world fades into the background and the real vibration of this land can be felt. And when you turn down the sound on all that contrived nonsense and turn up the sound on the land, it's a beautiful symphony.

What brings on this bout of philosophising? Well, a dear friend of mine gave me a parting gift of some of his 'home-grown', cultivated in the lush tropical highlands of the Gold Coast hinterland. Though I rarely indulge these days, I have been saving it for just such an occasion, to savour it in a pristine natural environment. Once the children are in bed, I roll one out and enjoy it in front of the open fire. Soon, I am on my hands and knees in the dark photographing Vivi's fairy shrine with my iPhone, marvelling at its intricate detail, congratulating myself on producing such an enlightened child. Kirst regards my reverie with amusement before retiring to bed and leaving me to it.

At some point in the following days, as the blissful camp site works its magic on me, I realise it has been quite some time since I have even seen my own reflection. I catch sight of myself in the mirror behind the cupboard door in the van, and wonder who this wild, disheveled, unshaven bush man is staring back at me. The weather is cool, and by immersing myself in the ocean most days I barely miss showering. I wear the same clothes for two or three days. It is, in a word, liberating. Strangely, at the same time, I am becoming fastidiously houseproud of our little van. Lacking a broom, I get down on my hands and knees and sweep the floor with dustpan and brush, even attending to the groundsheet outside our door, chastising the children if they forget to remove their shoes before entering.

I feel alive. The bush speaks to me. Days unfold however we choose, making them up as we go. In the midst of my bliss I almost dare not wish for waves, as if such ingratitude might break the spell. Even so, a tiny pilot light of hope flickers. After several mornings of pointless early surf checks, I trot down the beach at dawn and am greeted by solid but lumpy beach breaks closing out the length of the cove. At the southern end, small waves splutter and roll down the point, barely resembling a surf spot. I race back to the van, don my wetsuit, grab my board and paddle out in the beach break close-outs, wanting only to feel the ocean's energy and find a few short rides amid the random peaks. And then as I paddle back out I spot a set looming at the point. From the side view in the water, I watch in awe as it peaks and throws into an inviting, almond-shaped tunnel. I scratch my way closer to investigate and soon another set peaks and peels down the point. The closer I get the better it looks, and before I know it I find myself in the midst of a proper, full-blown session on an empty point break. It's not perfect, a bit like Angourie with too much south in the swell, a little fat and pushing wide of the reef. But there are fast, rearing drops, big bowling sections and the occasional smaller one that hugs the Point and runs cleanly for a hundred metres or so. It is astonishing.

I have it to myself for maybe half an hour before four blokes from Phillip Island paddle out, apologising profusely for inter-rupting my solitude. I don't mind a bit – with schools of fish and a pod of dolphins zipping through the line-up, I am actually glad for some human company.

The conditions hold up for the next couple of days, and I happily take my fill – sometimes alone, sometimes with a handful of fellow campers, often with dozens of dolphins sharing the waves, crisscrossing under my board as I ride. It may well stand as the high-water mark of my surfing life. Then the swell gradually evaporates, and it is time to move on.

To find one's goal at the very beginning of a quest is a delightful but unsettling surprise. What can possibly match or exceed this? Will everything that follows be rendered an anticlimax?

I'm ready to take my chances . . .

4

TURNING THE CORNER

As we approach the Victorian border, I am gripped by a particular excitement: this is the confluence of my childhood and adult surfing lives.

I grew up surfing the rugged Victorian east coast, where there always seemed to be swell and we just waited for the wind to turn offshore. Weather systems roared through like steam trains, and you'd see them coming on the synoptic chart, moving through from WA to South Australia to Victoria, that trailing edge of a high-pressure system delivering the longed-for northerlies. It could blow onshore for days on end, Antarctic sou'-westerlies that reduced the ocean to an unsurfable mass of whitecaps. These storm systems would whip up the swell, then the offshores would groom them into some sort of order, usually providing a one- or two-day window of quality conditions before the swell subsided and the cycle would start over with the approach of the next low.

It was a revelation to move to Sydney as a 21-year-old to discover the east coast conditions were so radically different – the ocean generally smooth and the winds a gentle offshore, most mornings at least, unless there was some dramatic local weather event. The missing ingredient was swell, and the east coast surfer waited patiently for an obliging offshore low to bring the desired wave energy to the party. The ocean here was altogether more tame, orderly and predictable than its southern counterpart. With the east coast's vast surfing population, every swell was eagerly anticipated, forecast, analysed, the precise angle of its direction carefully calibrated to gauge where it might deliver the most pleasing waves. They were almost diametrically opposed worlds.

Surfing was largely a rural experience in Victoria. Once I left school, got my driver's licence and landed a job at a newspaper, I worked weekends and had days off during the week. If conditions looked promising, I'd drive an hour or more down the coast and surf all day, returning home in the evening without having spoken to another soul, only a few disinterested cows as witnesses to my wave-riding. Surfing was a detour from my everyday routine in which I donned a suit and tie and caught a train to the city with all the other commuters, a secret, indulgent double life. In Sydney, surfing was on your doorstep, something you did before work, in your lunch break, even after work if you resisted the lure of the pub. The beach was somewhere you called in as you went about your daily business, a bustling village square where people came and went all day.

As a southern surfer, I had never ventured as far east as the New South Wales–Victorian border, had no idea what secrets its rich national park coastline held. As an east coast surfer I had never ventured this far south, rarely travelling beyond Ulladulla from Sydney to the true far South Coast. The surf media paid little attention to this remote corner of the country. There were few big-name surf breaks, no local surf stars or home-grown surf businesses or media. It was, in almost every sense, an unknown.

WHAT'S IN A NAME?

Even the placenames are foreign to me. Ben Boyd National Park? Who was Ben Boyd, and what had he done to deserve having a national park named after him? The park brochure is vague but respectful, describing Mr Boyd as a 'nineteenth-century entrepreneur who played an important role in the development of the local area'. I ask a friendly park ranger about Mr Boyd and he is more candid: 'He sounds like a bit of whacko. He founded Boydtown in his own honour, and he was a big fan of slavery.'

Wasn't there an Indigenous name for the region they could have used instead, I ask?

'We looked into that but nobody can agree on it,' he reckons. This strikes me as both odd and sad, but it did whet my appetite to find out more about Boyd.

Benjamin Boyd, it turns out, was a spectacular failure whose dubious business dealings left debt and unfinished building projects in his wake. A former London stockbroker, he sailed to Australia on his yacht, the *Wanderer*, in 1842 with ambitious plans to make his fortune. He had already floated the Royal Bank of Australia and raised some £200,000 in capital, which he wasted no time in grandly investing in the new colony. He quickly became one of the largest landholders on the South

Coast, launched three steam ships and three sailing ships into service up and down the coast, and made an aggressive entry into the local whaling industry. Short on cheap labour, he sailed into the South Pacific gathering slave labourers for his various enterprises. And he founded the settlement of Boydtown in his name. With visions of it becoming a major city, he built a church, brick storehouses and a hotel. He also commissioned a lighthouse, which became known as Boyd's Tower, but it never operated as such and became a look-out tower for whalers.

It all went horribly wrong for Boyd when one of his ships was wrecked and he lost a resultant lawsuit with his insurance company. His slave labourers were returned to their island homes after protests by local labourers and humanitarians, and his investors became disillusioned with his grandiose plans. He left the colony in the *Wanderer* in 1849, £80,000 pounds in debt and headed for the Californian goldfields. He faired no better there, and in 1851 he sailed to the Solomon Islands, where he went ashore with a native to shoot game and was never seen again. It is assumed he was killed soon after he landed, but his body was never found.

I like to think of Boyd as an early ancestor of modern-day corporate cowboys like Christopher Skase and Alan Bond, ambitious empire-builders who bit off rather more than they could chew. And if Bond can have a university named after him, despite a stint in jail, then why can't Boyd have a national park, a decaying ghost town and a street in Neutral Bay, Sydney, named in his honour?

The nearby town of Eden, a former whaling port, has an even more colourful history to impart. Its fascinating whale museum documents the long-running, now defunct, whaling industry that was once the town's lifeblood. Local lore has it that a pod of killer whales assisted the whalers by herding their prey into Twofold Bay, like cattle dogs rounding up livestock. They'd then alert the whalers by slapping their tails and, as reward, would receive a share of the catch. The skeleton of 'Tom', the leader of this pod of killer whales, is still on display in the museum. The Davidson Whaling Station was the hub of whaling operations for three generations of the Davidson family, the longest running shore-based whaling operation in Australia, a dynasty that only ended when Tom and his pod of killer whales passed away. Modern political correctness might judge the whalers' exploits harshly, but there is no questioning their bravery – jumping into longboats at a moment's notice, often in the dark of night, and rowing out to sea to hunt enormous whales with simple harpoons.

Eden today is a curious mix of new and old, still celebrating its whaling history long after it's been deemed unseemly elsewhere. The local bait and tackle store is distributing 'Stop the Extreme Greens' bumper stickers on behalf of the Shooters and Fishing Party. Meanwhile, a young dreadlocked Greenpeace representative patrols the main street with a clipboard, recruiting members. The young man who serves us at the local café is sporting black nail polish and heavy eyeliner, like a young Robert Smith from the Cure, a display of alternative fashion sense that must take some nerve in a small country town.

We push further south, across the Victorian border and on to the fishing port of Mallacoota. We mark the crossing of the New South Wales–Victorian border by bursting into a succession of AFL football club songs. The winding drive into Mallacoota, bordering the spectacular Croajingolong National Park and the intricate, meandering waterways of Mallacoota Inlet, is magnificent. I have composed a jingle for the local tourist authorities before we've even arrived in town:

I just want to sing a long,
When I'm in Croajingolong,
Why don't you bring along,
A smiling face . . .

The children howl me down in protest, insisting I am taking my obligatory daggy-dad humour to uncomfortable extremes.

Mallacoota has attracted my interest for several reasons. It's the scene of a twenty-year-long environmental battle to save the main local surf break, Bastion Point, from a massive breakwall and boat harbour development that would destroy the wave. It is also the hub of the abalone industry, a favourite seafood delicacy of mine since childhood, which is normally prohibitively expensive because of its demand in Asia. The local abalone divers are rumoured to harbour some other rich secrets: numerous mysto surf breaks only accessible by boat.

While the town centre consists of only a dozen or so shops, it does feature reputedly the largest foreshore caravan park in the southern hemisphere, its 700 plus camp sites enjoying majestic ocean and inlet views. Here, Grey Nomads from all corners of the country congregate, gathering in circles of camp chairs at fivesies each afternoon to share drinks, nibbles and fishing tales. Local restaurants offer seniors' discounts, while fishing charters and river cruises do a brisk trade. All this is much as you'd expect of a popular seaside holiday town.

What is less expected is the culinary find of our trip so far – the wondrous delights of Lucy's Café, where a Chinese couple produce their own homemade rice noodles and dumplings, grow their own vegetables and combine it all with the area's fresh seafood. The result is some of the most delectable, authentic Chinese cuisine you will taste this side of the Xianchou Province. Lucy is an officious, bustling presence in the open kitchen, producing bowls of noodles and plates of dumplings amid clouds of steam. It is an eccentric little business that started its life as a second-hand bookstore, somehow acquired a video hire library on the side and then mutated into a busy café while retaining its former revenue streams in overcrowded backrooms.

The Lucy's Café crew of locals reminds me of a cold-climate

Byron Bay thirty years ago, or an Australian coastal version of the US television series *Northern Exposure*, a slightly off-beat ensemble of disparate characters who seem to coalesce into a charming and fascinating whole. This is never more evident than on their weekly open mic night, when local musos come out of the woodwork. We turn up acutely aware of our outsider status, me with my guitar case under arm, and are immediately made welcome by a charming young guy named Angus, who encourages me to get up as soon as possible. The vibe is warm and we are instantly made to feel like locals. Another couple is playing a pretty good line of blues with an impromptu ensemble, all gelling magically.

They are a tough act to follow, and the guy who does plays a bit of rough-and-ready slide that mercifully doesn't set the bar too high. I am up next. Angus gets on bass and another young local guy, Aaron, climbs behind the drum kit and we seem to come together, playing a few of my three- or four-chord, white-boy funk originals without mishap. Vivi says she wants to get up and sing backing vocals, but when the time comes she is gripped by an uncharacteristic bout of shyness and refuses, until my fourth and final tune, when she creeps her way towards the stage, takes a seat next to me and very gradually begins to chime in. The last thing I want to be is a stage dad and so I have not pushed the issue, just tried to leave the door ajar for her to walk through if she chooses – and I'm thrilled when she does. She stage whispers for me to sing the first verse again because she knows the lyrics, and I begin to pull back on the vocals and let her lead, and it is the sweetest sound imaginable. The crowd is just as enchanted, and afterwards she is inundated with expressions of appreciation and encouragement. I am thrilled for her, and she tells me later that she wishes she'd got up sooner.

The pretty young waitress at Lucy's gets up next. She has a phenomenal voice, one of those delicate, wavering female voices so in vogue at the moment, but with the guts and sensitivity to make it unique. She does a couple of standards, 'Fever' and a great all-in jam to 'Hit the Road Jack'. Her father, Tony, joins in with his own very handy Tom Waits impersonation. Later, the waitress takes the time to point out to Vivi that there have been two father–daughter acts this evening.

It is a magical night out; Mallacoota has embraced us. I meet Jeff, one of the lighthouse keepers who alternates a month on and a month off on nearby Gabo Island — as quiet, bearded and brooding as you might expect a lighthouse keeper to be. I also meet Jim, who came to Mallacoota for the former Easter Arts Festival ten years ago and never left. There is a visiting older couple; they do a convincing set of rootsy blues to the great approval of the crowd and later pronounce that they are moving to Mallacoota. It seems a common response to its small-town charm.

THE BATTLE FOR BASTION POINT

But not all is well in paradise. It's one thing to read about the plight of the latest endangered wave in some remote corner of the country, in the token environmental column of your favourite surf magazine. It is quite another matter to actually clap eyes on the place, meet the surfers whose main source of recreation is to be destroyed and see the impassioned, handwritten protest signs tied to front fences throughout town.

At first glance, Bastion Point reminds me of Snapper Rocks back home on the Gold Coast: a jagged, rocky finger that provides the take-off spot for a long right-hand wave that peels through multiple sections of varying length and character. On a good day at Bastion, the ride extends almost 500 metres from the outside section, known as Broken Boards, through the Point itself and onwards towards the beach breaks that extend to the east almost as far as the eye can see.

The proposed breakwall (known as Option 3b) — at

2.8 metres high, 130 metres long, constructed of 8000 tonnes of rock and costing around $6.5 million – would cut the break in half, preventing swell from reaching the Point and creating backwash and other unknown effects, which would render Broken Boards unsurfable.

From the end of the breakwall, boats would emerge completely unsighted and with no clear view of oncoming boats, swell or surfers. Worse, boats would come out travelling side-on to approaching swells, a scenario that has raised alarm bells in almost everyone but those who have approved the project. The recent death of a surfer at my own home break of Currumbin Alley, run over by a fishing boat coming in through the break, has cast a harsh spotlight on this dangerous mix of surfers and boats.

The case in favour of the breakwall is based on an expected increase in recreational boating and improved efficiencies for the lucrative local abalone industry, worth around $20 million a year. Yet many in the abalone industry are also surfers and say they don't need such a large, expensive and intrusive piece of infrastructure. It was approved by the previous Labor government and its planning minister, Justin Madden, despite an independent panel appointed by the minister advising against it. Four-hundred and eighty-two submissions were received by Planning Panels Victoria in July 2007, of which eighty-seven per cent were opposed to the planned breakwall. The independent panel sat for two weeks and heard submissions from seventy-two individuals. The panel's comprehensive 178-page report left no doubt that it was totally opposed to the plan:

> The Panel concludes that the economic case for the proposals based on increased recreational ocean boating is flawed, and that the economic prosperity of Mallacoota rests on sustainable, nature-based tourism.
>
> The Panel considers that the impact of the breakwaters

in the new proposals will have considerable impact on the wilderness and landscape values of Bastion Point and an overall net detriment to tourism.

The Panel has concluded that the case for the development options is not strong. Weighing up all the different issues and considerations for ocean access at Mallacoota, the Panel has concluded that on balance the development proposals should not proceed.

Despite all this, Madden approved the controversial plan. Several of his other high-profile planning decisions have since been exposed as flawed, and the Labor government was voted out at the last election. The local Independent MP, Craig Ingram, another staunch advocate for the project, was also turfed out at the last election. Yet the East Gippsland Shire Council recently voted 5–3 for the proposal to go ahead.

A new Liberal government has promised a thorough review of the case, and opponents of the breakwall are putting forward an alternative plan for a low-key upgrade to the boat ramp, one which will not threaten the surf break, at a quarter of the cost.

Feelings are clearly running high in the town. I stop to photograph one Save Bastion Point sign that reads, 'Great Walls like Break Walls belong in China', and an old lady wanders out to see what I'm up to. When I explain my interest, she invites me in for a cup of tea and a chat. She has had her signs taken down by supporters of the breakwall, she claims. 'We just don't want it,' she tells me, echoing sentiments I am to hear over and over again during my time in Mallacoota.

A younger woman, presumably her daughter, joins in. 'They want to spend six million dollars, for what? There are other things we need, like a swimming pool or a library. They think it will bring lots of money and visitors to the town, but we have our tourism market – and it's for nature and wilderness.'

Though we encounter plenty of beautiful places on our travels, Mallacoota has given us a rare experience and instilled a feeling that there would be a ready-made place for us here tomorrow, and these complete strangers we have met over the course of a few days could become good friends. The kids love the van park, too, meeting up with a gang of kids each day in the playground, tearing around on their bikes, disappearing to each other's vans, which then forces Kirst and me to go and befriend their parents.

One old-timer, who looks like a regular here, drives past our site, observing the kids on their bikes. He stops and winds down his window, and I imagine he's going to have a go at me about their being a danger on the roads. 'If anyone drives too fast around here, you have a go at them,' he instructs sternly. 'This place is for kids and bikes more than cars.' It strikes me as a beautiful sentiment, one that should apply to more of our public spaces.

WHERE THE WILD THINGS ARE

We are sorry to leave Mallacoota, could have easily stayed longer, but are excited about our next destination, plunging deep into the natural splendor of Croajingolong National Park. I had never heard of the place before we began researching this trip, but Kirst has it ear-marked as a must-visit location early on. And she's not wrong – I didn't know my country was this beautiful.

Prof Short has recommended this little out-of-the-way campground by a beautiful estuary. Surprisingly, it is a good two-kilometre walk to the beach – more a fishing spot than a surfing spot, to be honest – but I imagine Andy has sent me here because it harbours either secrets, tests or lessons. Perhaps all three.

If it's a test, the road in provides the first one. We are

bumping along the narrow, rough dirt road through thick forest when we pass a curious road sign. It is diamond-shaped, yellow and shows a large truck taking up much of a narrow road, with 'UHF 40' in large black type. I am led to believe this is a friendly suggestion to tune your CB radio to channel 40 so you can hear if there are any logging trucks barrelling down the road towards you, as they are apparently prone to do here, so you can slow down, pull over and avoid a calamitous head-on with a fully-laden eighteen-wheeler. *If* you have a CB radio. Funding for ours, as you may recall, was slashed during the infamous razor-gang cost-cutting measures back at our local ARB outlet. It seems a curious circumstance that you can encounter a logging truck speeding out of a national park with recently felled trees. We are forbidden to take so much as a skerrick of kindling from the forest floor to light a fire. Of course, they are not logging national parks, but this road does provide the only access to neighbouring logging operations. Given that most campers in these sorts of pristine, bush camping grounds might be considered a fairly deep shade of green, it is an odd culture clash. And there are no prizes for guessing who'd come off second best in a collision.

Still, what are the chances, I figure, as we rock and sway our way down the road. Sure enough, as we round a bend we are confronted with a massive logging truck bearing down on us. I'm only going 40 km/h anyway, but I slow down, pull over and he races by without touching the brakes. My senses are tingling with the near miss.

It takes us forty-five minutes to wind our way through the forest to the campground, and it feels even longer when you are constantly wondering if your destination will appear around the next corner. Finally, we make a steep descent into a gorgeous bush setting that trumps even Knacklehho. Camp sites are nestled between large gums. There's a magnificent estuary with a small timber jetty. A handful of campers are spread among a couple of dozen sites and communal fireplaces. The van barely fits between the trees, and it takes some reckoning to find a site that will accommodate us. Our few neighbours are all in simple, utilitarian tents or camper trailers, and again I feel as if we are cheating a little with our mod cons. Within half an hour we are all set up and Alex and Vivi are tuning in their 'kid radar'. They're happy, and our neighbours are a friendly bunch. They say your kids pick your friends, and so it goes.

It is unfathomably gorgeous, but it's a thirty-minute round-trip bushwalk to the coast, and I find this inability to gauge the ocean's mood unsettling. We are not about to turn around and retrace the long drive in, but I need to get my bearings. 'Walk' has quickly become a four-letter word to our kids, yet we herd them reluctantly along the bush track, which gives way to a spectacular timber boardwalk that follows the banks of the estuary to the ocean. Alex and Vivi give up just short of our destination and stage a determined sit-in, refusing to go any further. I send Kirst ahead to check out the beach while I stay and play with them by the water's edge. She returns and heads back to the camp with the kids while I get a moment to myself with the ocean, even if it's without a surfboard.

You can hear it well before you see it, the rumble growing to a roar as I wind through the forest, climb a steep dune and emerge through the bushes onto a large, sweeping beach.

At the eastern end, a large fur seal colony inhabits two rocky offshore islands a short distance outside the mouth of the estuary. And we all know the main natural predator of the fur seal. It is a spectacular stretch of beach, but I do not imagine I'll do any surfing here. Even a small chomp and you would bleed to death before they even lugged you up to the campground. I write the place off for surfing purposes: too sharky, too remote, too . . . wild. And I am thus confronted with the limitations of my own bravery. I had fancied myself the fearless wave-hunter, scouring the vast Australian coast for unridden waves – yet I want nothing to do with this. It's solid and onshore; foamy close-outs pound the length of the beach. On a different day, however, that river mouth and cove at the western end of the bay suggest potential.

On our first morning here, I rise early and walk the track to the beach at pace, eager to see what the ocean is doing. I am again confronted by huge, wild, windswept close-outs from one end of the beach to the other – perhaps ten feet, but without any scale it is impossible to tell. It is a classic collection of 'almost' waves. At the western end, there is an almost right-hand point break, pitching and barrelling on dry rock off the end of the headland, then quickly filling up into a fat swell. Another section unloads on reef halfway along the point and turns into an ugly close-out on another rock ledge. All the way along this stunning headland it does this infuriating dance. It is dry or it is fat, with none of the perfect geometry in between so beloved by surfers. But what if the sand were packed into that western corner after a big sou'-east blow? It's a tantalising thought.

On the beach breaks, the odd one reels and spits, about one makeable barrel for every ten deathly close-outs. The odds are not inspiring. It is a slightly maddening predicament – not knowing this coast, I face a one-and-a-half-hour round trip just to drive out and check elsewhere or a major hike of indeterminate length over the headland to see if the next bay might house a rideable wave. I decide to just let it go, soak up the wildness of it all and forget about chasing surf for the day. There is a sweet relief in this decision, just to be with the family, wander the beach, marvel at the might and scale of nature, watch the seals swimming and surfing and diving in the mouth of the inlet. An occasional reform left-hander breaks across the sandbar like a mini-Mundaka, tubing and spitting for a hundred metres or so. I watch a lone seal at play in the surf, just waiting for a massive pair of jaws to explode from the water and bite it in two. It doesn't happen.

The wind is howling from the west, and only the most protected corner would harbour a rideable wave today, and consequently would be sheltered from the brunt of the south-west swell. I have the gnawing suspicion that somewhere must be going off. Still, all is right in the world, and the memory of Knacklehho sustains me. I get through the day without undue trauma.

There are also fresh oysters to pick off the rocks, mussels to dive for, abundant fish for the anglers among our fellow campers, and I realise they have found their own idea of paradise. I ponder what a limited view of the coast and the ocean we surfers sometimes have, assessing it purely for the existence of an evenly peeling wave that might lend itself to riding. For today, my boards remain dry and I try and find peace in my predicament, but that uneasy equilibrium cannot last.

By the time the sun works its way through the forest canopy and rouses us from our slumber, it is already eight o'clock. I involve myself in cobbling together some breakfast for the kids – the ocean a faint rumble, thoughts of the surf as distant as the beach. I can glimpse the river mouth from a particular vantage point at the back of our camp site, and it looks to me like the swell has dropped. Where yesterday the river mouth was filled with mountains of whitewater, today it appears smooth and flat. Eventually, I extricate myself from familial duties and pound the bush track to the beach in quick time to confirm the conditions. I trudge over the final sand dune and am struck dumb by the sight. The ocean is sheet glass, the wind a light offshore, and the entire beach from east to west is one colossal close-out – but ruler-edged and smooth. It looks like photos I have seen of the huge Easter swell at Bells Beach in '81. I know instantly that somewhere must be going absolutely bananas. But where?

I weigh my options. I can return to camp, grab my board and wetsuit and hike either east or west to see if a neighbouring bay is handling the swell any better. I can jump in the car and brave one of the rough four-wheel drive tracks, risk creek crossings and fallen trees and who knows what else, to explore a couple of headlands and river mouths to the west. Or I can hightail it the hour and a half back to Mallacoota and check the conditions at the endangered Bastion Point. A couple of park rangers are in the camp, cleaning toilets and fixing signs, and I ask one of them if he knows anything about the local surf conditions. He confirms that Bastion had been good the day before and is apparently doing its thing again today. My mind is made up. I made a pact with myself at the beginning of this journey to try to avoid backtracking. There is enough driving to get around the country as it is – some 25,000 kilometres of it – without adding distance, but the circumstances are compelling. I can stumble about this unknown coast hoping to chance upon a surfable wave, or I can race back to Mallacoota where I know there is a quality point break awaiting me, a surfing experience that may not be available to me or anyone else for much longer.

Kirst, bless her, is encouraging. 'You should go,' she urges. My fellow campers observe my state of distraction with curiosity. I grab a board, wetsuit, a bottle of water and a couple of pears and jump in the car. It is already 11 am by the time I get my shit together. Without the van the trip to Mallacoota maybe closer to an hour. Two-hour round trip, two hours of surfing, something to eat – I should be back by four this afternoon, I estimate. It is an odd feeling, tearing out of this secluded, tranquil bush campground on a frantic surf mission, leaving my family behind. What if something happens to them in my absence? Or something happens to me in the surf? There is no phone reception here, and I entertain grisly scenarios of misadventure as I speed along the winding dirt track back towards the highway. I find a lone melting moment biscuit rolling about the front passenger seat, seize on the unexpected treasure and scoff it quickly. I am in the car park overlooking Bastion Point within the hour.

My first impression is one of anticlimax. I had hoped it would be reeling for hundreds of metres. The Point itself appears to be barely breaking, almost bang-on high tide. Further out, Broken Boards occasionally springs to life with a wobbly set. It's not hard to see how it earnt its name. The foreshore is a veritable minefield of jagged rocks. In the days before leg-ropes it must have been a surfboard graveyard. The wave is a little uninspiring. On the high tide it looks fat, kind of wonky, the line-up full of weird boils, clumps of seaweed and large kelp beds. What's more, there is not a soul out. I had imagined the entire townsfolk might have gathered to witness their mighty threatened point break come to life, but there are only a bunch of Euro backpackers loading their boards and wetsuits into their Wicked campervan.

I sit watching it for a while, weighing my options, the accumulated adrenalin of the speedy drive here awaiting an outlet. A couple of locals I recognise from an afternoon at the beach here a few days earlier are checking the surf. I strike up a conversation with one, Lenny, and he tells me – inevitably – that yesterday was really good. Of course it was. As we talk and watch the line-up, a couple more regular sets and a hint of sunlight begin to make it look more appealing. I ask him where the paddle-out spot is and he describes a keyhole in the reef at the top of the point. I can't go home dry. 'I'm keen for a paddle,' I announce, desperate for a companion.

'I'm going out. I'll show you where to head out,' he replies cheerily. I could kiss him. Another local surfer joins us and soon we're a cosy trio out in the pitching line-up. The other bloke, would you believe it, is from Burleigh Heads on the Gold Coast, about a ten-minute drive from where I live. He met a local girl and moved down here five years ago. Lenny's a surfboard shaper, part-time abalone diver and carpenter –

he experiments with timber boards. We strike up an instant rapport.

It is an odd but challenging wave. It peaks outside on a kelpy rock shelf, angry boils marking the take-off spot. Halfway down the Point, a second ledge gurgles and boils, throwing a warp into the wave face, and you must ride high on the face to miss it. Make it through that section and you are surfing towards a wall of rock, or what might soon literally be a rock breakwall.

You can't link it up to surf through from Broken Boards to the Point today, but a couple of the larger sets get close. It is a spectacular bit of coastline, sandwiched between two of the most stunning patches of national park I have ever laid eyes on. It is astonishing that all this natural beauty is still not enough for some people, that the urge to re-engineer, interrupt, attempt to improve upon this grand design still persists.

Lenny works on the abalone boats, so he sees both sides of the argument, but he reckons the current plans are overkill.

'We just don't need it,' he tells me.

When he and his mate head in, I'm suddenly left alone in the line-up – this Victorian Snapper Rocks with its boils and kelp beds. I catch a wave into the Point and enjoy a few long peelers into the beach breaks as the tide drops, paddling back out on my own in brilliant sunshine. How long might this experience exist?

Back at camp, I return safely to a happy family and decide there is almost no better feeling in the world, to have both a surf adventure and domestic harmony, to not be forced to choose between the two.

BALI FLASHBACKS

This routine, a week in a remote bush camping ground with only the basic amenities of pit toilets and non-potable water, followed by a few days in a small town with the mod cons of a van park, reminds me of my early forays to Indonesia twenty-five years earlier.

I first went to Bali in 1986 and thought I'd already missed the glory days of surf discovery. Yet, when I look back, I realise with some surprise that we were only the second group into the newly opened Sumbawa Surf Camp, founded by swashbuckling surf explorer Paul King, which was until then a closely guarded secret. We enjoyed a week of empty waves, living in bamboo huts, existing on rice, rubbery chicken, banana pancakes and Bintang beer. The locals stood around and watched in stunned amazement as we screened the slapstick debauchery of *Bachelor Party* on video cassette, upsetting generations of Muslim tradition. Then we returned to Kuta to shower, shave, buy new shirts and go out on the town looking for a shag, crazy on *arak*, the local rice spirit, and over-the-counter speed pills, like diggers on R and R in Manila, Bangkok or Cairo.

Then I headed off to the famed Grajagan Surf Camp, which only a few years earlier had been the exclusive preserve of eccentric surf pioneer Mike Boyum, funded by his global drug-trafficking operations. I was twenty-one and it was the beginning of my surf travel adventures. It still stands as a high point, which I have only come to fully appreciate years later. At the time I felt guilty, saw myself as the soft surf mag guy taking the easy option of the fully-catered surf camp, following well-worn trails beaten by the true pioneers and blabbing their secrets to the surfing world. But looking back it seems like adventure enough for a kid from Blackburn, who had only recently moved out of the family home.

Back in Kuta, I bumped into some of my old footy club mates from the mighty Forest Hill Zebras in suburban Melbourne, along with their girlfriends – all sunburnt, the boys in Bintang singlets and the girls with their hair freshly braided. I passed myself off to them as the bold surf adventurer, regaling them with ripping yarns of my fearless travels to the outer islands of

Indonesia. One of those old footy mates, Darren 'Henry' Lawson, died recently, without warning, from a brain aneurysm. His widow, Rhonda, sent me a photo of the three of us together back then at the Sari Club in Kuta, since destroyed in the Bali bombings. We look so fresh-faced and expectant, awaiting life's grand adventure, with no idea of the various fates awaiting us. Henry was a top bloke, a talented, tough footballer, and he and Rhonda had been sweethearts since their early teens. It seems too cruel, too sudden.

It's odd that this family road trip should conjure memories of those self-indulgent Indo days. Except now, instead of a mad *arak* and speed bender, I might invest in a six pack of Boag's Light and take the family out for a slap-up Chinese feed or fish and chips on the beach. The spirit of appreciating a remote destination with few frills, followed by the sweet indulgence of power, laundry, a hot shower and a shave is so strongly reminiscent of those Indo adventures all those years ago – except it doesn't seem that long ago.

THE HUNTER-GATHERER

Throughout our travels I seem to continually make the acquaintance of men who are adept at, quite literally, putting food on their family's table, no matter where that table might be. I always find it a humbling, confronting experience meeting these bold outdoorsmen equipped with tinnies and kayaks and numerous fishing rods and large tackle boxes. I don't even own a tackle box. Old Doug Mackenzie's charitable sinkers and 'ends' are rattling around in a plastic zip-lock bag in a kitchen cupboard in the Jayco. These men disappear in the wee hours and return with a brace of bream or several salmon or a bag of mussels, all without appearing to raise a sweat.

At our latest camp site you can pick abundant oysters off the rocks at the mouth of the estuary. Surely picking oysters is one task I cannot bungle, yet I have gathered no more than half a dozen, clumsily opened and consumed a couple with the aid of a screwdriver, before I very nearly put the end of the tool through my thumb. I stem the bleeding with a tissue and curse my incompetence. I am ill-equipped even for this most basic food-gathering task.

What good am I if the shit hits the fan, when the system collapses and we are all forced to return to primal hunter-gatherer skills? In my case, it seems, they have been dormant too long to be awakened.

And yet, when we eventually move on from the Wild Coast to the rather more tranquil waters of Cape Conran, a short hop to the west, something is indeed awakened in me. As a boy, on my first childhood forays to the open ocean at Point Leo and Flinders, along the Mornington Peninsula, a family friend had introduced us to the joys of diving for abalone. It was a task I had taken to with relish, amazed that food could be plucked from the wild like this, *au naturel*. On calm days we would snorkel in tidal rock pools with masks and screwdrivers, gather bags of the succulent shellfish, gut and clean them, pound them for tenderness and slice the meat thin. Rolled in flour and fried in butter with lemon and pepper, they were one of my first experiences of a true delicacy. Cooked quickly at high temperature, they were a little like calamari but with a more substantial, almost nutty flavour. I had no idea then that Asian markets paid vast sums for abalone meat, or that illegal poachers would soon force the introduction of strict rules and bag limits governing their collection.

Cape Conran is a beautiful stretch of beach draped around a large headland. A simple bush campground is nestled among the coastal banksias. On an exploratory drive around the cape, I stumble upon the most idyllic cove on the western side, known as Salmon Rocks. A small jetty and boat ramp mark a popular fishing spot. Tiny swells cap on a left-hand point, exhibiting all the telltale signs of a quality surf spot in larger swells. Small rock pools provide the ideal environment for the kids to snorkel, and I resolve to return with the entire family.

It is gloriously warm and sunny on our last of three days at Cape Conran, and I finally convince the family to join me on my return to Salmon Rocks, presumably named not just for the local fish population but also the deep-orange lichen that decorates the rocky point. We swim, rock-hop and beachcomb, spot crabs, starfish and sea urchin, the children delighting in the simple, nature-based play, and their parents delighting in the children's delight.

And then I spot a familiar orange, oval-shaped shell in a crevice below the water's surface: abalone. It is probably twenty years since I last collected abalone and, until our visit to Mallacoota, it was probably that long since I'd tasted it. Here is my chance. I will be a hunter-gatherer. I have come ill-equipped for the task, expecting only to get the kids snorkelling in the rock pools. I find an old screwdriver in the car and let out the strap on Vivi's goggles to its maximum length, stretching it around my boofhead. Kirst has recently acquired a fishing licence from Parks Victoria for $24 but, with our complete lack of experience and one primitive surf rod, we pose little threat to the fish stocks of the Southern Ocean. 'There is always a cost associated with fish you catch yourself,' one camp neighbour, John, informed me around his campfire one night. 'I'm running at about eight hundred dollars a kilo,' he told me. I had recently purchased fresh local flathead, boned and filleted, for $32 a kilo, and it had been so delicious, prepared simply in seasoned flour, that I had scoffed at the need for fish caught by my own hand.

But abalone. This is a different matter. This is a nostalgic trip into my childhood, sharing a bit of our family history with my children and asserting one of my few survival skills in the wild.

While at the car, I retrieve the fishing guide Kirst has acquired with her fishing licence to make sure I am doing it, literally, by the book. We are allowed a limit of five abalone. They are to be a minimum of eleven or twelve centimetres long, depending on which section of the Victorian coast you're on. Central Victoria only has sixty allocated open days for collecting abalone, and today just happens to be one of them. This is all clearly meant to be. I hop about the rocks with my child-size mask and snorkel, screwdriver in hand, stumble about the rock pools, swim through thick forests of kelp and, eventually, come across a good-sized abalone. I have never been particularly good at holding my breath for long periods, a weakness that has further heightened my lack of bravery in big waves. When it comes to abalone diving, this results in a rather comical performance, thrashing and kicking in shallow water while I try to wrestle one of the stubborn mollusks from its crevice. It must be quite an entertaining spectacle to behold.

I retrieve my first abalone and hold my trophy aloft. 'I AM HUNTER-GATHERER MAN!' I bellow before diving again to find another, taking several subsequent plunges to separate it from its perch. Over the next half hour of thrashing about I manage to fill my quota, and I'm euphoric with my morning's manly work. We will dine on fresh abalone for lunch.

We enjoy this delightful cove for most of the morning and into the early afternoon, traipsing over the rocky point with the kids, taking photos, swimming, lolling about like so many sun-baking walruses. Kirst comments that it feels like Europe, the Greek Isles or some secluded Italian seaside hideaway.

'Except if this was Europe,' I comment, 'there'd be some delightful trattoria just up the road where we could dine on exquisitely prepared local abalone at a reasonable price and drink good wine served by a convivial host.' It has struck me throughout this leg in the south-east of the country, where so much spectacular fresh seafood is harvested, that we have come across only one establishment serving local abalone, or abalone of any sort for that matter, and that is the remarkable Lucy's Café. It has taken a Chinese couple to recognise the virtues of the local produce. This region should be dubbed the Abalone Coast, with a giant abalone built of chicken wire and papier-mâché perched above a local roadhouse, the local eateries offering abalone chowder, abalone sushi, abalone pies, abalone pasta. But this delicacy is whisked away promptly to Asian markets, where it can fetch such outrageous prices that it has barely a chance to land on local tables. It's a damn shame and a large part of what is wrong with Australian tourism. Why can't we partake of this great natural bounty, embrace a sensibility so evident in European cultures and make the most of such magnificent local produce? It would save me the trouble of splashing about, acting a fool on a sunny afternoon.

I cut the meat out, careful to collect and bag the shells and guts for proper disposal, as advised by my Victorian fisheries guide. Another successful amateur abelone diver strolls off the beach with his bag of five, beaming with his good fortune.

'Beautiful day,' I comment.

'It's always a beautiful day when you get abs,' he effuses.

We are just gathering up our things when a man dressed casually in shorts and a T-shirt approaches. He whips out an official ID and introduces himself as a fisheries officer. I feel no alarm – I have my requisite five – and happily display the bagged remains and meat. He measures them studiously and sets two of the shells aside. They are each a centimetre under the required twelve-centimetre minimum, he informs me. I have used a screwdriver, which is illegal, he adds sternly. I have been diving in the 'intertidal zone', in less than two metres of water, another no-no. He produces a notebook and dictates my movements and behaviour for most of the morning. He carries binoculars and a walkie-talkie – I have been under surveillance the entire time we've been here. It is like something out of a

Pink Panther movie. He asks for my driver's licence or other ID, which I do not have on me. He announces he will follow us back to our camp site to confirm my personal details.

I am dumbfounded. My total catch of abalone in the last twenty years stands at five. I am clearly not a serial poacher, I point out. There was nothing surreptitious about our activities. I had not set out to dive for abalone. I had used my daughter's mask and snorkel, brought no gear, no flippers or wetsuit. If I have been observed all morning, and this is about the protection of a valuable and fragile species, why was I not stopped from inadvertently committing an offence? The fisheries officer maintains that I am being let off lightly. He could fine me well over $1000 for my misdemeanours, seize my bounty of abalone and confiscate my screwdriver. Abalone is considered a 'high-priority industry', he says gravely, and thus rigorously policed.

He issues two warnings and just one penalty, for collecting undersized abalone, an offence which carries a fine of $358. That works out to $70 per abalone. I am heading towards my camp neighbor John's $800 per kilo catch. So much for the bold hunter-gatherer. The fisheries officer takes down my statement, warning that it could be used as evidence against me. Where on earth was the *Sea Shepherd* while this carnage was being carried out, I wonder?

I accept my fine without protest, apart from the calm observation that an educational approach rather than a punitive one might be more helpful, but I hold little hope that fisheries are interested in correcting this criminal behaviour. It is clearly far more profitable to punish unwitting wrongdoers.

ORBOST OR BUST

But there are other law enforcement offers to deal with before we depart the delightful East Gippsland Shire. Pulling out of

Cape Conran, Kirst has decided she'll have her first go at towing the van. I did the Cape Conran-to-Orbost drive a couple of days earlier to take myself off to the Orbost Public Library in a desperate bid to find a quiet work space. It was perfect for about two hours; then they suffered a blackout and my quiet work space was plunged into darkness. But I am able to report that the meandering drive along the banks of the Snowy River to Orbost would make an ideal caravanning debut.

And so Kirst takes the wheel, excited to open her innings. All goes well for thirty kilometres or so until we approach the outskirts of Orbost and a siren starts up behind us. We'd lost our extension mirrors on the bumpy dirt road out of Croajingolong and haven't found anywhere to replace them, so Kirst has been blissfully unaware that a member of the local constabulary has been trailing us most of the way from Cape Conran.

We pull over in the main street of Orbost and Constable Plod gets out and surveys our rig suspiciously. I have no idea the absence of extension mirrors is an offence in Victoria. When I'd gone shopping for them, one salesman had assured me they were unnecessary, but I'd wanted to err on the side of caution. Plod informs us that we could be liable for a $110 fine for towing a van without extension mirrors. He'd pulled in close behind us and put his lights on to see if we could see him, and thus convinced himself we posed a danger to the law-abiding road users of this sleepy country hamlet. I sigh and try to remain calm. This is turning into an expensive couple of days. I tell him our story of losing the side mirrors on a dirt road, but he isn't buying it.

'What, both of them at the same time?' he snaps. Well, no, I explain patiently, on consecutive days. And what days had this happened? he demands. I run over the past week in my mind, but the days of the week have happily become an indistinct blur. My delay only rouses his suspicions further. I start getting huffy, never a good move with hard-arsed country cops, and tell him we've driven all the way from Queensland and I am not about to take risks with my family's safety. He ignores me and asks Kirst for her driver's licence, studies it carefully then looks over our rig again.

'So, how come you have a Queensland driver's licence, New South Wales car registration and Victorian rego on the van?' This guy doesn't miss a thing; he's clearly convinced he has stumbled upon an interstate caravan-smuggling operation. Kirst explains that I'm a writer; the car and van are on loan from their respective manufacturers as a form of sponsorship. His attitude seems to soften a little and he tells us curtly that he'll let us off with a warning this time but to replace the side mirrors as soon as possible.

Vivi has been observing the tense scenario with concern and breaks into a smile at this sunny news. 'That's lucky,' she chirps. 'We've already been fined three hundred and fifty-eight dollars for taking an undersized abalone!'

The cop seems to reconsider his position, regarding us with new suspicion as serial law-breakers, a kind of cross-country Bonnie and Clyde, clearly breeding a new generation of back-seat delinquents. But he's already put his little pad and pen away, and the exertion of pulling them out again is obviously too much. He lets us go.

With relief, we inject a little more wealth into the Orbost economy with a cooked breakfast at the local café, devouring big plates of scrambled eggs with smoked salmon and sipping good coffee. Alex is a reassuring constant during every dining experience, ordering ham and cheese toasted sandwiches wherever we go – from the fanciest café to the most basic greasy spoon roadhouse. All seem charmed by him and happily oblige even if no such item exists on their menu. He will be able to write the definitive guide to finding the best ham and cheese toasted sandwich in Australia at the end of this trip.

THE PROM FACTORY

Wilsons Promontory is unlike any other national park camp-ground we have been to. First, it's size, at 450 sites, is more like the larger van parks. In peak periods, with three or four campers per site, that makes for a total population of 1200 to 1500 people, larger than a lot of the small towns we have passed through. Serious infrastructure and a large staff are required to cater for this many visitors. It boasts a general store, café, visi-tors' centre, medical centre, police station, outdoor cinema, hot showers, laundry, yoga classes, numerous cabins and its own generator and water supply. I imagine this would attract the contempt of the hardcore bushwalkers who first colonised this area, trekking vast distances into the wilderness with Spartan provisions, carrying their turds out in plastic bags and endur-ing the harsh elements. These days, visitors to the Prom like their creature comforts. I observe the women who run the take-away food store putting out signs to announce that closing time is changing from 6 pm to 5 pm to mark the end of summer. 'There'll be riots at five o'clock,' she warns staff.

Also, the Prom's relative proximity to Melbourne and its amenities means it attracts a different type of camper to the more remote and basic national park campgrounds. Litter is an issue, as is noise at night. Signs warning against feeding the wildlife are ignored. A charming old man near us is delighting our children by feeding the lorikeets milk arrowroot biscuits and getting them to land on his bald head for a photo-op. A group of young French travellers in an old van have set up camp in one of the toilet blocks, powering their laptops in the elec-trical sockets and cooking crepes for dinner on their electric frypan on the bathroom bench. Alex thinks it is the funniest thing he has seen all day when I take him for his bedtime wee.

Then there are the animals. Now, I am all for the preserva-tion of rare and endangered native species, but there is a certain arrogance about the modern national park critter that is more than a little disconcerting. It mirrors the age of entitlement and wilfulness seen in our children in an era free of corporal punishment. Generations of national park wildlife have grown up with no fear of humans; it's unnatural. At one time, possums, kangaroos and goannas would have been hunted. These days, they will saunter into your camp site, stare you down and steal your food without blinking, supremely confident that you will do them no harm or else feel the wrath of the Native Species Act.

I used to think possums were cute, but the Prom possums are overweight, lard-arsed caricatures of possums, bloated by dumb, unwitting human food suppliers who have been stripped of any means of self-defence. I've always thought of wombats as the most delightful of creatures, ambling along on their stumpy legs with imagined dopey, deep-toned cartoon voices. At the Prom, stern warning signs alert campers to the necessity of keeping all food inside their cars lest rogue wombats tear open their tents and steal it at night. The wombats here are like lawless bikie gangs.

I am woken one night from a deep slumber by the most bloodcurdling screams and a violent shaking of our entire van. I sit bolt upright and leap out of bed, ready to defend my family to the death. Then, when no crazed intruder can be found, I assume it is Alex having a nightmare. But he is sleeping soundly, despite the commotion. Eventually, I realise it is the sound of possums wrestling on the roof. I grab a torch and stumble out into the night and shine the light on them; they stare back at me accusingly. In a fit of rage I hurl a banksia cone at one of them and it lands loudly on the roof of a neighbouring caravan, so I switch off the torch and duck back inside. I lay awake for hours while the possums make a dance floor of our van's pop-top. Finally, in defeat, I get up at two o'clock in the morning and start writing about the incident. Last night we were kept up by a screaming baby nearby; tonight it's aggro possums – the peace and tranquility of nature.

Despite all this, and the near-arctic temperatures in February, it is possible to have a thoroughly engaging time at the Prom. The scenery is breathtaking: an ancient, alpine-flavoured vista of towering mountaintops decorated with huge boulders and forests that spill to the sea. Sweeping bays and rocky headlands define the winding coastline, while tiny offshore islands speckle the stunning seascapes. On a late-afternoon drive, as the sun finally breaks through a grey sky of intermittent drizzle, we round one bend in the road and are greeted by a pure white crescent beach bordered by massive boulders tinted orange with lichen and ringed by wooded hills, the sun glinting off the turquoise ocean.

The surf, however, is woeful for the duration of our stay – small and onshore, the howling winds not even succeeding in whipping up much serious swell. I have fond memories of exercising my newly acquired surfing bug during family camping holidays here in my early teens. I vividly recall bobbing happily in the southern corner of Norman Bay for hours on glorious summer days, catching wave after wave with just me and a mate. It was where I first felt like I was able to manoeuvre my clunky old Island single fin with a reasonable degree of control, where I could size up an approaching wave and confidently anticipate a successful ride. I remember telling my eldest brother and first surfing mentor, Pete, that I had done three re-entries on one wave, and he howled me down in disbelief, assuring me that I had never done a proper re-entry in my life. He was, of course, right.

The kids love the Prom. For them, it strikes the perfect balance between the natural charms of bush camping and the modern indulgences of the van park. They adore the shop, poring over naff trinkets, postcards and books for hours. There is a roaming gang of kids playing in the playground and riding bikes. But when the weekend ends and the families return to the city, the only kids in the park are school groups. The sight of them happily roaring around the park en masse, their delighted shrieks and peals of laughter, only exacerbate Vivi's homesickness.

We cross the footbridge over Tidal River just as a school group of nine- and ten-year-olds come kayaking down the river. They are splashing and jovial, hopping out of their kayaks to haul them over shallow sandbanks. Vivi stands in the middle of the bridge looking at them in silence, tears trickling down her cheeks. She is a social creature, our daughter, and to watch a group of peers having so much fun and not be able to participate is torture. We encourage her to try and talk to some of the school kids when the opportunity presents itself. 'I tried,' she says sadly, 'and they looked at me like I was an alien.'

WHERE PENGUINS FEAR TO TREAD

Phillip Island is where my surfing life really began. As a teenager in suburban Melbourne, it was the first place I considered myself a quasi-local, courtesy of a mate's family's beach house we frequented every school holidays. It was a pretty mild form of localism we practised. 'If you don't have a mate with a holiday house here, don't surf,' was our good-natured catchcry.

So, it is with a nostalgic, rosy tint to my eyes that I tow the Expanda across the bridge from San Remo onto the island. The rest of the family are not so enamoured. It is cold, grey and windy, and there's not much for them to do while I go sniffing around for a marginal surf in uninspiring conditions. But taking the Rav down those familiar dirt roads, unhitched from the van . . . I'm in heaven. It is also Kirst and my tenth wedding anniversary, so we go out to dinner at a smart wine bar, the sort of place you once would never have found on the island, then take the kids to the Penguin Parade.

I have fond memories of the event as a kid, rugged up in blankets, watching the achingly cute little fairy penguins waddle up the beach. But times have changed. The Penguin Parade has grown into one of Victoria'a biggest and most lucrative tourist attractions. It has been inducted into the Australian Tourism Hall of Fame, presumably for services to the art of separating chumps from their money. A huge visitors' centre and the inevitable gift shop full of crap souvenirs marks the entrance to the beach. You can buy paper bags of chocolate-coated peanuts marketed as 'Penguin Poo'. Asian tourists are brought in by the busload to ogle the tiny creatures. It's $60 for a family of four to get in, or double that if you want to splurge for the 'Premium Penguin Viewing Platform'. This cordoned-off area is where sixty per cent of the penguins make landfall for the exclusive amusement of around twenty per cent of the crowd.

Humans appear to outnumber penguins by about five to one. Why the penguins continue to return to their roosts in the face of this wanton exploitation is beyond me. They must stuff heroin down their burrows. There is something acutely disconcerting about the whole thing. The parents come ashore from their day's fishing at sea to vomit up fish smoothies for their young and waddle up the beach, blinking in the face of enormous floodlights and a tiered gallery of humans. They struggle up the dunes, following the desperate bleating of their young, trying to locate their nests amid the raised timber walkways, fences and milling crowds. Besotted tourists stalk them as they scramble to find their offspring. Meanwhile, flocks of seagulls stand around on the beach looking pissed off, thoroughly ignored: *What's all the fuss about? We have beaks, feathers and webbed feet, too, but no one cares about us.* The kids last about half an hour and they're over it.

The next morning I find myself returning to the Penguin Parade, as its sheltered bay offers about the only decent wave to be found. I spot two dead penguins on the side of the road as I check the surf. The surf is three feet, clean and protected in the sou'-wester, a reasonable right breaking nicely for a hundred metres or so – and not a soul to be seen. I scamper down the hillside and wade across the reef, unsure of the paddle-out spot. I am suckered too far along the point by the mirage of large, shapeless swells that feather way out and promise a long ride, only to fill up and vanish before your eyes. I am soon joined by an older local guy, who knows the line-up better than me. He waves, indicating the proper take-off spot.

He's a friendly bloke but full of bad news. 'Heaps of mako sharks around,' he says, 'because the water's so warm.' Did he say, warm? And, sharks? I was already shivering from the cold, now I'm also quaking with fear. 'I thought you were pretty keen, paddling out by yourself,' he says.

He's spotted the New South Wales rego plates on the Rav. 'What are you doing here? Did you take a wrong turn?' he quips. He joins in the chorus of disdain I have heard from Victorians everywhere, that they have had no summer this year. We have a good chat and I tell him a bit of my story, including the bit about us spending our tenth wedding anniversary on Phillip Island. 'It's a wonder she's still talkin' to ya,' he marvels.

It's a fun, though unspectacular, session, and I don't last long. The spectre of the mako sharks and the realisation that we are just round the corner from one of the largest fur seal colonies in Australia begins to gnaw away at me. I am starting to think the state's fur seals are stalking me. And Kirst and the kids are awaiting my return. It's on to Melbourne to see family, then on to the *Spirit of Tasmania* to explore more cold-water delights.

It's already time to pack away the lightweight rubber and shorts and T-shirts and pull out the vacuum-packed winter gear. And it's only early March. Researching camp heaters suddenly becomes a pressing priority.

WRONG WAY, GO BACK

It's about one month into our trip and I'm googling up some factoid when I stumble upon the drivingroundaustralia.com website – and I am rattled to discover that we are doing this all wrong. Author Dave Jeanes has written a comprehensive guidebook to driving around our country, available as a downloadable e-book, and in his introduction he cuts to the chase:

'Although it may seem a trivial matter, the direction to tour around Australia during your Australia tour is a critical issue. In a nutshell, you go around anti-clockwise,' he states emphatically. 'Why is this critical? Because you take advantage of the prevailing winds, which will be east to south-easterly when driving up the east coast, easterly when travelling westwards across the top of the continent, north-westerly when driving south down Western Australia, and generally of a westerly component when finally heading east from Perth towards the east coast.'

Damn, why hadn't I, the bold wave-hunter so finely attuned to the elements, thought of that? With the wind at our tails, Mr Jeanes advises, we could expect to use around sixteen litres of fuel per 100 km/h towing an average-sized van in a standard six-cylinder family car. Against a headwind, it is likely to be more like twenty litres. Thank God for our fuel card.

The other element I hadn't fully considered was the true nature of the southern seasons, as idiotic as that sounds. Twenty years on the subtropical Gold Coast has lulled me into the notion that autumn is a charmingly benign time of year, a gentler, milder extension of summer, a time of all-day offshores, consistent swells and comfortable daytime temperatures. It has long been my favourite time of year, the real surfer's season. Legendary filmmaker Bruce Brown's 60s surf movie epic should have been called *Endless Autumn* in my book. So, what better time to explore our nation's wave-rich southern coastline? February in Wilsons Prom has already comprehensively kicked my arse.

Early March in Melbourne isn't much better, until a late out-break of summer heralds our journey across Bass Strait.

How will we fair in Tassie in March, or the Great Ocean Road in April, or Ceduna in May, or Albany in June? There is clearly a good reason why all those arthritic Grey Nomads follow the sun north in winter. But our course is set, and there is no turning back now.

5

THE SPIRIT OF TASMANIA

I HAVE DEVELOPED A deep, irrational fear of the early-morning drive through Melbourne traffic to board the *Spirit of Tasmania* ferry. After my father-in-law's driveway back in Tugun, it stands as my next great van-towing hurdle. Actually, perhaps the fear isn't irrational at all: I must tow a 1.5-tonne caravan across Australia's second-largest metropolis through peak-hour traffic to the inner-city bayside hub of Port Melbourne. The ferry departs at 9 am and we must be there at least forty-five minutes beforehand or we forfeit our $700 fare. They could not have scheduled this any worse, as far as I can see. I have rallied the family to be up before dawn so we can traverse the city before the worst of the morning commuter crush hits.

I toss and turn all night, have set the alarm on my phone and booked a reminder call as well, just to be safe. I wake repeatedly during the night to check the time, and eventually get up well before my alarm, get dressed, rouse the wife and kids and get the van packed up and ready to go. The kids are strapped into the back seat, bleary eyed and half awake, still in their pyjamas. We pull out of the driveway at 6.10 am. Mercifully, the traffic gods are kind and we make it to Port Melbourne in less than half an hour without incident. The streets are almost deserted, and we arrive near the front of the queue to get on the ferry.

The *Spirit of Tasmania* is an impressive old barge, done up smartly in a fresh red-and-white paint job, its enormous bulk towering over us like an office block. Lifeboats hang from its perimeter, and I try and dispel the thought of the circumstances in which they might be necessary. The kids are wide awake now and excited, our collective mood buoyant as we contemplate the sea voyage across Bass Strait and the month ahead in Tasmania.

Surf information on the Tasmanian coastline is fairly scarce, apart from the big-wave mutant monsters of Shipstern Bluff, but I'll give that particular horror a miss. Its grotesque, multi-stepped waves provide a dramatic photo studio for career big-wave chargers, who tow into these unthinkable beasts behind high-powered jetskis. These images have been beamed around the surfing world and have made surf stars of some of these fearless, down-home Tassie boys. It's about as far from what I know of surfing as cage fighting is from tai chi.

When I'd booked our ferry fares, I'd thought $1400 return sounded a bit steep. We are doing the day trip over and the night trip back, just to experience both. By day we have booked what's called 'ocean recliners' to travel in comfort, and a sleeping

cabin on the way back. For the four of us and our car and caravan to be safely transported on a ten-hour ocean voyage both
ways across the treacherous waters of Bass Strait, $1400 sud-
denly seems like extremely good value. I'm thrilled to discover
our fare is subsidised by the Federal Government to the tune
of $758 – yet more of our tax dollars won back in what seems
exceedingly generous middle-class welfare.

Most people touring the country and doing the ferry trip
with their $100,000 LandCruisers and Jaycos are not exactly
hard up. The rationale is that if you travel anywhere else within
Australia, the government pays for the roads out of your taxes.
Thus if you have cause to travel to Tassie, to compensate for
the lack of a road the government helps you out with the cost
of the fare. Very decent of them, I must say. We are among
several hundred passengers this day, and if that's a fairly average
day over the course of the year, a quick bit of maths suggests it
might be cheaper for them to build a bridge across Bass Strait
than for the government to continue to stump up the subsidy,
though my rough estimates of building costs for the world's
longest bridge may be a bit out.

I like the *Spirit of Tasmania* immediately. Even the security
staff are friendly and jovial, almost apologetic for the intrusion as they cast a cursory glance over our car and van for any
forbidden fresh fruit and vegetables, fish heads or abalone offal.
They ask if our fishing gear has been thoroughly cleaned, and
I can assure them that it has been nowhere near any fish, alive
or dead. The ship is clean and comfortable, our ocean recliners
are splendid and provide a spectacular view out over the stern
of the ship as we watch our wake and the Australian mainland
recede into the distance.

We steam past Port Phillip Heads and I dash outside to
take in the moment, gripped by a sense of another threshold
crossed, a new stage in our journey. A mysto surf spot lies out
here somewhere near the heads, and I catch a glimpse of the

line-up, which isn't breaking today but is known to throw up long, dreamy, Indonesian-style reef-break barrels in prime conditions. Its existence is under threat from the current dredging of the channel through the heads to ensure safe passage for large cargo ships. The survival of a treasured surf spot seems like pretty small change compared to the powers of international commerce and shipping that inevitably prevail here. Local surfing and environmental groups put up a brave fight to halt the dredging, but they never stood a chance.

On board, we eat a bad, over-priced breakfast and settle into our recliners, Kirst and I take turns ushering the kids around to view the ship's attractions. Alex befriends a small Aboriginal girl from Alice Springs, and they dash off through the crowded ship, hand in hand.

I take the kids to the onboard cinema, allegedly to see a kid's movie, *Beverly Hills Chihuahua 2*, but I have misread the schedule. Instead, we have turned up just in time for a talk by a national parks officer on the unique flora and fauna of Tasmania. This fails to impress the kids, but I try to get them excited with grisly descriptions of the habits of the dreaded Tassie devil. They bear it bravely and the young presenter is engaging and full of interesting facts. Who knew one third of Tasmania is devoted to national parks, or that one fifth is World Heritage listed? We hear the poor Tasmanian devil's tale of woe: already slow, nearly blind, a terrible hunter and butt ugly, it's now being decimated by the hideous Devil Facial Tumour Disease (DFTD), a contagious parasitic cancer that threatens its very survival. Its only saving grace is its ferocious jaw strength and success as a scavenger, enabling this 'vacuum cleaner of the bush' to devour every morsel of roadkill and other dead or injured wildlife it comes across – beaks, claws, bones, skins, feathers, the lot.

Mercifully, the Devil Facial Tumour Disease has not yet reached the remote south-west corner of the island due to its extreme isolation, and 'insurance' colonies of devils are being kept in quarantine to allow them to be repopulated should the disease wipe out the wild population.

In other startling revelations, we learn a wombat's poo resembles those square packages of mini-Violet Crumbles so they don't roll away – a wombat uses them to mark its territory. And when attacked or frightened, the otherwise poorly armed wombat will defend its burrow by blocking it with its bum, which is comprised of thick cartilage and can ward off almost any attacker, much like Winnie the Pooh when he becomes lodged arse-first in Rabbit's burrow after eating too much honey. I can now also dazzle dinner party guests with the news that baby echidnas are called 'puggles', and the amusing spectacle of five or six male echidnas following around a female on heat is known as an 'echidna train'. Expectant kangaroos, clever things, can determine the gender of their offspring and delay or accelerate its birth according to the needs of their mob and the availability of food.

We learn of the extraordinary migratory journeys of the humble muttonbird, or its far sexier alternative name, the Shearwater. My daughter sticks up her hand and wants to know why we saw so many dead muttonbirds on the beaches of Victoria. The answer would be funny if it wasn't so sad. Muttonbirds, it turns out, have been almost as short-changed by nature as the Tassie devil. With poor eyesight, lousy judgement and badly balanced physiques, they almost inevitably crash-land on their descent from their epic migrations from Siberia. It seems an almost inconceivably harsh fate – to have successfully flown thousands of kilometres from the frigid environs of Siberia and made it to their southern Australian breeding grounds, only for their bloodline to be cut short by an ill-judged landing. Enough of them survived these ungainly arrivals to become a staple diet for Indigenous Australians and early settlers alike.

Less fortunate was the long-extinct Tasmanian tiger, which

was mercilessly hunted for decades by farmers protecting their flocks of introduced sheep and cattle and bounty hunters who were generously remunerated by successive governments for delivering their pelts. It was eventually declared a protected species on 10 July 1936, fifty-nine days before the last known tiger died in captivity. Undeterred, our optimistic offspring remain hopeful we might spot one.

LOST IN THE NORTH-WEST

The ten-hour journey passes smoothly and happily enough, and we disembark in the northern port of Devonport on dusk and make for the nearest inn. We have booked lodgings for the night, rather than having to find a van park and set up in darkness. Even this mid-range motel feels like luxury after our first month in the van, and we make the most of the hot showers, crisp clean sheets and a decent counter meal before retiring. After consulting a couple of local contacts and carefully studying the weather map, I succeed in convincing the family that we should first strike out to the rugged north-west coast of the island and the little town of Marrawah.

I'd been here twenty years earlier on a surf magazine trip with a gang of big-wave surfers ready to charge the region's famed reefs. But we had been comprehensively skunked, and so I have something of a score to settle. I've tried to prepare Kirst for the empty isolation of the west coast with descriptions of Marrawah's one general store and rough-and-ready brown brick pub.

'It may have come along a bit in the last twenty years,' she offers optimistically, imagining perhaps that the tide of sea-changers has swept through here, too, spawning an outbreak of cafés and gift shops. Yet, as we traverse the north-west's lonely country roads through windswept fields and only the occasional farmhouse, I can sense the family's faith in my stewardship waning. As we pull into Marrawah it is immediately apparent that this is the one coastal town in Australia that has not changed a skerrick in the past twenty years.

I've been recommended a free beachfront camp site at Green Point, close to the surf and the area's only general store, but when we arrive late in the afternoon it is packed with caravans and campers, all squeezed into one small patch of grass next to a small besser brick toilet block. It seems mad and slightly depressing that, in the midst of all this vast emptiness and great natural beauty, all these travellers should huddle together in one unremarkable parking lot simply because it's free. It is a grey, wet afternoon, the ghostly silhouette of an army of wind turbines slowly rotating in the distance. There is nothing here but a fairly nondescript stretch of beach and a children's playground. We could barely park the Expanda in its crammed confines if we tried. The Grey Nomads have infested the place, drawn by no other attraction than the absence of camping fees. Clearly, it is time to increase the old-age pension.

We decide to press on, having come too far to try and squeeze our van into a crowded car yard of campervans on a barren, windswept paddock. We pass another cluster of Nomads congregated at a roadside rest stop, gathered round in their camp chairs, exchanging the day's news. It has only just occurred to me that those hundreds of vans that come trundling off the *Spirit of Tasmania* every day have to go somewhere, anywhere it seems. We are like a plague of locusts descending on the island. We drive on and check out another national park campground, one with modest camping fees, and it's entirely deserted. Somehow it just doesn't feel right so, even though it is getting late and the kids are starting to protest, we promise we'll find a much nicer spot five minutes down the road. We pull into the last of the three camp spots listed in our guide as dusk settles, and it is also utterly empty, its cosy camp sites nestled into the coastal bush. There are basic pit toilets and non-potable water taps but, with the comforts of the Expanda, it's all we need.

It's starting to mist, and the dark evening clouds are threatening so we set up quickly before the heavens open. Kirst and I seem to have settled into fairly traditional, unspoken gender roles. I handle the outside – unhitch the van, open up the bed ends, wind down the stabiliser legs, detach and stow the sway bars, light a fire in a rusted old drum with some wood left by the last occupants. Kirst works her magic inside and soon has the beds made up and a homemade chicken noodle soup on the stove.

Both kids are complaining of sore throats. Kirst is convinced the complimentary ice-cream with chocolate topping at the hotel restaurant last night was the tipping point. And the damp weather isn't going to help. We hustle them into bed early and I go for a quick walk before it's completely dark, keen to find the beach and orient myself.

This coastal scrub all looks remarkably similar, with few landmarks, only one or two species planted en masse, presumably to hide the scars of some earlier sand-mining operation. It would be easy to get lost in the fading light and the pervading grey mist, I muse. I follow the campground dirt road as far west as it seems to go before it loops back around to the main road. The ocean is getting louder, but there's no way through. I spot an old four-wheel drive track through the sand, almost overgrown and decide to give it a crack. I trudge on for a while, but I am getting no closer to the beach; I seem to be running parallel to it. An even more overgrown track off to the right beckons, so I give that a go. I run over the directions back to our camp site in my head to ensure I don't get lost – *turn left at the four-wheel drive track, then right onto the campground road*. It is a featureless dusk now and I toss up whether to turn back, but the track seems to open up on a rise ahead, and I am convinced the beach is just over it. I clamber on to the top, panting, only to be greeted by yet more dunes stretching off into the greyness.

In the distance, I can't tell if I am looking at sky, ocean or the all-pervasive mist.

Entranced in my boy's own adventure surf fantasy, I boldly press on, eager for redemption after my abject failure as a wave-hunter on Victoria's Wildcoast. I imagine stumbling over the final dune to the sight of perfect, empty beach breaks stretched out in both directions. The reality is somewhat duller: it is getting dark and my family is curled up in a little van back somewhere in the bush. I figure it is time to turn back. As I trudge along, I am becoming increasingly damp and my mind begins playing tricks. *Is this the way I came? I don't seem to remember this large overhanging gum tree. I don't recall the sand changing colour here.* I am retracing my footprints and there have been no forks in the track, so this must be the way, but I have to stop and actually place my foot in one of the prints to convince myself that the fit and tread pattern are identical, to calm my rising nerves. I am starting to sweat, despite the evening chill. *Did it really take this long to get back to the four-wheel drive track?* When I do find it, the track is now a dark tunnel with some faint smudges of light where the canopy thins out. It takes forever to reach the campground gravel road. What would my panicked wife do if I was stumbling out here all night, lost and disoriented – leave the kids, grab a torch and look for me? Drive into the nearest town and raise the alarm? Curl up with the kids for a sleepless night? What started as a simple evening stroll is quickly morphing into a flight of paranoia. I am very happy when I finally glimpse the pure white of our van through the bush and slip eagerly into its protective cocoon.

THE EDGE OF THE WORLD

I am standing at an ocean lookout grandly titled 'The Edge of the World'. It lives up to the name. Head due west out here across the Southern Ocean and you won't hit land until Argentina, over 11,000 kilometres and three oceans away. The mouth of a broad river has stained the sea black, as a large unruly swell collapses across the sand bar. Crazily oversized driftwood – entire mature trees – bleached white by the sun and salt, are deposited on the beaches in piles like matchsticks. A howling onshore and bitter cold assaults me with the legendary force of the Roaring Forties.

A poem by local legend Brian Inder has been immortalised on a bronze plaque bolted to a rock, reminding me of my fleeting mortality in the face of these timeless elements.

> *I cast my pebble on to the shore of Eternity*
> *To be washed by the Ocean of Time,*
> *It has shape form and substance*
> *It is me*
> *One day I will be no more*
> *But my pebble will remain here*
> *Mute witness for the aeons*
> *That today I came and stood*
> *At the edge of the world*

I am feeling quite small and insignificant enough as it is, thanks very much. The family is bored and miserable back in the deserted campground, staving off colds. There is no rideable surf. The onshore wind is relentless. I have no clue as to the whereabouts of any local surf spots that might work in these conditions. I bump into a park ranger who, inevitably, informs me that this mass of whitewater at the river mouth offered perfect waves yesterday afternoon. I want to interrogate him for local knowledge, but don't want to look like a clueless tourist. And he is off to clean the toilets, taking his mop, bucket, rubber gloves, disinfectant and secrets with him. I am just starting to appreciate that the humble national park rangers of this fair land are the gatekeepers to some of the last remaining secret surf spots we have. They know every inch of the coastlines they patrol, and have access to four-wheel drive tracks and beaches not open to the general public. The pay is apparently lousy but the pay-off is potentially great.

Remarkably, I do have mobile phone reception, and so I find myself, during a fruitless drive around the surrounding coast, able to watch the final day of the Quiksilver Pro at Snapper Rocks, back home on the Gold Coast. It is a surreal experience, taking in the hype and clamour of the pro surfing circus from this remote region.

North-west Tasmania is the polar opposite to the Gold Coast. There you can drive down the main highway, taking in views of one world-famous point break after another without getting out of your car. 'If there isn't a car park out the front and a McDonald's over the road, they won't surf it,' was how one old-timer described the softness of the young Gold Coast surfers to me. Am I suffering a similar condition? These remote, cold-water waves aren't looking too appealing, especially on my own. You have to drive for hours just to check a handful of obscure surf spots, a thirty-minute round trip down bumpy dirt roads just to get to the coast, then a hike over dunes to catch a glimpse of the ocean on the remote chance it may offer a good wave.

In the absence of surf, desperate and disoriented by the elements, I make a dubious decision to embark on a spot of video blogging. The disturbing results, posted on YouTube, inspire a flurry of emails from friends, alarmed by my clearly deteriorating mental state.

Despite these conditions and my family's misery, I am quite taken with Tassie's west coast. She may be a poor cousin to the more popular east coast, with its famed Bay of Fires making Lonely Planet's top ten travel destinations, but even the fruitless driving, the potential discovery around every bend, is an endearing if slightly maddening trait. If the Gold Coast gets about in a bikini with all its assets on show, the Tasmanian west coast is shrouded in multiple layers that must be carefully and delicately peeled away in a deliciously slow reveal. I'm just not sure I have time for her slow-motion striptease.

I do find one spectacular vantage point to survey the surrounding coast: the concrete foundations of an old lighthouse, long since demolished according to another park ranger. Standing atop this strange concrete box on the crest of a hill, I can see for miles in all directions – the craggy coast to the south, a great outcrop of wind turbines to the north and the low coastal heath all about. A small bay to the south seems to hold a borderline rideable wave, and I watch it for a while. Maybe with an offshore wind and a bit of sun, but not today.

I return to our empty campground and the kids, having done a bit of morning school work, are riding bikes while Kirst reads a book. It's a cosy domestic scene and I count my blessings. They are amazed I've been gone two and a half hours and haven't surfed and I try to impart some of the excitement and wonder I've been experiencing for the surrounding coast. I am keen to take the family for a drive and reveal the spectacle of the west coast to them but they are not convinced. I goad them into the car to take them on a tour of some of the most scenic coastal vistas, but the kids seem unmoved by all this majestic natural splendour, the sense of marvellous isolation, and want to return to the van and watch a Harry Potter DVD instead.

STANLEY TO THE RESCUE

Two days are enough. The kids are damp and cold and require some basic creature comforts – a warm shower, a laundry, flush toilets, a café – and so we retreat to the impossibly quaint charm of Stanley, only sixty minutes' drive but a world away.

En route we decide to check out the inauspiciously titled Dismal Swamp, a giant 640-hectare sinkhole, the largest in the southern hemisphere, in which a magnificent blackwood forest has thrived for millennia. The early explorers, who tried to survey its dark, damp depths back in 1828 and had to perch on tree branches above the swamp to sleep, gave the area its name. It must have been inconceivable back then that the source of their suffering would ever become a tourist attraction. Re-branded as the Tarkine Forest Experience, there is now an enormous 110-metre steel luge that allows you to slide down into the sinkhole at astonishing speed. For $60 for a family of four, we each get to experience this thrilling ride twice, except for Alex, who is deemed too young and happily accepts the offer of a quad-bike ride to the bottom. Some of us think he's gotten off lightly. The rest of us wait at the top of the luge, fitted with ridiculous polystyrene foam helmets and hairnets, and are one by one fitted into large vinyl sacks. Kirst screams the whole way down, a spectacle that has become a minor – very minor – YouTube hit.

Vivi is nervous and dissolves in tears when it's her turn. Our guide wisely suggests I go next, rightly predicting that Vivi will find her courage once Mum and Dad are out of the way. She does, and gets to the bottom beaming with excitement, ready to go again. It's the best family tourist attraction we've come across and worth every cent. Incredibly, the proprietor is yet another Tassie tree-changer from the mainland, just around the corner from us in Currumbin

At the bottom, the soggy forest floor is explored via a series of winding wooden boardwalks, decorated here and there with interpretive sculptures and art pieces. It sounds like a dubious concept, but it all works in well with the natural surroundings. My only reservation is the timber company Gunns' forestry industry propaganda at every turn, incorporated presumably in return for their generous corporate sponsorship of the attraction. They have even managed to have a species of orchid named after the company and brag that forestry is Australia's 'only carbon-positive sector'.

Stanley is everything Marrawah is not – a popular yet relaxed, historic seaside town whose every dwelling appears to be heritage listed. Perhaps it is just the pleasing contrast to Marrawah's isolation, but we all fall in love with the place immediately. The day we arrive it is a brilliant, cloudless afternoon as we follow the narrow promontory out towards the Nut, the spectacular plug of an ancient volcano that rises from a sparkling blue ocean like a large cake, Stanley's old cottages clustered about its flanks. An old fishing port decorated with cray pots and suitably weathered old tugs completes the picture.

Vivi is about to turn nine and she has asked to celebrate in some of the small-town attractions. We ride the chairlift to the top of the Nut and wander the misty plateau, pretending we are lost in the Scottish moors. She buys homemade nougat from the old-fashioned sweet shop. We visit the Seaquarium, a modest collection of sharks, crayfish, seahorses, fish and mollusks housed in a large steel warehouse by the wharf.

We take the high road out of town to the Highfield Historic Site, the well-preserved home of the former head of the Van Diemen's Land Company, Edward Curr. I'm not normally a huge wrap for historic homes, but this one is engagingly presented, and snippets of letters and articles on display offer an insight into the times.

For instance, it's remarkable how unattractive these early settlers found the same surroundings that we are so charmed by. Edward Curr wrote *An Account of the Colony of Van Diemen's Land, Principally Designed for the Use of Emigrants*, in which he observed of the all-pervasive eucalypt:

Nothing could be more unsightly than the generality of the tree, thinly clothed with leaves, and the trunks and huge branches covered with long shaggy strips of dead bark . . . In our Australian paradise, our highest aim is to exhibit on a small scale something like the beauties which rise at every step in the land to which we have bade adieu, well content if we can here and there produce a corn-field surrounded by a post and rail fence, or a meadow of English grasses clear of stumps.

And the cultural life of the colonies was hardly an attraction for these early settlers. A Mrs Adey wrote a letter to her family in London in 1828, which was published in a London newspaper and later in Hobart, in which she declared:

In the first place, you could hardly imagine that a country like England could produce such an illiterate club as this Colony. Who would not have expected to find by this time a library at least? They had one at South Carolina before it was established twelve months. Saturn is not more remote from the sun than Hobart Town from all Science and Literature.

IT'S ALWAYS FIVE O'CLOCK SOMEWHERE

Despite the fulfilment of this dream to travel the country with my family, surfing and writing as I go, I find I am subject to some odd bouts of moodiness. It is something of a let-down to realise that even this supposed Utopian existence is not going to banish my darker musings – or teeth-grinding, for that matter.

What's prompted this searching self-analysis? I have just had my first alcohol-free day of the trip, nearly six weeks in. It's an easy trap to fall into. You're on holidays. So are all the people you run into in camping grounds and caravan parks. You've been driving, setting up the van or herding kids about all day. It seems the most natural thing in the world to have a beer, or two, or three at the end of the day, and then – sure, well, alright – just a small glass of wine. If someone goes to refill it, why protest? It would not be difficult to get on a mild bender for weeks or months on end without anyone raising an eyebrow. I wonder if this is part of the lure for many of the Nomads, happily getting sozzled in their fivesies circles in van parks around the country. And I guess there is no great harm in that. Except, for me, I suspect it is manifesting in a little shortness of temper, a slight darkness of mood in daylight hours. If I'm honest, I've been a bit of a grouch through much of the early stages of our journey, despite some delicious highs. So, why am I needing to gently sedate myself at the end of each day?

The Stanley van park encapsulates the simple beachside cara-vanning holiday enjoyed by so many average Australians, the sacred Working Families our politicians seem so enamoured with. The sight of a family kicking an old Aussie Rules footy with the bladder almost bursting out the laces sends a wave of nostalgia through me. On the Saturday night, management has even organised a little on-site entertainment in the form of veteran showman Wayne Lunson, the 'One-Man Band'. He's an old-school country-and-western singer well into his sixties, dressed in black from head to toe, who throws in a bit of rock-and-roll to keep the young ones happy. He sets up in the camp kitchen at dusk for a sound check and breaks out a bit of Johnny Cash's 'Folsom Prison Blues'. It's quickly apparent that he's the real deal. He reminds me of legendary Hawaiian shaper Dick Brewer, a dignified, silver-haired gent, immacu-lately groomed and politely spoken off-stage. I compliment him on his choice of music and he marvels at the enduring power of Cash. 'Even the young ones will get up to dance to

Johnny Cash, even when they won't dance to rock-and-roll,' he observes.

There're only the kids and me around to appreciate his sound check, and I worry that he's not going to have much of an audience. I needn't. By the time we get back from dinner, the Stanley Caravan Park is rocking. Almost the entire population is gathered around in camp chairs, sipping beverages, the kids riding around on bikes, a few unsteady dancers stumbling about the cement dance floor. It goes on well into the night, until I am no longer charmed by Wayne Lunson, the One-Man Band. Instead, I wish he'd shut the hell up and that the now well-lubricated crowd would stop yahooing.

The family is in no hurry to leave Stanley for another spartan surf mission, but I am getting restless. I've had my two surfless days in Marrawah, and I've done my three days of being a mug tourist in Stanley – I need to get in the ocean. A trip like this can easily cease to be a surf trip altogether, the longer you go without getting wet. A few days sightseeing and you start to see yourself as just another punter lining up for the next attraction, driving from place to place, only pausing to pull out your wallet and hand over more cash.

I am starting to feel more like Bill Bryson than Bruce Brown – visiting historic sites and tourist attractions, scribbling notes of fascinating facts, exploring the curios at the local museum and chatting to the archetypal museum volunteer in his Led Zeppelin T-shirt, sampling the famous scallop pies at the Swinging Anchor Café.

While certainly fine attractions, they aren't what I've come for. Rick Miller and Jonnie Grant wouldn't have lingered over such rustic charms. They might have chatted up a comely barmaid at the pub, but they wouldn't have been photographing particularly cute cottages.

ON THE ROAD

And so, after careful, angst-ridden discussions, Kirst and I hit upon a compromise. We will depart Stanley and head south, where a new swell is brewing and I have a local surf companion keen to show me around. We will break up the marathon journey from the far north of the state to the far south with an overnighter in another historic seaside hamlet, Strahan, gateway to the astounding Gordon River. To make it easy on ourselves, we'll lash out on a comfortable holiday apartment to save unpacking and packing the van for a brief one-nighter. It seems a reasonable enough itinerary.

Yet, in the execution, several flaws reveal themselves. The rest of the family has come down with a cold, and so we're coughing, wheezing and sneezing the whole way. Driving from Stanley to Bruny Island, via Strahan, proves roughly twice as time-consuming as heading directly down the middle of the island – we could not have chosen a more winding, agonising route if we tried. This means we arrive in Strahan late in the afternoon and leave early in the morning, seeing none of the many sights and attractions – the magnificent Gordon River Cruises, the glorious national park surrounds, the succulent fresh local seafood, Australia's longest running stage play, *The Boat that Never Was*, performed nightly at the local visitors' centre since 1984.

Strahan is also distinguished, as I'd learned from Prof Short, for having the highest wave energy of any beach in Australia. And I can't leave without at least observing this phenomenon. Though not renowned as a surf destination, its rugged west coast is almost never without thumping Southern Ocean swells sent straight from the Roaring Forties. And so I drive out to Ocean Beach to watch the enormous beach break close-outs thump endlessly along a seemingly infinite stretch of beach. The waves are big, ugly and formless for surfing purposes – all this swell expending its energy at the end of a vast ocean voyage to no useful end. We've hoped to get away early this morning to make Bruny Island by nightfall, and the day is getting away from us. If I were to calculate total kilometres driven per wave ridden on this trip so far I would be horrified. We've been in Tasmania a week and I have yet to enter the ocean.

We eventually get away around 10 am and drive all day, with short breaks, until moods are frayed. The journey is staggering with its scenes of great natural beauty one moment and destruction the next – pristine forest butted hard against clear-felled plantations. I am starting to think of Tasmania as a state split between sharply contrasting personalities. There is the clean, green Tasmania of the '100% Pure Tasmania' tourism slogan, of Bob Brown and the birthplace of the Greens, of the stirring defence of the Franklin River, of ecotourism, eager tree-changers from the mainland opening handicraft businesses, boutique breweries, artisan food producers and organic farmers. The other is the Tasmania of old-school miners and loggers who'll terrorise demonstrators in their tree houses, of the Gunns Corporation tying up conservationists in long and expensive court action, of corrupt politicians doing their corporate masters' bidding, of clear-felled forests and lunar landscapes.

These two Tasmania's are no better represented than by the near-neighbours, Straham and Queenstown – one an ecotourism hub, the other a hellish vision of the effects of unrestrained mining. Kirst has been cautioning me that our intended route will take us right through the heart of Queenstown – am I prepared for this? At first I don't know what the fuss is about. And then we turn a corner along our winding mountain forest road and are confronted by a landscape laid to waste. I know people live here, raise families here, have civic pride and attachment to their town, but decades of gold and copper mining have stripped every last skerrick of vegetation from the surrounding hills for hectares. A barren, grey-brown landscape of bare stone and earth stretches off in all directions. Remarkably, Queenstown is enjoying something of a bohemian renaissance with artists and writers finding unlikely inspiration in its bleak landscape. The next moment, we round another bend in the highway and are back amid glorious, rolling forest, as if Queenstown were just a nightmarish mirage.

BRUNY ISLAND CALLING

But I have a date with a swell, and damn the World Heritage listed forests, wild rivers and stunning national parks. My family can only watch nature's wonders fly by as we speed on to our date with the Bruny Island ferry. My local contact in Tassie, Ryan, a marine scientist by trade, has suggested that conditions look favourable for this remote, unspoilt island outpost and has offered to take a couple of days off work in Hobart to show me around and unlock its surf secrets. It is a generous offer and, after blundering around the north-west, the prospect of some local knowledge is thrilling.

It's touch and go whether we're going to make the 5 pm ferry or have to wait another hour for the next one, a prospect that excites no one. I rush on, even when all hope appears lost, speeding through quaint little towns with names like Snug, Lower Snug, Tinderbox and Oyster Cove, barely pausing to admire their charms or observe speed limits, and pull into the ferry terminal a few minutes after five. Thankfully, the ferry is running late and we have time to spare. I take this as a good sign and, after our two-day road marathon, I'm invigorated by the prospect of the short ocean voyage to an island destination. The kids befriend a local family on the ferry and I take this as another good portent. When they learn I am a writer, the kids' mother encourages us to call in to the local school so the kids can meet again and suggests I might like to talk about my books to the students. I think we're going to like this place.

It's only a short, fifteen-minute ferry ride to North Bruny Island, but I underestimate the drive to our camp site at the far end of South Bruny, joined to the island by a narrow land bridge. I'm in a celebratory mood and convince Kirst we should stop at the pub for tea, an unremarkable besser brick structure blessed with the most sublime views over the water to the Tasmanian mainland. The food is average but a cold beer never tasted so good. By the time we leave, the sun is going down and I'm alarmed to discover my estimated ten-minute drive to our camp site turns into thirty. The kids are exhausted after two long days in the car and a bit spooked by the dark bush setting; we set up hurriedly to get them to bed. It has been a mad two days on the road and it's taken a toll in brittle moods and dark expressions; I vow never to schedule such a gruelling road marathon again.

I have a day before my local host arrives and I'm itching to explore the island, so I opt to give Kirst a break while I take the kids for a surf check. It seems cruel to stick them back in a car, but Kirst needs to go to bed and convalesce from her stubborn cold. I fall in love with South Bruny immediately. We go to the lighthouse and look out over some enticing beach breaks peeling away in a distant cove, while Alex is simply delighted to find a flat surface on which to ride his scooter.

At Cloudy Bay we run into another family on the beach. 'Digital Odyssey' is professionally written on the side of their LandCruiser, and I'm curious to know what it means. The guy's a similar age to me and it turns out he's a visual artist, touring the country presenting his video installations projected onto natural surfaces. His name is Craig Walsh, and he and his wife and two-year-old daughter have been travelling the country presenting his work for the past eighteen months. Their little girl knows no other life. He's taking part in the Ten Days on the Island Arts Festival, which has events scheduled all around Tasmania during our stay. It's serendipitous. When I mention we're from Currumbin, he explains that he's been invited to our local Swell Sculpture Festival, but admits he has reservations about the whole 'sculpture by the sea' public art movement, because of its artificial imposition on natural landscapes. He likes light, his chosen medium, because it leaves no footprint. I make a mental note to check out his work when we're in Hobart. When I explain I am on a surfing road trip around the country, he mentions that he's recently read and enjoyed, *Occy*, the biography of surf champion Mark Occhilupo. I'm immodest enough to admit that I wrote it. We both marvel at how blessed we are to be travelling the country with our families while practising our respective crafts. He's plugged into the arts funding scene and corporate sponsorship. We are both the beneficiaries of an incredibly wealthy society and system that will allow a couple of middle-aged family men to earn a crust exercising their artistic impulses.

We drive to the local school so the kids can meet up with their new friends from the ferry. I go to the office, explain our situation and am ushered in to meet the principal, a charming man who seems delighted to make our acquaintance. The students are on lunch break and he whisks Alex and Vivi into the playground while he asks if I'll speak to the Grade Fours after lunch. I give them my spiel about pursuing dreams and the power of story, and they seem to enjoy it. Our kids are welcomed into their respective grade levels and made a part of the afternoon's classes. When I'm finished, I go to collect Alex and they are being taught to give each other massages. The kids are thrilled with the company and don't want to leave. On the way back to our camp site, we stop to pick blackberries by the side of the road and gather wood for a campfire. It's a brilliant, impromptu day of chance encounters and happenstance that leaves us all on a high. We return to camp to find Kirst rested and well on the way to recovery. Everyone wins.

STRANGER IN THE NIGHT

By now our kids have charmed senior citizens across the eastern states, but I'm almost pleased to discover a pair of crusty old fishermen in our campground who prove immune to Alex's cuteness. He's quickly learned that the oldies are easy prey who hand out treats to performing children, but this pair of old fishos next door are a tough crowd. They give Alex short shrift despite his best efforts and clearly want to be left alone. They're a funny pair and have pitched two tents at diagonally opposite corners of their spacious camp site, I assume because one of them is a snorer. By the end of our first night, I am able to confirm my theory.

They sit in their camp chairs round a large fire mainly in silence, broken only by the occasional fart or grunt of conversation. They look like a pair of walruses, donning their waterproof fisherman's overalls for each expedition out in their tinny, moored just off the nearby beach.

It's a glorious camp site, nestled among twisted coastal eucalypts, in the lee of a sheltered white sand beach. We cook chops, polenta and veg for dinner on our little roll-out barbecue, and sometime after dark my local contact, Ryan, turns up. He's a friend of a friend, a keen client of Gold Coast surfboard shaper Neal Purchase Jnr, but we have never met before. He impresses me immediately by parking at the far end of the campground and quietly approaching our camp on foot, not wanting to intrude on our cosy family scene. We all warm to Ryan instantly; he's a hard guy not to like. He's driving an old school LandCruiser ute with a canvas awning over the tray, all decked out for surf exploration with a mattress, a couple of Neal's distinctive shapes in the back and a little camp stove and provisions neatly stored away. He spends his working hours studying data from fishing boats to work out how our fish stocks are holding up and his leisure time scouring the Tassie coast for waves. I'm in good hands.

Ryan's an ex-Sunshine Coast boy, lured south by his marine science career. I know only a handful of people in Tasmania, yet over half of them seem to be marine scientists. There are more of these salty boffins per head of population here than anywhere else on earth, drawn by the abundant, pristine environment and its proximity to research stations in the frigid Antarctic.

'I'm better suited to this climate anyway,' says Ryan, referring to his pale skin and red hair. 'I used to fry at home.'

The next day he takes me on a tour of the island and is relaxed about showing me its numerous breaks. I ask if I should be wary of using the name of the island in anything I write, and he says to go for it. There are only about half a dozen surfers here, and its remote, cold, southern isolation and fickle elements means that is unlikely to change. He just seems happy for someone to surf with. The potential here is staggering, and it is a tantalising prospect that over the next couple of days we might score one or more of these places doing their thing. There is a river-mouth right that looks incredible, a long sandbar set against a magnificent headland of towering eucalypts. There's another wedgey left peak in the corner of a bay surrounded by cliffs, and a rare left-hand point that only breaks on huge swells into a kelp-lined bay, like a cold-water Padang Padang.

The first day there is no sign of our predicted waves and I am left pondering how a seven-metre swell can simply go missing. But I enjoy Ryan's company while bouncing down dirt roads in his LandCruiser. We stop to sample the award-winning pies at the little local store – I go the scallop and Ryan opts for the wallaby. We end up surfing the little wedgey peak, and we get a couple of glimpses of promise on the odd bigger set, but the fairytale swell doesn't materialise. A young couple appears on the beach and goes swimming, which seems slightly remarkable since I am shivering in a full-length steamer. The surf is average but the surroundings are sublime.

The family is off to the local berry farm today, and we pass them on a dirt road speeding in the opposite direction. It is a strange experience encountering them like this, by chance, on the road. To see them from from the outside makes me feel oddly protective. What a pretty picture they make.

'IF WE HAVE ABS, I'LL MAKE PILAF.'

Ryan and I meet the family back at our camp site in the afternoon and take the kids back to the bay to dive for some abalone for dinner. I've told Ryan of my ordeal in Cape Conran and he's determined I will enjoy some Tassie abs, unmolested by fisheries officers. The light is fading, and Ryan is into his wetsuit and away before I know it. He is an expert in and around the water, and the quickest changer into a wetsuit I have ever met. Normally, I am the one waiting for my surf companions to get ready, but I can't keep up with him. Viv and Alex hop across the rocks after us, Alex falling numerous times trying to keep up and howling like he needs hospitalisation with each minor bump. But it is great to see them free-ranging to their hearts' content, slightly soft city kids being gradually toughened up by this exposure to the elements.

Ryan has plucked a couple of abalone before I even get in the water. Alex is a bit concerned about Uncle Ryan's safety out there in the ocean on his own: 'What if he gets swept out to sea?' I tell him that Ryan works in the ocean and knows what he's doing. Later, after Ryan has collected five large abs and I have collected none — hear that, fisheries department! — Alex comments, 'Ryan really loves the ocean; he works for the ocean.'

I find the diving here challenging. It is cold, dark and we are in two to three metres of water. There are thick forests of kelp to be negotiated under water, and my ears throb in pain when I dive to the bottom. I soon give up. Alex has fallen again on the rocks and is calling for me. Vivi is further up the bay, having waited where we changed into wetsuits. Like seeing them in the passing car, it is an odd experience viewing my children from this vantage point, treading water out in the cold ocean. They appear incredibly small and vulnerable set against the rocky foreshore and the high sea cliffs that ring the bay.

Kirst has taken the rare moment of solitude as an opportunity to go bush walking and has left us a note: 'If we have abs, I'll make pilaf.' It sounds like the name of a Raymond Carver short story or an obscure art-house film. The abs are amazing rolled in flour with salt, pepper and lemon, shallow-fried and served straight off the pan with a cold beer. Kirst's rice pilaf is the perfect accompaniment.

The next day we are less optimistic about our alleged swell and take our time hitting the road but, when we eventually check, it has indeed risen. We head to the river-mouth right and it is breaking, but from the distance of the check-out spot it's hard to tell how big. 'There's only one way to find out,' says Ryan. We suit up and I jog down the track after him, again struggling to keep up. The track is littered with a millennia of accumulated oyster shells, the inlet being alive with huge rock oysters. It is easy to imagine the Indigenous population reclined around a fire under the big gums that line the water's edge, feasting on oysters, mussels, abalone and fish. Ryan reckons he and his mates often light a fire here and warm up around it between sessions.

We jump into the tidal current and are soon carried out to the line-up. The tide is running out and the line-up is a bit confused with the new rising swell. We get a couple, but Ryan reckons it will improve on the other side of the midday low tide, so we head in for coffee and another pie, have a bit of a scout around a couple other beaches and then return to the river mouth.

The wind has swung a little and it's more sideshore, the line-up still uneven and lumpy. It's frustrating to get this tantalising glimpse of the place without the full monty. There are small insiders hugging the bank and dredging over the shallow sand-bar, but they are too quick to make. The larger sets break wide and often close out. There are some in-between ones that go all the way through, but they are hard to find. I am willing the wind to swing offshore, the sun to come out, the tide to fill in a little with the brunt of the swell and ruler-edged barrels to start spinning down the sandbar. It doesn't happen. I feel like my expectations of perfect waves are killing the magic. I fear my years of working in the surf media have skewed my perceptions of these sorts of experiences – they call it surf porn for a reason. I sense there is some kind of Zen lesson for me in all this: dispense with expectation; give up the chase; calmly, patiently and joyfully meet my familial commitments, casting an occasional eye seawards to monitor conditions. It's a tricky balancing act to pull off, though. We leave tomorrow for Hobart, to prepare for the other wedding in which Vivi will be a flower girl. I may get a chance for a quick early, perhaps just as the surf is getting good. I have to surrender.

What's worse, I bump into a real-life, modern-day Jonnie Grant in the campground as we are preparing to leave – a young, good-looking bloke who is doing the round-Australia surf trip with a mate and their girlfriends. They've set off from Double Island Point on Queensland's Sunshine Coast and scored waves all down the east coast, he reckons. 'I've got all these cuts that haven't had a chance to heal. We've been in the water every day,' he enthuses. 'At least they're getting a chance to heal now.' Bastard.

THE WEDDING SWELL

After a couple of weeks dragging the tribe the length and breadth of Tasmania in search of surf, we have the wedding of dear friends to attend. Vivi will be fitted for her dress in Hobart, then it is on to the Tasman Peninsula for one of the most joyful weddings I've ever had the fortune to help celebrate. The magnificent location, on the edge of a bay on the surfless north coast of the peninsula, is dotted with historic convict lodgings and could only be improved by the miraculous appearance of perfect left and right point breaks peeling down both sides of the Bay.

It doesn't matter, though – I'm not even looking at the weather map. I am ready to enjoy the occasion to the full. And so I do, coming out of the blocks rather too fast for my own good and hitting the wall by 9 pm, whereupon I take a little nap, then re-emerge around midnight to rejoin the festivities. Not a bad effort, I think, for an old married bloke. I don't know what time I get to bed, but the kids are up at 6.30 regardless, which is just as well – a mate, John, has the good sense to knock on the Jayco door and get me up for the early around 7 am.

Hung-over, sleep deprived, clueless as to where the most favourable conditions might arise, I clamber behind the wheel of the Rav and simply drive as directed, with no expectations but to immerse my craggy head in saltwater. I drive down more winding dirt roads, barely daring to care what lies at the end of them. Inexplicably, in the middle of nowhere, a large pile of old shoes stands on the side of the road like a termite mound. More quaint Tassie eccentricity.

Finally, we swing into yet another dirt car park, trudge up more dunes, get to the top and catch a glimpse of the Southern Ocean and . . . well, what do you know? Long, straight swell lines make their orderly entrance into a wide bay, groomed to perfection by the most gentle offshore breeze. I can scarcely believe my eyes. A dozen or so surfers are enjoying a well-defined right in the western corner of the bay under sheer cliffs. In the middle of the beach, another peak is offering a handful of surfers quality lefts and rights. I am speechless.

It is a solid four to five feet and reminds me of Johanna, Victoria, with its neatly tapering banks separated by deep channels, its long, powerful walls and pinching almond barrels. We cannot haul on wetsuits fast enough. It's a long, meandering march down a narrow track, through encroaching coastal bushland, a short wade across a shallow creek and then a mad sprint down onto the wide, glorious beach.

I choose the less-crowded middle peak. Even though the right in the corner looks superior, I'm in no mood to wait my turn in a crowd. I discover I have the right of the peak virtually to myself, paddling out, picking off set waves, kicking out in the shore break and paddling straight back out into another set. I am exultant.

By the time we get back to the wedding site, a leisurely recovery breakfast is being served for the large crew who have camped overnight – bacon, eggs, hollandaise sauce, mushrooms, spinach, coffee, fruit, toast, pastries. The morning could not be more perfect if my father-in-law rang to say he'd just purchased the Boag's Brewery.

RETURN TO VAN LIFE

After the wedding festivities, life back in the van at our next bush campground seems awfully quiet. It's a secluded national park at the north-western tip of the Tasman Peninsula with barely a soul around, known as Lime Bay. There are no waves, but with an indifferent weather map I've decided to forgo the wave-chasing for a few days and just be. I'm enamoured enough with Tassie now, despite its trials, that I'm ready to be absorbed into this remote coastal bush and feel the sweet relief of my dissolving sense of self. The kids are less thrilled, riding their bikes around the clearing in a vain search for playmates.

There's one old guy camped at Lime Bay in an old-school

canvas tent; he's fifty-something and apparently quite content in his own company. I find Alex at his camp site one morning, and the guy is oiling Alex's bike chain with olive oil. He tells me he is from Brisbane, and his forest activist daughter lives in Hobart. He's waiting for a call to go and join her and her friends in their latest protest, a blockade of some threatened forest as loggers attempt to clear-fell as much old-growth forest as possible before new regulations put an end to the practice. He looks more like a blue-collar timber worker than a greenie. It's not the sort of backstory I'd imagined for him, and so I immediately catch myself concocting another – a distant, estranged father now trying to win back his daughter's affection by joining in her radical ecoactivism. But I could be miles off. Another afternoon he is preparing dinner, and Alex wants to know what he is having.

'The same every night – a tin of peas, Dutch Cream potatoes and either sausages or steak,' he says. 'Tonight I'm having steak.'

'Mmm, sausages,' Alex moans.

THE BIG EAST COAST LOW

The weather slowly deteriorates until we are just about blown and rained out of our camp site. I've seen the weather coming, a vicious east coast low that promises to bring both surf and foul weather, and I convince Kirst that we should vacate to more comfortable accommodation to ride out the storm and position myself to take advantage of the resultant swell. A stranger in a café overhears our conversation and recommends the Best Western Motel at Eaglehawk Neck. In a region thick with B & Bs and country cottages, I figure we can do better than a generic motel chain. But as we drive around looking for suitable lodgings in the pouring rain and howling wind, the Best

Western appears like an oasis out of the gloom. Formerly the Tuffra Hotel, it is situated on a hill overlooking Eaglehawk Neck with panoramic views of the ocean and surrounds. Sir Reginald Ansett apparently once claimed it had the best view of any hotel in Australia. We don't hesitate. As the elements rage outside, we each enjoy a spa bath and curl up in front of the gas fire and a movie. Kirst serves up a hearty Lamb Korma for dinner. I've procured a bottle of local pinot noir from nearby Richmond, where Kirst's granddad Max grew up, and a packet of Norfolk Bay smoked octopus. It could be Beluga caviar and French champagne at the Waldorf Astoria and I'd be no happier.

The east coast low that I'm counting on to bring swell is tracking south right over the coast, producing near cyclonic conditions on its leading edge, but hopefully at some point in the next twenty-four hours it will generate offshore winds from its trailing edge. Before darkness falls, I venture out to have a sniff around and check the ocean conditions. The swell is huge, but in the maelstrom it's hard to tell exactly *how* huge. The rugged sea cliffs to the south are marked by some spectacular geographic features – Devils Kitchen and the Blow Hole. I park the car and get out in the sheeting rain to marvel at the crazy, anarchic ocean smashing itself against these pockmarked cliffs. I don't think I've ever seen a wilder ocean. It seems preposterous that I'm going to paddle out into it tomorrow. The family couldn't be coaxed out of our cosy apartment this time, so I return with bug-eyed bluster about what I've just witnessed, but I'm alone in my excitement.

I've been in touch with some of the Shipsterns crew, the local big-wave chargers who are plotting a mission up the east coast to surf a little known offshore reef named Governors. I have in mind a nearby right-hand river mouth sandbar that's been described to me as a Southern Ocean Kirra. The Tassie boys are hoping to get down and surf the river mouth in the afternoon, then we've arranged to rendezvous back in Hobart for a slideshow of this and other recent surf adventures and a group interview with the core of the local big-wave clique.

Tassie has proven a confounding surf destination, and this is where I hope to hit paydirt. I'm like a poker machine junkie feeding coins into the slot, figuring it has to pay out sooner or later. I go to reception to request a late check-out. I'm off at dawn on my surf mission, but I don't want a 10 am deadline for my return. It's at least half an hour's drive to a shadowy location I've never been to before; I want to give myself every chance of success.

The hotel manager is another tree-changer, a panelbeater who divides his time between here and Brisbane. How long has he been here? I ask. A young bloke in his early twenties dressed up in a hotel uniform, presumably the manager's son, walks past and quips, 'forever'. He is clearly not enchanted by the area's social opportunities. I'm granted a midday check-out and have the family's blessing. Now I just need nature to cooperate, but she's proven to be an unaccommodating mistress.

As night falls and the wind and rain rage outside, I stand on the balcony, willing the wind to swing offshore, but my faith is fading. I finally surrender: Tassie has beaten me. Its meteorology and geography is too confounding. Like a Rubik's cube, it just seems too complex trying to get all the elements to align. If most stretches of your average coastline are 2D, with one generally favourable swell direction and one prevailing offshore wind direction, Tasmania is 3D, with so many different facing coasts – not to mention bays, inlets, nooks and crannies – and so many different wind and swell directions, that there is simply too much information to process. Surfers take a lifetime to learn its tricks and moods, and still get skunked. What hope do I have in a month, with a family and a van in tow?

When I wake early the next day, still harbouring some faint hope of partaking in the fresh swell and predicted offshore winds, conditions outside look no better. Crestfallen but desperate, I venture out into the maelstrom, drive for half an hour with barely 100 metres visibility along rapidly deteriorating roads until the path ahead is a muddy, potholed goat track leading to a rough, dirt car park. Incredibly, on this Thursday morning, kilometres from anywhere, the car park is packed. This, at least, seems encouraging.

I peer out into the haze, but it is hard to discern a thing through the fog, drizzle and spray. The wind, at least, is offshore and the swell is clearly up, but it is raw and wild. We are returning to Hobart that afternoon, the offer of a friend's house for the weekend too good to pass up. I've promised Kirst a day off in the city as compensation for her tolerance of my swell-tracking. This is my window.

And so I suit up to paddle out, hoping for the best. On the beach, a young bloke comes staggering out of the shore break, wide-eyed and panting. 'I just saw the biggest fin out there,' he wheezes. 'I thought, bugger that.' What do I do now? Walk back to the car park dry and change out of my wetsuit? I bump into a pair of fishermen and they reckon there've been plenty of dolphins about, so I choose to believe them. I've come too far to turn back now. I paddle out nervously, scouring the all-pervading shades of grey sea and sky, trying to discern any sudden movements of large marine creatures. It seems mad.

I get to a spot about half a kilometre out where the ragged swells seem to stand up into rideable walls. There is not a soul about. I've never been so disappointed to have the surf to myself. Where is everyone? I look out towards the horizon and see someone kick out of a wave another 500 metres out. I am only halfway to the line-up, after thirty minutes of determined paddling. These guys are nuts, I decide, and steel myself to the mission ahead.

Once, I've been told, this place broke all the way through from the outside take-off spot to the beach, like Tassie's own Superbank. Someone had published a line-up photo in a surf magazine and, as if in protest, it had never broken like that again. It is a shadow of its former self, chopped up by deep holes, hopeless close-outs and fat sections.

It is a grim battle to try and make position out here amid the madly rearing peaks, but I'm determined to salvage something from this wild ocean. I bow my head into the sleet and spray and keep paddling seawards, hoping some benevolent force might reward my foolhardy endeavours. I find a couple of wide, fat walls before getting comprehensively cleaned up by a rogue set and washed halfway to the beach, defeated.

When I get back to the hotel just after midday, the cleaners are already going through our apartment and the family is nowhere to be seen. I head to reception sheepishly and there they are, waiting patiently, the van already packed, the kids playing on the pool table. Kirst is reading a magazine quite contentedly. Fortunately, spirits remain buoyant on the Good Ship Baker.

THE SHIPPIES CREW

It's another cold, wet evening in the quiet suburban enclave of Clifton, just south of Hobart, and the Shipsterns crew have gathered at their unofficial clubhouse. It's a squat concrete dwelling on a quiet street that's home to three of the lads, but functions as a regular crash pad and gathering place for the entire crew. Old boards are strewn throughout the house and unkempt backyard. A rusted barbecue that's seen better days leans against the fence. Surf mag posters dominate the walls. There's plenty of beer in the fridge and chips on the coffee table. Rather surprisingly, someone is whipping up a tangy Asian salad in the kitchen.

The boys have been chasing a massive east coast swell at a notorious offshore slab up the coast. The last time they surfed the place eight months ago, Billabong XXL Ride of the Year nominee Mike Brennan broke his back. He's only just got back in the water, and this is a fairly extreme exercise in 'getting back on the horse'.

'That was scary driving up with Marti,' Mike says. 'I started getting all these weird feelings in my toes and my back. I thought it was going to be twenty-five foot, but today it was nice – a good day to get back into it. I'm stoked. That was my biggest fear, getting back out there.'

'Nice' is not the adjective I would use to describe the nightmarish death slab the boys have been towing into all morning.

There's a rowdy post-mortem of the day's surf adventures over a few beers as the boys drift in one by one from various points on Tassie's south-east coast.

With a mainland surf journo in town (me), they've pulled together a few of the Shippies regulars to talk story and explain what it's like growing up with one of the world's most monstrous waves in your backyard. There's the unofficial spokesman Marti Paradisis, along with Mike Brennan. There's big, blond, softly spoken Tyler Hollmer-Cross and the diminutive Dustin Hollick, a smiley bloke who shows enormous ticker in beastly waves.

'Tyler gets the bombs every session, but because he's, like, seven feet tall they don't look that big,' laughs Marti. 'They're fucking huge, man. You're thinking, *if that was Dustin on that wave it would be in the XXL.*'

And then there's Iain 'Wombat' Chalmers, the entrepreneur of the group with his own sports marketing business, trying to engineer a big-wave event at Shippies.

After watching mainland surfers come down and launch big-wave careers off the back of a few waves at Shipsterns, the local crew decided it was time to step up and lay claim to their wave.

'It was like, this is it, this is in our backyard. This is what we want to get into it. Let's make it happen,' says Marti with obvious passion. 'And we made it our goal to be locals out there. Other crew from the mainland started coming down and surfing it, and we were like, fuck, if we don't do something soon this isn't going to be our wave anymore. So, we just started chasing it, made sure we were onto it in every swell and started pushing limits.'

Now, half a dozen of the local crew have attracted sponsorship and established serious big-wave cred from their dedication to Shipsterns. Several of the boys have earned nominations in the Billabong XXL Big Wave Awards, untold magazine covers, their images at Shipsterns plastered on the side of buildings.

'How's Hollmer's wave? It's on the side of this six-storey shopping centre, his Shippies bomb,' says Wombat. 'One of our mates in South America, he was on a bus and was like, what the fuck? There's Hollmer on the side of a shopping centre.'

Next, they are planning a big-wave contest there, pitting the best local guys against the top big-wave surfers from around the world. To some, this may sound like sacrilege, the final indignity for a once-secret big-wave spot that has been turned into a photo studio. But the Shippies boys say if they don't do it, someone else will.

'If anyone's going to benefit from the commercialisation of our wave it's going to be us. It's not going to be anyone else,' declares Wombat.

'The hardest thing is going to be who you cut out of the local guys,' says Dustin.

'If there's a comp at Shippies and I'm not invited, I'm paddling out there and telling every cunt to fuck off, so that's not going to happen,' Mike adds.

Marti Paradisis was the first of the current Shippies crew to be introduced to the place, as a naive seventeen-year-old straight out of school, by Shipstern pioneers Andrew Campbell and James 'Polly' Polanowski. The pair showed him footage of a wave that blew his young mind, and promised to take him along the next time it was on. It was another six months before that day arrived and, when Campbell took a heavy wipeout, injured his back and came up screaming, Marti decided he was out of his league.

'I hadn't really travelled around, had only been surfing a couple of years, so it was all pretty new to me. I'd never seen waves over six foot,' he says.

But another six months later, Marti got his first good barrel out there and the fire was lit. Dustin Hollick; the Hollmer-Cross brothers, Tyler and James; Jye Johansen and a few others started charging it regularly, and photographers Andrew Chisholm and Stuart Gibson were always on hand to record their exploits.

The next step was to get the machinery to allow them to surf the biggest days. 'A couple of big swells came through and we were walking in, sitting on the rocks, trying to paddle the sets that weren't the big ones, and there were these fucking nuggets coming through, the biggest barrels we'd ever seen, like, fifteen-foot-plus,' recalls Marti. Despite being on the dole, Marti managed to get a $10,000 bank loan to purchase a jetski, which has proven a wise investment, enabling them to surf the biggest days and placing the Shippies crew squarely at the leading edge of big-wave surfing. 'Then we'd go down and it didn't matter how big it was – we'd be frothing. And the bigger it was the more frothing we were, because we've got this machine that's going to get us into these things.'

Then Marti tells a little story that convinces me never to so much as paddle out at the place. 'Brook Phillips, a local board shaper round here – I towed him out the back, and it was the first time he'd really whipped, so he was like, "Just get me into a small one to start with." Just jokingly I said, "You get what you're fucking given, Chooka." I was thinking, *I'll just get him into a small one*, and then I turn around this fucking set of the day rolled through, just rose on the horizon. I said, "Dude, there's a fucking bomb coming. Any one of us would kill for this wave.

You've sort of got to go, ay." And he says, "Righto, get me into it." So I towed him in perfectly, and he slightly overcorrected his line. It was on a big wave, twelve to fifteen foot, and he went down on take-off. I thought, *fuck, alright*, and started doing a few circles, looking for him to pop up. I turned around and the next wave behind was probably even bigger, pushing twenty foot, the biggest wave I've ever seen out there. I'm like, *fuck, Chooka hasn't popped up yet*. I can't see his board. I can't see nothing. And this thing just mowed him down, two-wave hold down, and then he pops up two hundred metres down. You watch the video and see his nose pop up just before this thing mows him down – he didn't get a breath or anything. Copped it sweet. And that's why that day is memorable, because that was fucking heavy.

'I went and picked him up, and he jumped back on the ski. He chilled out for a minute, and I went, "Fuck, dude, you're not going to get worse than that. You may as well have another dip." And, same deal: got out the back, no small waves, then the horizon went black and I went, "What do you reckon?" He said, "Fucking do it." I whipped him in and he got the barrel of the day, got the bomb, made it out, wave of the day, loved it.'

Marti finishes his tale with a smile of satisfaction.

HOBART IS A SMALL PLACE

I love Hobart. It is so small that you don't actually have to arrange to meet up with anyone – just wait a while and you'll inevitably bump into them. We'd met a lovely lady in our campground on Bruny Island who had hit it off with the kids. We'd been hoping to catch up again in Hobart and, lo and behold, cruising around the beautiful inner-city harbour front at Salamanca one day, we walk into a bookstore and there she is behind the counter. I do a double-take when I enter and see Vivi happily conversing with her. Later that week, again in Salamanca, I bump into the video artist Craig Walsh and his family having dinner, and we organise to catch his installation. Before I left home, I'd asked my publishers whether I might be put in touch with renowned local author Richard Flanagan. He and I had met at the Sydney Writers' Festival and share the same publishing house, so I thought it would be valuable to gain his insights into Tasmanian society and culture. I hadn't managed to get in touch with the great and private man before we left, but I walk into a Hobart bookstore and there he is, chatting to the proprietor.

We all adore Hobart, a rapture only heightened by the spoils of having our newly wedded friends' house available while they are honeymooning at North Stradbroke Island, near our Gold Coast home. But on our last day in Hobart I am faced with a tough cultural dilemma. We have planned to visit MONA, the stunning Museum of Old and New Art that has the art world, and most of Hobart, buzzing. Admirers of this vast, privately owned art museum, made possible through the largesse of professional gambler David Walsh, speak of it as a life-altering experience. But the day before our visit the boys from Shipsterns inform me their wave looks likely to be on. Would I like to come down and surf it?

A trip to Shipsterns will involve hiring a car so my family aren't stranded in Hobart, then driving an hour and a half down the coast, walking for two hours into the break, paddling out into waves that I have neither the fitness, ability or desire to tackle, where I might very well drown or maim myself. MONA involves a fifteen-minute drive with my family or a leisurely ferry ride up the Derwent River, free entry and the chance to gawk at the largest private art museum in the world, built at a cost of around $100 million, showcasing around $75 million worth of art. Both are likely to be awe-inspiring, to challenge and confront. I think of Marti's story of whipping his hapless surfboard shaper into the biggest wave of the day, of the two-wave hold down, the sheer rock cliff that fronts the break, the shallow rock ledge that forms hideous and unpredictable steps in the wave face. At MONA, the greatest horror I face is being confronted by a wall-sized depiction of genitalia.

In the end, I choose MONA, shameless coward that I am, but feel edgy and unsettled all day. Still, the museum doesn't disappoint. Just wandering the building itself would be worth the price of admission, if there was an admission price. Remarkably, Mr Walsh has made entry to this vast temple to his eclectic art tastes entirely free, despite annual running costs estimated at $7 million. (MONA has since announced a $20 entry fee for 'Non-Tasmanians'.) A former croupier and alleged maths genius, Walsh has become the wealthiest man in Tasmania by formulating the complex mathematics to beat the house in a range of gambling pursuits. Some conservative elements in Tasmania seem alarmed by this mixing of art and gambling, they think it unseemly for lofty cultural pursuits to be bankrolled by something as crass as games of chance. Yet I think of him as a modern day Robin Hood, taking from the rich casinos and bookies of the world and giving this gift of art to the great unwashed. Rumour has it that he has his own apartment within the building, with a one-way mirror as a floor so he can look down at the masses filing through his museum.

I walk into one exhibit, a bizarre installation in a darkened room that looks like a science laboratory. A hushed crowd is gathered around a large apparatus comprising glass jars, tubes, metal piping and pumps that claims to replicate the human digestive system. It is called Cloaca, Latin for 'sewer'.

'Cloaca is being fed,' an attendant whispers to me.

'I beg your pardon?' I ask, thinking she has me confused with someone else.

She repeats the statement in an urgent, hushed tone. Lo and behold, another attendant has a silver tray laid out with lunch for this strange science experiment/art installation, consisting of a salmon salad to be washed down with a dark ale. This meal is ladled into a funnel, which then makes its way through the elaborate system of tubes and chambers, its progress clearly visible. 'You should come back at five and watch it poo,' the attendant recommends seriously. 'It will blow your mind.' Apparently, in some other galleries where Cloaca has been exhibited, its poo has been sold for vast amounts.

David Walsh is not selling poo, but he is promoting his wine and boutique beer, Moo Brew – 'Not for bogans' is it's appalling slogan. I'm not much of a wine buff but I can report that the dark ale is one of the great beer-drinking experiences of my life.

It occurs to me, observing the studiously hip young things patrolling the museum floor as attendants, that perhaps this whole thing is an employment program for hipsters who would otherwise be sitting forlornly in inner-city cafés discussing the experimental short films they are trying to get funding for, or the movie roles they just missed out on.

Later, we go into town to view Craig Walsh's 'Digital Odyssey' in one of the city's many gardens at the appointed hour on dusk. I'm not sure what to expect, but when we turn up at the allotted place and time it appears nothing is happening. There is just a quiet garden on a Sunday evening with a couple of skateboarders loitering around, bludging cigarettes off a suspect older gentlemen in a sports car.

I look about more carefully and spot a large black box installed at one end of the park, with openings for video projectors and an explanatory notice about the art event we are about to witness. Gradually, as darkness falls, more people drift into the park. The video projectors flicker to life and the vague image of faces can be seen on two large trees. As it gets darker the images become more distinct, until you can clearly see the faces staring and blinking at you and each other. This seems to me a wholly original art form. There is no clearly defined start or finish, no physical space that we enter or exit to partake of it, nothing that announces its presence if you didn't already know about it. And when daylight returns there will be little indication that it ever transpired. I like it enormously. As the oversized faces look down at us, mouthing silent conversations, I am reminded of Christo, the French artist who drapes material over huge objects, though Walsh does the wrapping in light.

UP THE EAST COAST

In many ways, we've saved the best until last. The east coast is stunning – the weather milder, the beaches more family friendly, the roads better and the charming coastal towns closer together. We head first to the rightly renowned Freycinet National Park, home to the ridiculously picturesque Wineglass Bay. Our camp site at nearby Coles Bay is perhaps the best value of the trip – $22 a night for an exquisite position on a protected bay surrounded by towering, rocky mountains. Wineglass Bay's unspoiled natural environs are protected by an absence of vehicle access. It's a forty-five minute uphill hike just to glimpse it from the lookout, and a three-hour round trip to actually set foot on its white sand. It is possible to camp at its far end, but you must pack in and out everything you require. We only succeed in herding the kids the forty-five minutes up to the lookout, and that is quite an achievement. When you get to the lookout you might think you are being witty when you make some quip about expecting there to be a glass of wine waiting for you as reward. I know I did, but after hanging round the lookout for about twenty minutes I realised that every middle-aged dad who reaches the top makes a similar quip.

Your neighbours can really make or break a stay at any camp site. We meet Jim, an old surfer from Yallingup in southern WA doing the Big Lap with his wife, Marg. He has designed and built his own small runabout with twin outriggers and a tiny outboard motor. Constructed out of an old sailboard, the runabout is carefully configured to fit onto his roof racks alongside a quiver of boards. I'm hugely impressed, and when he takes the kids for a brief spin in it they are ecstatic. He's knowledgeable about the local breaks and latest swell and weather forecasts, as fit and keen a surfer as I'd aspire to be at his age.

Col and Jenny are another pair of Nomads in a vintage van, who adopt our kids with boundless kindness, playing their preferred card games for hours. Steven and Renee are taking their young son, Riley, around the country for a couple of years, paying their way partly through Renee's hairdressing, which she advertises on little flyers on the toilet doors and a sign out the front of their camper trailer. Our entire family gets haircuts for a grand total of $40, while our kids play together during Riley's carefully scheduled breaks in a strict homeschooling regime. We feel slightly guilty for our own informal educational approach, our kids less so.

A FAREWELL TREAT

The surf forecast, however, looks grim – gorgeous weather, light winds and mild temperatures, but almost no swell. I sense the surfing component of our Tassie leg is over, without it ever really hitting great heights.

I concede that it's all a part of the adventure. I have loved almost every moment being in Tassie, despite the frustrations of tracking down waves amid the swirling, ever-changing southern elements. It is still possible to have a true adventure here, to feel as if you are beating paths to little-known coastlines and discovering hidden gems. It is a wonderfully liberating feeling, a million miles from the mainland masses.

But, there is also a hint of regret that the weather has con-
founded me and I haven't made the most of our stay. As we
make our way up the east coast, I am painfully aware that just
a few days earlier this whole stretch of coast was lit up with a
stunning east swell that I have missed. There are tiny waves
peeling down dozens of inviting set-ups, and the idea of scoring
them at size is a torment.

It is all so beautiful, though, that it would be ungrateful to
sulk. One sunny day the kids even swim in the chilly waters
at our doorstep, and I take the chance to investigate a couple
of beaches to the north that have been recommended to me in
hushed tones.

The swell is small, but the coast is awesome – miles of empty
beach without a soul around. From a high coastal lookout, it
appears almost completely flat – a sheet-glass ocean sparkling
under a brilliant blue dome, the tiniest fringe of whitewater caress-
ing the beach. As I descend the winding dirt road, it becomes
apparent there are some fun peaks to be had. A little cove houses
a right at one end, a peak in the middle and a left at the other
end. It is an entirely unexpected treat. If this was the Gold Coast
there'd be a hundred surfers scrapping for those peaks.

Still, it is a slightly eerie sensation paddling out entirely on
my own. Is there some deadly peril I don't know about? I stroke
into my first wedging right and quickly discover one minor
hazard. I kick out of the small close-out and find myself hopelessly entangled in a thick bank of kelp. The stuff wraps about
my legs and leash so tightly I can barely wade out of it. Every
ride ends in the same struggle to free myself from its clutches. I
am just about fed up. If it's not the wrong wind or tide or swell
direction, it's the damn kelp. The little wedging peaks are fun as
hell but paddling back out each time is like pulling teeth.

I eventually give in. There's a little southerly pulse predicted
in a couple of days' time, and I resolve to return then and see if
the weed has been dispersed. As I drive out I see a busy gang of

national park workers preparing for a controlled burn, reducing the fuel load to lessen the bushfire risk.

⌒

When I return, on a crisp, cool morning a couple of days later, the entire foreshore is smoldering. Little plumes of smoke rise out of the blackened forest here and there, and small flickers of flame are still dancing on fallen logs. The smoke is choking, and it's a surreal drive through the hazy, charred forest down to the beach. The swell is indeed a touch bigger, the weed appears gone and the beach break looks like an inviting skate park of peaks and bowls and ramps. If I was Chippa Wilson, I'd be in heaven. Even as an old cruiser, I still manage to have a ball, pausing out the back to contemplate the apocalyptic scene along the foreshore.

One heavy plume of smoke is rising from the midst of the forest and, as the offshore wind freshens, I begin to wonder what would happen if the fire sprang back to life. At what point would I be well advised to paddle in, jump in the car and get the hell out of here? Tassie surfing definitely serves up some interesting dilemmas.

I watch the plume closely in between rides as it rises above the forest, but the waves are too much fun to leave. As it turns out, this will be my last surf in Tassie, and a suitably strange and symbolic one – a see-sawing wrestle between delight and anxiety, exhilaration and frustration.

BAY OF FIRES

I'm ready to be unimpressed by the legendary Bay of Fires, if only because I dislike the kind of 'Top Ten Travel Destinations of the Next Five Minutes' hype that travel guides generate these days, but as we cruise towards the north-eastern corner of the state it becomes clear this is a truly exquisite slice of paradise. The nearest town, St Helens, gives little indication of the coastal splendour that lingers just outside its city limits. It's just another sleepy country town with a pretty harbour, a non-descript main drag of petrol stations, supermarkets and take-away joints. We completely miss the discrete sign for the turn-off to the Bay of Fires.

As we head out of town, though, things quickly take a turn for the beautiful. Binalong Bay, the gateway to the famed bay, welcomes visitors, quite inexplicably, with a saucy statue of a fine-figured lass in a bikini sitting atop a large stone pedestal on the side of the road. Being from the Gold Coast, I'm accustomed to girls in bikinis being used for tourism promotion, but I'm not sure when a real one was last spotted in these chilly environs.

Undeterred, we push on through a series of stunning bays and bush campgrounds, all entirely free. That someone isn't trying to profit from this area's sudden vogue seems remarkable. The fact that we can take our pick from half a dozen unspoiled bush settings is a boon. We settle on a prime beachfront site at Cosy Corner, out of the wind but with a perfect white sand beach and its aqua-blue waters literally at our doorstep.

I feel like my insistent, gnawing surf lust has quieted, the overwhelming beauty of this place humbling me. Still, I can't help looking at that shore break. What miniscule swell there is comes out of deep water, hits the shore, stands up abruptly and collapses in one final gasp. It reminds me of Ke Iki in Hawaii, an ideal body surfing wave. I fantasise about what it might produce with a bit of a swell, imagining Hossegor-style beach breaks. But I content myself with long beach walks and rock-hopping with the kids over the boulders that litter the corners of the bay, exploring rock pools and rambling through the foreshore bush, gathering round an evening fire and sharing the last of our wine with delightful camp neighbours.

A billion stars decorate the night sky. The gentle woosh of the shore break punctuates meandering campfire conversation. The serenity of the moment is only marred by the accursed generator of a fellow camper. The lowest form of life in the caravanning world, I've decided, are those who insist on travelling with a generator. They are hopelessly hooked on a steady supply of electricity for their TVs and air cons, but not content to confine themselves to the mains power of the van parks. And so they insist on imposing their noisy, diesel machinery on their fellow campers, thumbing their noses and blowing raspberries at the tranquility to be enjoyed just outside their van door, if only they switched off their stupid appliances. It is quite unbelievable.

EXIT THROUGH THE GIFT SHOP

On the way to Devonport, on our final day, it is obvious this is a well-worn road by those departing Tasmania at the end of their holiday. Road signs pointing to the *Spirit of Tasmania* ferry terminal begin appearing on the side of the highway at least a hundred kilometres out from the ferry terminal. The highway is dotted with quaint establishments designed to wring the last few dollars out of the departing tourist. It's not until we board the ferry and bed down the kids in our cabin that I get a quiet moment to reflect on the past dizzying month.

This is written on the top bunk of our four-berth cabin as my family slowly drifts off to sleep around me. A predicted two-metre swell gently rocks them as they toss and turn and the ship's engine provides a faint background drone. The past four weeks have provided many lessons, some breathtaking highlights and severe tests. At times I've felt stretched to my limits, trying to juggle family life on the road, my myriad work commitments and the stubborn, indulgent pursuit of a few memorable surfs.

At times I've felt like I wasn't meeting any of these commitments very well. Certainly, in the early stages at least, I've been unreasonably grumpy and short-tempered with those I love the most. I've been confronted with the naive optimism of my original vision for this trip. If I wanted to surf all day, chase each new swell, have my movements governed by wind and swell and tide, I should have done all this when I was young and footloose like Rick Miller and Jonnie Grant. This is a different type of undertaking, more complex, with four sets of agendas, moods and personalities, needs and desires to take into account.

In some ways I feel like I have blown Tassie. I was so determined to hunt down waves that I was blinded to the needs of my family and a broad, long-term view of the unfolding weather patterns. I am also reminded of a bit of advice Pipeline legend Gerry Lopez gave to fellow Hawaiian Johnny Boy Gomes before he paddled out for the final of the 1997 Pipeline Masters. 'Let the waves come to you,' the calm, Zen-like Lopez had coached the notorious hothead Gomes. 'Don't chase them,' he'd urged as they'd surveyed the Pipe line-up from the balcony of Gerry's beachfront house before the final. Lopez had waved positioning signals from the balcony, and Gomes had gone on to win the final.

Of course, Gerry was talking about a thirty-minute contest heat at a legendary Hawaiian reef break he knew every inch of, not a month-long family road trip around a frigid, unfamiliar, wind-swept island. My strategy, I reasoned, would have to involve really putting the family first – read the weather, make careful judgements about where good waves were likely to arise, position us where everyone's needs could be best met, and then wait for the waves to come to me. I'd been chasing the surf, always arriving a day or two late, or leaving a day or two early, somehow fundamentally out of sync with the elements.

The only way, I figured, to get back on track was to sacrifice the surf for a while, surrender, give myself over to the family holiday, get us all back on track and then start again, hopefully this time in a better rhythm with the ocean and life.

6

GLIDING THROUGH VICTORIA

IT'S A FITFUL NIGHT'S sleep on the *Spirit of Tasmania*. The crossing is only mildly bumpy but the ship creaks and groans, and I toss and turn and drift off for only short intervals. Eventually, the faint light of dawn creeps through our porthole, just as an announcement comes over the PA system that we are approaching Melbourne. The kids jump out of their bunks and cram around the porthole for a view of the city lights.

Even though I've loved Tassie, returning to Melbourne is

sweet relief – an extended family pit stop at Mum's, with home cooking, an on-site babysitter, laundry, proper beds, hot baths and central heating. There's footy, family and a familiar coast-line. As we trundle off the ferry with all the other vans and cruise through Melbourne's eastern suburbs in the opposite direction to the morning peak-hour traffic, the kids are burst-ing at the prospect of being indulged in ways only a grandparent can.

Mum, bless her, always cuts out and keeps newspaper arti-cles she thinks will be of interest, usually surfing-related, and she's left a pile of them by our bed in the spare room. There's an interview with Richard Tognetti of the Australian Cham-ber Orchestra, whom Kirst and I are going to see that evening. There's an article about the rise of 'retro' surf fashion and cul-ture, cool urbane surfers with tastes for vintage single fins and a disdain for mainstream surf brands. And there's a bunch of clippings about the wild weather, floods, landslides and mass evacuations that hit Wilsons Prom only a week or so after we were there. Tourists had to be airlifted out by chopper, bridges were washed away, roads are still closed. It's unlikely they'll get it open again for the Easter crowds. The sense that we are only narrowly avoiding extreme weather events, staying one step ahead of disaster, only intensifies.

THE GLIDE

Tognetti is performing one of his more experimental concerts with the ACO, another of his explorations into the synergy between surfing and classical music. Surf photographer Jon Frank is presenting his artful still images and film as accompani-ment to the ACO's soaring soundtrack, and it's a collaboration I don't want to miss. Frank, ever the artistic perfectionist, triggers each individual image manually on a laptop to ensure they sync precisely with the music as it is played that particular evening. They are haunting, sometimes abstract images that blur the boundaries of art, music and surf cinema – extreme close-ups of a curling lip of whitewater, a chocolate-brown tidal bore in a Sumatran river, rough chunks of ice on a beach in Iceland as a heavily wetsuited surfer paddles out into a chaotic northern ocean. It is a memorable evening – old surfers in beanies rubbing shoulders with regal gents in bow ties and young urban hipsters dressed in black. All stumble out into a chilly Melbourne evening unsure what they've just witnessed, perceptions thrown wide open.

I'm gripped by a conviction that we've been present at a significant moment in the evolution of surf culture, one that has lifted it into the realm of high art. Frank's an old mate and he's been widely hailed for his unique perspectives on the ocean. I'm inordinately proud of his achievement, flushed with excitement as he bows awkwardly on stage with the orchestra, the packed concert hall offering thunderous applause.

This concert series, titled *The Glide*, has been made possible by the patronage of long-time ACO supporters Janet Holmes à Court, one of Australia's most successful businesswomen, and Jan Minchin, director of the Tolarno Gallery. I wonder how each of these disparate characters – Tognetti, Frank and their generous patrons – was convinced this was a project worth pursuing. Over the ensuing days, I'm determined to speak to each of them to gather their particular perspectives.

I ask Tognetti what it is about Frank's work that caught his eye.

'Mystery and depth of field,' he replies simply. 'That famous shot of Mick Fanning that Jon has taken in the barrel at Teahupo'o, you get the whole perspective. I don't get to travel to Teahupo'o, let alone surf it, so I want context. I want to be taken into the mysterious undertow of psychological narrative, and Jon's work does that.'

'Astonishing. His images are astonishing,' Ms Holmes à Court says when we speak by phone. 'To a non-surfer, it's quite fascinating how surfers do what they do, let alone how a photographer captures those moments . . . You can also see there is music and dance and spirituality in surfing, it seems to me, as a non-surfer.'

Jan Minchin, who has exhibited some of Australia's foremost artists and photographers, is no less effusive.

'Perhaps because I'm not a surfer and don't "know" waves, four days after seeing *The Glide*, I'm thinking about the sheer beauty of seas from King Island to Iceland,' says Ms Minchin. 'I'm thinking about the magical images of oceans, waves and surfers that Jon Frank captured. His presence is so palpable in those unexpected shifts from one sequence to another that I'm beginning to think that maybe the real subject of *The Glide* is filming itself.'

And so Frank has suddenly found himself the darling of the arts world, presenting his work to audiences from Slovenia to New York to Noosa, and taking a bow alongside Tognetti and the ACO to packed houses in Sydney and Melbourne.

Jon worked as a cinematographer on a documentary film that Tognetti collaborated on with surfing identity Derek Hynd and director Mick Sowry, *Musica Surfica*, and a close creative rapport was born. 'Richard just threw it at me – "We should do a concert together",' says Frank. 'He doesn't really give too many details when these things pop into his head. He doesn't want to restrict any creativity I might bring to the table. You go away and think, *Where do we start?* I've got a bunch of surfing footage and stills. There's all this music. How do we make the two work together without it being trite, without it looking like a surf movie, so it's a bit of its own entity? I had never done anything like this before.'

Frank is a private, reclusive figure, more comfortable bobbing in a wild ocean than in a concert hall, and finds the whole business of public performance completely nerve-racking. 'Melbourne, I was a fucking mess, a basket case,' he confesses. 'Live performance is not what I really do. I'd rather swim across a kilometre of open sea with sharks and twenty-foot waves. It wasn't that much fun. The way technically we have to trigger these images; you're running out of a laptop because the musicians play at a different tempo every night. It's like live TV. Honestly, if nothing goes wrong it's because a whole lot of stuff goes right. The potential for technical mishap is quite large. I'm holding my breath the whole time.'

After toiling in the commercial environment of the surf industry for most of his working life, Jon found the unfettered artistic focus of the project enormously refreshing. 'It means a lot to me, just to find people who appreciate what you do, who aren't running in the same circles,' he says. 'I'm essentially a surfing photographer, and I'm okay with that. It means a lot to me to have that support from people in different areas of life. To spend time with these successful, positive, really excited, very clever people – women and men who just want to help the arts and other areas – it's pretty inspiring.' He laughs. 'We need help. I applied for my first-ever arts grant this year, and it was a nightmare.'

LONG LIVE THE KING

After a few days supping on the urbane charms of Australia's cultural capital, Kirst and I have booked some much-needed couple time. Grandmother, uncle and aunt have agreed to take on child-minding duties for a long weekend while Kirst and I head off to King Island. This tiny speck at the western entrance to Bass Strait enjoys a unique standing in the surfing world, an open secret as a secluded wave haven that manages to escape any hint of crowds or commercialism. Its isolation, relative expense of travel and accommodation, and swirling, fickle weather patterns ensure that the surf masses will pick Indonesia ahead of King Island every time. Which suits us just fine.

Purely by chance, our visit coincides with King Island's legendary Long Table Festival, a celebration of local produce organised by the community to showcase the Island's treasure trove of fresh seafood, beef, lamb, cheeses, organic vegetables and unlikely delicacies, such as muttonbird.

Our transport to King Island is with King Island Air out of Moorabbin Airport on a tiny, twin-prop eight-seater Chieftain. Space is at a premium. I have to deliver my surfboard to the terminal several days before we fly to ensure it gets there for the weekend.

After two months together in the cosy intimacy of the Expanda, it's odd to wave goodbye to the kids and head off on a long weekend, but they're in good hands. We fly out on a gorgeous, sunny afternoon. Bass Strait is a shimmering blue blanket stretched out ahead of us, and then a little patch of green appears on the horizon. It is almost completely flat but ragged at the edges, like a torn scrap of fabric. Swell lines are clearly visible, wrapping around both sides of the island. We are only here for three days and the chances of scoring surf seem slim but, gazing down from the Chieftain, it looks an unimposing size to explore in the time I have.

Everything about King Island seems relaxed. We stroll across the tarmac to the small terminal and collect our bags a short time later from a trolley. Our hire car is waiting for us in the car park with the keys in the ignition. We're a short drive from KI's only town, Currie, and my first port of call is to pay my respects to legendary local and unofficial gatekeeper of the island's waves, Jeremy 'Wire' Curtain. Wire's a third-generation local, one of an elite club actually born in Currie Hospital, and a pioneer of many of the island's twenty or more quality surf spots. These days, however, a series of heart attacks has kept him out of the surf. He requires constant medication and his hopes of a return to good health hinge on the uncertain search for a heart transplant donor. He lives in a small flat above the chemist, which is fitting as boxes of pills and tablets occupy most surfaces. His enforced exile from his beloved waves has led to new interests in painting and music, his seascapes decorating the walls, guitars and amplifiers filling whatever space isn't occupied by furniture.

Wire has become close friends with many of the celebrity surfers who've passed through. There are signed posters on the walls from Kelly Slater and Pearl Jam lead singer Eddie Vedder. The pair flew Wire to Melbourne for one of Eddie's concerts recently. Signed surfboards from other visiting pro surfers hang from the walls or are piled up in corners. Wire pulls out a map and happily indicates a few of the main breaks likely to offer sport over the next couple of days. 'Some I won't tell you about,' he tells me with a sly grin. King Island is no secret spot these days, with surf movies and magazine spreads showcasing it to the world, and the local surfing population of around two dozen are generally keen for company. But they are not about to reveal their entire hand.

I want to hear more of Wire's story, but the afternoon's fading and we're keen to settle into our accommodation at Boomerang by the Sea before nightfall. Nowhere's far from anywhere in Currie, and we've soon installed ourselves in our ocean-view cottage, the heater already cranked up for us, with just enough time for a quick surf check before dark.

British Admiral is Currie's nearest surf beach, named after a shipwreck on its treacherous offshore reefs in 1874. *British Admiral* was on its maiden voyage from Liverpool to Melbourne when it hit the reef at 2.30 am on 23 May. Only nine of the eighty-eight on board survived, taken in by kangaroo hunters on the island. The dead were buried by hand in shallow graves on the beach, only to be uncovered by the tide and savaged by wild dogs. It must have presented a gruesome scene, hard to imagine on this golden afternoon as small, perfect beach breaks peak and peel along the length of the beach. It's small, cold and too late for a paddle, but the forecast looks promising – a growing south-west swell along with some wild weather.

With an island that can be driven end to end in an hour, a sturdy Toyota HiLux four-wheel drive, no kids and an understanding partner who pines only for a sleep-in, I'm like a dog off a lead. Despite a warm bed and a chilly morn, I'm up at dawn and out the door, board slung in the back of the ute, map laid out on the passenger seat with Wire's notes scrawled all over it. The small swell is building, the wind's nor'-east and there's an obvious protected corner that should house a wave. I drive down winding country roads, past farms and wind turbines, cows and kangaroos. Tognetti told me to wave at every car I see, and I now know why – they are all waving at me.

As I head out of town the road narrows, devolves from bitumen to gravel to dirt until finally a couple of overgrown wheel ruts run off into deep, soft sand, forking into numerous indistinct tributaries. A road sign warns it is four-wheel drive access only from this point on. The prospect of locating my wave out here suddenly seems like finding a needle in a haystack. The island looked so compact and navigable from the air, but down here it's a maze of farm gates, rough tracks and high dunes. I pick a sand track through the coastal scrub, more or less at random, throwing my fate to the wind. It leads to a dead end and a rough car park at the foot of high dunes that might only accommodate two or three cars. I park and survey the scene, trudging up a steep sand track over the crest of the dunes. Lo and behold, I'm confronted by a reasonable facsimile of North Narrabeen – a well-defined left peeling for a hundred metres or so in the corner of a long stretch of beach. The only other hint of humanity is a couple of motorbikes buzzing over the dunes in the distance. It's only small – two to three feet with the occasional bigger set – but it's drawing hard off the bank into spinning, dredging tubes. I have it to myself for a couple of hours before I've had my fill. After all the hoops Tassie had me jumping through, I feel like KI has given itself over to me with remarkable ease.

But I know there are more gems this coast has to reveal and one grand prize that I almost dare not hope to enjoy. With the swell predicted to rise rapidly, and the wind and weather to close in, there is a slim chance I may yet witness a rare oceanic phenomenon on the north-east coast of the island. Here, in huge seas, swell lines wrap around both coasts and intersect at a stretch of beach known as Marthas, producing a wide, bobbing field of A-frame peaks. As far as I know, it's the only surf break of its kind in the world and on my list of waves to surf before I die, but the odds of scoring it on a pre-scheduled long weekend are miniscule. Surfers lie in wait for months monitoring conditions for the right combination of wind, swell and tide to get this place on. In the meantime, I watch my footy team, Hawthorn, smash Richmond by ten goals in the afternoon game. All is right in the universe.

I return to my own private Narrabeen the next morning, but the wind has swung, the swell has built and there is no trace of the left I surfed yesterday. I try and find my way to the other end of the long beach where it looks more offshore, via a series of rough tracks, but nearly become bogged before I give up. As I head north up the east coast, the swell is cleaner but smaller the further I go, and this time I can't find the needle in the haystack. It's not big enough for Marthas and eventually, after three hours of fruitless driving down dirt roads, I give up and head to Wire's place to hear a bit more of the island's folklore.

Wire's grandparents moved from England to KI just before the start of the Second World War, as a safe haven from the mounting hostilities in Europe. His grandfather was an analytical chemist, making explosives for the mining industry, and could see trouble brewing – he knew he'd be seconded into the military for his expertise. 'So I think he brought the family here as a refuge while he was away in Europe,' says Wire.

He started surfing in 1964, after he and a friend saw the movie *Gidget* at the town cinema and figured the waves that ringed their tiny island home could be put to a similar purpose as the long, perfect point surf of Malibu. They built a crude board based on plans they found in an old book in the school library and lugged it down to British Admiral. 'It was the only place we could carry this board, it was so bloody heavy,' he says.

He eventually bought a longboard off one of the older surfers in town when they headed to the mainland for high school. 'And then I virtually had the place to myself for years,' he says. He discovered many of the island's surf spots by bush-bashing his way to inaccessible stretches of coast.

'We haven't been all that bloody good on the conservation side of things, but you had to do it,' he laughs. 'Most of them have been made into tracks now. It's quite funny seeing some of the corners in roads, and that was just where we used to have to go round bogs and they just kept going that way . . . We've had some pretty amazing surf vehicles. We used to just build cars up so you could get through.'

Marthas remains their greatest discovery. 'We found Martha just going up there one time fishing, that was with another guy who still lives here, Pete McLean, probably '71, '72. Just walked over the hill and saw these perfect A-frames. We didn't have boards with us that day, and it was a hell of a mission to get in there. There weren't any tracks.'

He recalls the 70s and 80s as the golden era of KI surfing, when the handful of surfers on the island earned good money working in the local tungsten mines. They explored the island for new waves and could afford to travel to Indonesia three or four times a year to escape the oppressive winters.

'It's been strange, really, because I thought, being so close to Torquay, we would have been invaded years ago, but it's probably fifteen to twenty years ago that people started coming,' he says. 'You get a few crew, but it's still not crowded, mainly because of the expense of getting here and the fickleness of it. Guys will spend thousands to come over and not get a wave . . . I know I'd rather be spending my money to go to Indonesia or somewhere, knowing you're going to get waves, and it's warmer.'

KI's waves started making their way into the surf media in the early 90s when Tasmania-based photographer Sean Davey first documented the alluring A-frames of Marthas, but he kept the location a secret. Still, word soon spread and pro surf team visits became a regular occurrence. In 2000, Red Bull sponsored a big-wave tow-in event on the island that got thoroughly skunked for surf but well and truly put KI on the map.

Since then, the pro team trips have become more frequent, and surfing identity Derek Hynd has become a regular visitor and bought the old dairy. Sean Davey has published a book of surf photography from King Island, and Wire has released his own surf video showcasing his home surf. *Musica Surfica* was shot here, and the film went on to win nearly every surf film festival in the world, spreading KI's reputation globally. Yet its empty isolation has proven immune to all this promotion.

Wire even hosted enigmatic California legend Miki Dora for two weeks. 'It was really good because he was the guy who surfed in *Gidget* when I first saw surfing, and I got to surf with him at the break that I used to frequent all the time,' recalls Wire. 'One of the last decent surfs I had before I got sick, about '97.'

Wire's travelled widely himself and, ironically enough, had made up his mind to leave the island's isolation for good when he passed through the US, just as the September 11 terrorist attacks took out the World Trade Center and nearly 3000 lives. Suddenly, KI's isolation seemed like a blessing. 'Seeing the panic in people's eyes – it was horrible. I just decided to come back and resettle here.'

It's time for me to head on to the King Island Golf Club for the Long Table Lunch, but Wire's stories of Marthas are swimming in my head. With the swell forecast to peak late in the afternoon, I figure I can sample the Island's produce for a couple of hours then duck off for a spot more surf exploration before dark. But I've underestimated the length of the Long Table Lunch. It's a convivial gathering of locals, and a few visitors like ourselves, many of whom have participated in a weekend of workshops, tours and hands-on preparation for the lunch – visiting farms and dairies to see where the meat and cheeses come from, picking vegetables, diving for crayfish and abalone. This is the slow food, pasture-to-plate ethos at its most grassroots.

We are seated with a charming bunch of locals who immediately make us feel at home – farmers and fishermen and their wives, and big-city refugees who came for a holiday and never left. Executive chef Lucinda MacDougall heads the kitchen team, and she emerges to give a good-humoured account of the smorgasbord we are about to experience and the food-gathering delights the weekend has already offered up. There are enormous platters of wallaby burgers, crayfish salad, abalone, muttonbird, lamb, beef, homegrown organic vegetables and the island's legendary cheeses. Three hours in and there's no end in sight to the parade of dishes, and despite the good food and company I'm getting restless.

We're on the 9 am flight out the next morning and, though the weather looks foreboding outside, I can't resist a Marthas mission. I make my excuses, leaving Kirst in the hands of the locals, and jump in the HiLux. It's a forty-five minute drive through sheeting rain out to the other end of the island and a bewildering labyrinth of narrow dirt roads that lead off towards the coast. Some parts of the road are already under water, and with no let-up in the rain I wonder how long it will remain passable. I take a couple of wrong turns, nearly get bogged, backtrack and finally emerge into a muddy car park overlooking a vast ribbon of beach. The rain lets up but light is already fading, and it's immediately clear the swell isn't quite big enough. Even so, a dancing field of tiny peaks bobs and sways in front of me. It isn't hard to imagine the aquatic playground these waves would offer with a bit more size. I can only watch with hungry eyes in the final rays of sunlight.

It's dark by the time I get back to the golf club, but incredibly lunch is still going, more than five hours after it started. I've checked another couple of beaches on the way back, and I'm ready to start looking at real estate. Kirst has a gaggle of friendly, interesting women for company, and the mother of all cheese boards is laid out on a snooker table to cap off a monumental feast. I'm just in time to sample the muttonbird and slow-roasted lamb. I'm a happy man.

CONTESTS CAN BE FUN

The surf city of Torquay is our next stop, and it could not be more of a contrast to KI. The massive pro surfing extravaganza that is the Rip Curl Pro is on, and I have to admit to a slightly ambivalent relationship with the pro surfing world. Despite a long career in the surf media, I've always remained a bit skeptical about the validity of surf contests – the subjective nature of the judging, the artless straining of the hardened comp performer, the babbling commentary and thronging masses peering out to sea. As a form of entertainment, I generally find it only slightly more interesting than the organised tedium of Test cricket.

So, it is ironic in the extreme, after nearly three months on the road and some 7000 kilometres behind us, that I should score the best waves of the trip so far at a surf contest. And not just any surf contest but the fiftieth anniversary of the world's longest running surf contest. The Rip Curl crew must have sacrificed a whole herd of goats in the lead-up to Easter, because the surf forecast for their milestone event at Bells Beach is as good as it gets. And you can see it coming a week out.

So I leave the family in Melbourne for a couple of days, rise two hours before dawn on the Thursday before Easter, tow the Jayco across town, over the West Gate Bridge, past Geelong and down the Surf Coast Highway to join the great 'meeting of the tribe'. The car park attendant doesn't know what to make of the Expanda, flagging me down and dispatching me to a remote corner of the car park/paddock, where its girth will not disrupt traffic flow.

The sun is barely over the horizon and the waves are firing – four-to-six feet and ruler-edged, that familiar corduroy stacked up out to sea, a chilly nor'-west breeze working its magic. The first bit of surfing I see is two-time world champ Mick Fanning going to town on a long, gleaming Winkipop wall with devastating intent.

Past Bells winners are in plague proportions, flown in from the four corners of the globe to help celebrate the historic anniversary – and the surf gods must be pleased with this assemblage of legends, blessing them with a week of swell and offshore winds. I join the Winki logjam and jag a couple of set waves amid the scrum. And when they move the contest from Bells to Winki, I enjoy firing six-foot Bells with a cavalcade of champions all afternoon. At one point, Paul Neilsen, Terry Fitzgerald, Pam Burridge, Lynne Boyer, Tom Curren, Martin Potter, Richie Collins and Trent Munro are happily sharing the line-up. It's like some weird surfing time machine where you can spin the dial to your favourite era.

Later in the afternoon, Occy and Joel Parkinson go to town on the Bells Bowl as the ocean takes on a steely grey, metallic sheen. As I paddle out, I witness Parko perform the tightest, most critical hook in the pocket – fast and sharp as the crack of a whip. He paddles back out, almost hyperventilating with excitement. 'This is like snowboarding,' he nearly screams.

I surf three times in a day and can't recall the last time I engaged in such a mad binge. The next day I return to Melbourne to collect the family to spend the rest of the Easter weekend in the rowdy environs of the Torquay Foreshore Van Park, right over the road from the busy pub.

WAYNE'S WORLD

With the strains of AC/DC's 'Hells Bells' and all the hoopla of the Bells fiftieth event still ringing in my ears, I feel a palpable sense of relief as we head west of Torquay. Bells at Easter, despite the pumping waves, is a test for any surfer. Back when I worked for *Surfing Life* in the early 90s, we had a fiendishly talented cartoonist named Paul Collins, who produced comic brilliance every month for a relative pittance, including an occasional series entitled 'If Surfers Ruled the World'. It showed wave ski riders tried and condemned to death, tanned and dishevelled young men with sun-bleached hair ushered to the front of nightclub queues. It was an adolescent fantasy back when surfers were still socially unacceptable. Now, it could be argued, at least in Torquay, that surfers do in fact rule the world, yet the process of climbing to that lofty position has changed them more than the world, if the enormous surf emporiums on every street corner is any indication. At one point during the event, the commentators announce that they have received a congratulatory message from 'acting Prime Minister' Wayne Swan, filling in on official duties while Julia Gillard tours quake-racked Japan. 'As a surfer myself,' Swan's message begins, 'I can appreciate the great milestone of fifty Bells events.'

As a surfer myself? Perhaps surfers really do rule the world, or at least the country, but neither Swan nor the budgie-smuggling

Tony Abbott quite fits the Collins caricature. And there's nothing in our coastal management policies or commitment to marine reserves to suggest they're any more enlightened. I'm still thankful to have Prof Short on-call.

The drive west on the Great Ocean Road is a winding course carved out of sea cliffs. Every bend seems to deliver stunning vistas of a seemingly endless succession of almost-waves – tantalising reefs and points that peak before fattening out, or zippering beach-break barrels that peel teasingly but inevitably close out.

Victoria's west coast is defined by the V-shaped protrusion of Cape Otway, which neatly separates two almost entirely different worlds. East of Cape Otway, you have the bustling, fashionable, seaside hamlets of Torquay, Lorne, Apollo Bay, frequented by holidaying city folk. West of Cape Otway is inhabited by an altogether hardier, less-manicured breed of coastal dweller. Fishermen, farmers, underground surf maniacs who despise everything the industry hub of Torquay represents. They are vigilant in preserving the low-key, unexposed, secretive culture of their surf breaks, and are often hostile to outsiders – especially the surf media. I have drilled into the kids not to mention what their daddy does for work or the nature of our mission, as they are prone to do within the first minute of meeting any newcomer. Tell the wrong person around here that daddy is a surf writer and you might come back to a car with no air in its tyres, a rock through its windscreen or a turd delicately deposited on its bonnet. A certain section of the Port Campbell surfing community refer to themselves as PCLC – Port Campbell Loose Cunts, making it absolutely clear that they are capable of just about anything when it comes to protecting their surf spots. Not that there is any surf at all around here, mind you. Barely a rideable ripple is to be found anywhere between

Cape Otway and the South Australian border. I know, because I take the opportunity at Bells to ask Victoria's top-rated professional surfer, Adam Robertson, who hails from Portland on the far west coast. 'Nah, no waves at all,' he advises me. 'You may as well take the inland road and keep on driving through. It's quicker.'

Fortunately, I don't take his advice and find my way to a delightful bush campground recommended by a colleague, but from here on in geographical references will have to become absurdly vague.

The legend of this coast was largely forged by enigmatic Victorian surf pioneer Wayne Lynch, a man who defined the new shortboard surfing in the late 60s with the most accomplished tube-riding, wrap-around cutbacks and backhand re-entries the surfing world had seen till then. Lynch became disillusioned with surf contests and the industry early on, despite winning four Bells junior titles and starring in the seminal surf movies of the day, walking away from competition and taking up the country soul ethic along with Nat 'the Animal' Young. But Wayne had some compelling reasons for going country, disappearing into the remote western Victorian wilderness to avoid the Vietnam draft, only emerging after Whitlam's amnesty allowed him to step out of the shadows and claim some of the big bucks on offer in the new pro era of the Coke Surfabout in the mid-70s.

If the far south coast of WA is Tim Winton country, I've always thought of Victoria's west coast as Wayne Lynch country. The joys of remote wilderness surf adventuring were vividly captured in the classic short film *A Day in the Life of Wayne Lynch*, as he careered around dirt roads through lush rainforests and leapt off sheer cliffs into boiling seas to surf booming mysto breaks. Wayne has kept his secrets ever since, railing against the increasing commercialisation and crowds of modern surfing, and the rules and regulations of Victoria's national park rangers

as they seek to curtail his free-ranging surf adventures by closing forest tracks and prohibiting fires.

These are just abstract theories, however, until I arrive at
our next camp site and follow a forest track a couple of kilometres towards the coast to inspect a stretch of beach breaks I've
heard about. We've arrived late in the afternoon, too late for a
paddle, and as I walk the half hour in through the thick coastal
forest to check the surf I contemplate the issue of secrecy. Am
I breaching the unwritten 'surfers' code' by writing about my
travels? Am I adding to the pressures already mounting upon
our remote coastlines by inspiring others to visit them? Should
I just bite my tongue? Or do the militant locals have it wrong,
exercising their own form of elitism, seeking to exclude others
from their private wave havens as surely as the real estate developers? I'm going to have to resolve these ethical dilemmas in a
hurry, because as the ocean comes into view above the coastal
heath and rolling dunes, clean groomed swell lines are immediately visible. I've stumbled upon my own secret spot. I feel a
nervous rumble in the pit of my stomach. The track drops away
towards the beach and, as far as the eye can see, huge beach-
break peaks peel away in both directions. A booming left reels
away in the eastern corner against a craggy headland. Immediately in front of me, a well-defined right throws out, barrels and
spits. More peaks stretch off into the distance against the glare
of the setting sun to the west. I haven't even brought my board
or wetsuit, knowing full well that any time in the water this
late in the afternoon would mean a walk back on dark through
a maze of unfamiliar forest tracks. It is sweet agony. I snap a
few shots and short clips with my iPhone just to preserve the
astounding spectacle and stand dumbly trying to gauge the size.
Six? Eight feet? Bigger? With no point of reference it is almost
impossible to tell, but it is certainly solid. I'd be reluctant to
tackle it on my own. Wayne Lynch, I'd wager, would paddle
out without a second thought, even on dusk.

I trek back to camp, contemplating the next morning's session nervously.

The kids are up early and I'm feeling oddly nervous about the long walk in and the vast, unknown Southern Ocean with only puny little me to tackle it. Though our camp site is busy with holiday-makers enjoying their extended Easter/Anzac weekend, I have not spotted another surfboard or wetsuit in the camp. A surf partner now couldn't be more welcome. I've been craving this, the great solo wilderness surf experience, my own Wayne Lynch moment, but I am starting to think surfing alone is overrated. Still, I'm not going to be denied.

I get the kids breakfast, have a cup of chai, make myself a daypack with a water bottle, a couple of apples and my camera. I kiss each member of my family goodbye in turn and tell them that I love them. Melodramatic? Perhaps. Kirst can see my excitement and quiets the kids' protests as I head off with a stern decree: 'This is daddy's time to go surfing.'

It's a chilly morning and I have layers of clothes and a beanie ready, but as I grab my board, towel and wetsuit, sling the backpack over my shoulders and stride off through the campground, I feel strangely warmed. There's a sign on the outskirts of the camp pointing to the beach, and a couple of other signposts and little orange markers along the route, but there are a multitude of tracks crisscrossing through the dense bush and I can't tell which one I took yesterday. Some are wide, four-wheel drive tracks, others are churned up with hoof prints and horse manure. Others almost peter out altogether, overgrown by coarse bush grass and shrubs so that you have to duck and scramble through overhanging tunnels. The knee-high bush is wet with dew, and my pants are soon soaked through.

Up until now I feel like I've been stumbling about, making often painful compromises in the name of family harmony, other times I just got it wrong and missed out on surf through sheer ignorance. Here, on this south-facing coastline, I finally feel like I have my bearings. I know what a favourable weather map looks like, and I have positioned us well.

But, what will I find at the end of this long march? I walked away from heaving six- to eight-foot beach breaks yesterday afternoon trailing rationalisations: too late, too lonely, too distant. Deep down I felt a twinge of cowardice. Despite my best efforts, I still lack the deep well of confidence, ability and fitness to tackle serious surf alone, kilometres from anywhere. I'm a forty-six-year-old family man, for goodness sake, a desk jockey most of my working life, a latecomer to the waves who'd made do with weekend and school holidays at the beach until my twenties. Who am I trying to kid, playing the bold surf adventurer?

Most of the other Baker men are off at the football today, to see our beloved Hawks go up against their archrivals, the Geelong Cats, at the MCG. I could have backtracked to Melbourne and joined them, and it's a wrench to pass up the great male-bonding ritual with my father and brothers. I'd once been destined for the life of a newspaper football writer, many years ago, but somehow I'd stepped out of the existence mapped out for me back in suburban Melbourne and stepped into a new, less likely one as surf writer. That I wasn't at the MCG with the rest of the Baker men was a measure of how much my old life had been swamped by this new on. Instead, I find myself here, on this long stretch of coastline, trudging through the coastal bush, board under arm, looking for surf. Two days ago I'd been part of a crowd of 10,000 people who watched Joel Parkinson and Mick Fanning surf in the final of the Rip Curl Pro at eight-foot Bells. This morning, I feel just about as alone as I've ever felt.

Eventually, I encounter a bushwalker heading back from the beach. How's the ocean looking, I ask? 'Oh, pretty flat,' he insists. I have no idea if he is a surfer or not, but this is devastating news. I quicken my pace, desperate to refute his assessment. After yesterday's round trip, this is my third time along this track, and I swear I haven't followed the same route twice. As the track starts to descend towards the beach, the sand grows thicker, softer and lighter in colour, my feet sinking deeper. Soon, the vegetation opens up and the ocean comes into view. It does indeed look like a remarkably calm, flat, brilliantly blue expanse of water. I try to hold disappointment at bay until, finally, I can see the beach and only the gentlest fringe of white-water appears to be breaking on the sand. This is too cruel. I'd been so confident of getting waves this morning, had wagered everything on the long walk in.

Yet, as I traverse the dunes down to sea level, it begins to dawn on me that those lines breaking on the beach are rather larger than they first appeared. A set looms and looks a respect-able three to four feet, the occasional set slightly larger. There is a left and right peak directly in front of me, and another left in the eastern corner. I take it all in, almost daring not to believe the evidence – I've stumbled upon my own Shangri-la. I can't get into my wetsuit fast enough. I perform a few rushed stretches and scramble down the dunes. There is not a single sign of civilisation in any direction.

With no one around to confirm and share the experience with, I find myself questioning reality: can it really be this good? I paddle out, watching glassy rights spinning towards me. I turn and scratch into my first wave, suspended in an instant of disbelief as I'm momentarily held in its crest, then descend into the undeniable bliss of the moment. I'm surfing perfect waves. Alone. I might have preferred someone to hoot and holler and exchange incredulous expressions with, and I'm reminded of that old line about a tree falling in a forest: if a surfer rides a wave and there is no one there to hoot, does it still create a buzz? Yes, happily, it does.

When I finally return to the family, high on the morning's adven-ture, I struggle to communicate the heights of my euphoria, the sense that the trip is now on track and that, after the glorious wave-riding fun at Bells, we are tantalisingly close to being on a bit of a roll.

The surf forecast looks astounding – offshore for another week – and I prepare myself for a wave-riding feast on this glorious coast. As usual, things don't work out quite the way I planned. I set off the next morning to drive to a nearby river mouth that the camp manager has recommended, but lose my way on a series of increasingly overgrown and daunting sand tracks. Exchanging solitude for certainty, I head to the more well-known beach break in the region. As I head west, I pull into a scenic roadside lookout where the ocean first comes into view and am greeted by swell lines to the horizon and one enormous close-out exploding across the length of this wide, cliff-lined bay. It looks a bit big for the beaches but not quite big enough for the reefs, one of the dreaded 'in-between' days that often plague this coast, when conditions look pristine but a surfable wave is hard to find. I press on to the beach break, keen to confirm my assessment.

Johanna is hardly a secret spot, so I'm hoping I can write about it without physical repercussions. It was, after all, the site of the world surfing titles way back in 1970 and has played host to the Rip Curl Pro numerous times when conditions at Bells Beach haven't obliged. It's a popular camping spot and an obligatory stop-off point for every surfer passing through. Even so, it retains its rural charm and laid-back, empty line-ups for most of the year without much sign of the fierce localism that characterises much of the surrounding coast. Few people live round here, so there are few genuine locals.

Incredibly, on this perfect, sunny, offshore morning, there is barely a soul around. A few campers are just stirring, oblivious to the magnificence lurking just over the dunes. I park, climb a steep track to a look-out and do a 180 scan of this wide beach, unridden peaks littered from one end to the other. At a glance, it looks like an inviting fun park. So why is no one out? I watch a bit longer and one of those close-out sets I'd spotted at the earlier scenic look-out comes through and obliterates the neat peaks I'd been admiring moments before. In their place, almost continuous rows of whitewater steam through the curdling line-ups and, once they've passed, furious rips carry all that water back out to sea. It's just gone high tide and, as the water drains off the banks, the currents between them look like rapids.

Eventually, another couple of cars pull up, rusted old utes with boards in the back, carrying the kind of weathered, older surfers in beanies and ugg boots I associate with the area. They're friendly enough, but none of them are too keen. I suggest that one right down the beach looks just about rideable.

'You'd end up in Tassie,' the imposing alpha male of the group tells me curtly. I marvel aloud at the impressive conditions. The local claims it's the first time they've had more than twenty-four hours of offshore winds since last August, nine months ago. Yet, we've just strolled into a week of offshores and brilliant sunshine.

I sense there must be a quality option out there somewhere, but they aren't giving anything away. We all watch on in silence as it becomes clearer and clearer, with the regular close-out sets and raging rips, that paddling out here is not a good idea. You can drive all day along this coast and not get wet, and I know I've had a pretty good go of it lately. There's no way of letting the family know back at the camp that I'm going to be gone longer than I'd planned, so I take the responsible option and pull the pin.

Kirst's keen for a bushwalk to the nearby lighthouse, and I'm happy for the opportunity to at least admire the ocean on such a day. Despite some protests from the kids, we pack water bottles and snacks into a daypack and set out on the forty-five minute hike. We manage to coax them along with a kind of false log of how far we have to go, much like Christopher Columbus goading his crew on to explore the New World. The track we are on forms a small part of the Great Ocean Walk, a pedestrian companion to the famed Great Ocean Road, along which keen hikers can roam this coast from end to end, with designated camping areas and water at regular intervals. We pass a few serious bushwalking senior citizens, and it strikes me as a wonderful way to spend one's dotage.

I do feel a few pangs, though, that this coastline is being turned into an industry, with ever glossier marketing and escalating admission prices for many of its attractions. At the end of our walk, we discover entrance to the lighthouse grounds will cost us $17.50 for adults, $7.50 for kids, or $43.50 for a 'family pass': two adults and four children. Who has *four* children these days! We'd settled on two children largely so we could get into tourist attractions on a family pass and get value for money, and now we're forking out for two children we don't have. If I'd known someone was going to shift the goalposts, we might have kept procreating. They've got us over a barrel. We're hardly going to turn around and walk back without checking out the lighthouse, and a high fence prevents us from even glimpsing it or the coast without sticking our hands in our pockets. The bloke on the till seems to know it's a bit of a rort and lets us off for the price of two adults.

I have to concede, though, it's an impressive spread, wandering the old lighthouse keeper's quarters, climbing the spiral, stone staircase to the enormous bulb at the top. But the whole operation all got off to an inauspicious beginning, I'm humoured to find out. The first lighthouse keeper, Lieutenant James Lawrence, was sacked from his position after only a few months, officially for carrying out repairs he was unqualified for. But according to a small plaque, 'his foul mouth, penchant for rum and all round ungentlemanly conduct ensured his tenure at the station was a short but dramatic one'.

MY WAYNE LYNCH MOMENT

The next day we are heading further west. It is another perfect day but I have decided to forsake a morning surf in the interests of simply getting to our next destination. I've learned it's always easier to sneak off for a surf once we are set up at a new camp site. We have promised the kids a café brunch at the next town after our few days in the bush, so the option of simply pulling over for a quick session isn't going to be too popular. Yet the idea of sitting in a café and eating eggs benedict and sipping on a latte on a day like today is torturous. It's gnawing away at me and eventually I announce to Kirst, 'I think I need to go for a surf.' I'm met with stony silence from the passenger seat and figure this news hasn't been well received. I am beginning to formulate an argument about a day like today being a rare event, a great natural blessing for a surfer that is not be passed up, when I glance over and realise Kirst has her earplugs into her iPod. I cough, repeat my news – louder this time – and she looks over at me impassively. I have decided it is wise to present her with a couple of options. They can drop me at the next beach, and drive on to the next town for brunch while I surf for a couple hours, or I can drop them off in town, unhitch the van and drive on for a surf nearby. She likes the first option, but when we get to the next beach the banks look indifferent and there is not a soul out. I um and ah, trying to decide what to do. Inside the car young tummies are rumbling. I don't know this coast well, could drive around all morning and not find another wave, but the day is so perfect I can't bear to spend it surfing close-outs. I decide to drive on.

I have a two-hour window in which to find waves, suit up, paddle out, surf, get back in and pick up the family. It is a tall order, and so I decide to phone a friend. Keith Curtain is the founder and publisher of *Australian Surf Business* magazine, a surf industry trade publication that goes out free to every surf retailer in the country. He is to be our host at our next destination and I figure he'll know where to go. I punch his number into the phone and, mercifully, he answers. I give him the scoop, describe the swell and conditions, and he directs me to a little reef. I must turn off at the speed limit sign on the western end of the next town and go down a dirt road to a small car park. This is a jealously guarded secret spot that had its only media exposure forty years earlier in that classic Jack McCoy surf film, *A Day in the Life of Wayne Lynch*. In one memorable scene, Wayne and his buddy Nat Young are shown jumping off a craggy sea cliff into a boiling ocean to surf one of Wayne's recent discoveries. If I want my Wayne Lynch moment on this coast, here it is.

I speed through the little town of squat fibro beach shacks and a few more opulent recent additions, get to the western edge of town and spot a speed limit sign. I turn down a dirt road but it leads nowhere, stopping abruptly in the middle of the bush, so I get out to scout around. I can see waves breaking further along the coast but can't tell how to get there. It's maddening. The family would have ordered brunch by now; the clock is ticking. I jump back in the Rav and scream out of the car park further west to the next speed limit sign, to another dirt track. Sure enough, it opens out into a car park dotted with half a dozen old utes and four-wheel drives. One surfer in a wetsuit and a board under arm is jogging down a track towards the coast. Good enough for me – without even checking, I jump out, haul on my wetsuit and grab my board. I regard the rest of our surfboards still on the roof, my guitar and other valuables in the car, our NSW rego plates. I wonder what I'll return to in this isolated dirt car park? I am past caring. I give thanks for my lockable surfboard straps and trusty padlock, and secure the car as best I can, jogging after the surfer I just saw disappearing down the track. In foreign waters, I want a bit of a hint how to tackle this place.

As I race down the pebbled track, the ocean comes into view

and I draw a breath. A perfect peak is standing up, unloading over shallow reef in the middle of a crescent bay bounded by sandstone cliffs. Other inviting waves break at either end of the bay. It's a picture-perfect surf fantasy, the kind of thing you'd draw on your schoolbooks as a kid. I watch the surfer ahead of me nimbly skip over the rocks, pause at the end of a protruding finger of stone and leap into the ocean as a swell rises towards him. It's straight out of *A Day in the Life*; I can scarcely believe it.

Out in the line-up, eight or so surfers are leaving few waves unridden, and I'm unsure what sort of reception a stranger is likely to get. I teeter out to the cliff's edge, look down at the water as it rises and falls, strap on my leg-rope, draw a deep breath and jump. Almost as soon as I hit the water, I think, *I wonder how you get back in?* As I approach the line-up, I feel like the out-of-towner walking into a western saloon. I hover on the outskirts of the take-off spot, not wanting to jump the queue. I let the pack take their turns on the next couple of sets and wait for an opening. The reef is shallow and the waves stand up abruptly, pitch and barrel, and the reef forms boils and surges in front of it. The locals are good, solid surfers who clearly know their wave, make few mistakes, take off late and deep and smoothly pull into the cascading tubes with a minimum of fuss. It's a tight take-off spot and even eight surfers form a bit of a crowd out here.

'Beautiful day,' I eventually comment to one surfer when we find ourselves sitting next to each other on the peak, after everyone else has ridden a wave. He looks at me, laughs and doesn't say a word, as if it's the silliest thing he has heard in a while.

I scratch around for a few leftovers, and the wave is as good as it looks – a fast, steep take-off with open barrels and an inviting shoulder. The locals seem intent on catching every single wave that comes through, dominating the sets and spinning around for the smaller ones on their way back out. I have to work hard for my waves and there's not a hint of camaraderie. I start thinking about the Rav in the car park, imagining sinister messages telegraphed back to land to deal with the interloper's vehicle and his quiver of boards. I'm starting to get paranoid. I manage to get my share of waves without mishap, though, figuring I'll get my fill and get the hell out of there. The family will have finished brunch by now and started wondering how long they're likely to be stranded in this little country town.

I watch one of the locals paddle in, scamper up onto the rocks and gently place his board tail-first up on a ledge while he scrambles up the cliff face. He clearly knows every foot and handhold of this vertical expanse of rock, and I wonder how I'll fare. After a brisk hour session, I head in, ride a surge up onto the rocks and manage to delicately balance my board on the ledge before attempting the rock climb. Another local has paddled in behind me, and there is only room for one at a time on this little ledge – he floats in the water, waiting. I can't for the life of me figure how I'm going to scale the rock wall, and eventually I step back to make room for him on the ledge, asking politely, 'Do you want to show me how it's done?' He chortles and quickly, expertly hauls himself onto the ledge, places his board on a small protruding rock above, heaves himself next to it and nimbly shuffles up the wall like a spider. He looks down over his shoulder and directs me to the most desirable footholds. I feel an enormous surge of gratitude and clumsily manage to mimic his route to the top.

When I get to the car park the Rav is safe and a crew of locals is standing about chatting. They are all blokes in their twenties, not the hardened first-generation locals who have given this stretch of coast its fearsome reputation. I get the sense these second-generation locals would like to be friendlier to a blow-in like myself, that they might actually enjoy a bit of conversation and cultural exchange with surfers from other parts of the country, but it's as if they feel honour-bound to uphold a tradition of stern localism. It's a lonely feeling as an outsider surfing in such an environment, and I guess the locals' routine serves its purpose. I have never seen a shot of this wave in a surfing magazine and, since the Wayne Lynch movie forty years ago, it has never appeared in another surf film, as far as I know. It's not the sort of wave that could handle a crowd – there aren't too many waves going to waste – and any mainstream media exposure could ruin the place. It seems right and proper that it remains a local stronghold,

But I can't help wondering how this coast will fair in the age of relentless tourism marketing. Every small town, every stretch of coast, every conceivable natural feature or local festival in the country is doing its darndest to attract visitors. In numerous other parts of the country, less remarkable surf than this forms a cornerstone of tourism marketing campaigns – surf spots are clearly marked on tourist maps and prominent street signs direct the visitor to the prime waves. If the marketers ever decide to make a feature of this coast's waves, there will be open warfare. In many ways, the locals have done a remarkable job of keeping their waves out of the media, but I can't help wondering at what price. People need jobs. Small towns need businesses. Businesses need customers. There is now plenty of credible research to show just what kind of economic benefits a popular quality surf spot can deliver to a community. How do you weigh up the rights of locals to have their waves to themselves and the need to deliver economic opportunities to small communities with limited employment options?

Underlying all this, of course, is the tragic irony that this hostile territorialism plays itself out in an occupied land, whose original inhabitants were forcibly, often viciously and illegally, displaced from homelands they had lived on for tens of thousands of years. One local break is known as Massacres, not because the wave is especially fearsome, though it is heavy enough, but because it is where the first Australians were herded off the sea cliffs to their doom. Another break in South Australia is known as Blackfellas for similar reasons. If prior occupancy really afforded preferential rights to an area then all those territorial local surfers would vacate the region and invite back the ancestors of those hunted and murdered Aborigines.

I return to my family and find them happily at play on a gorgeous beach in a protected bay after a hearty brunch. I have pulled off my surf mission without a hitch. All needs and agendas have been met. We hitch up, refuel and hit the road, pressing on deep into Gunditjmara Country.

TUNA AND HOME BREW

In Port Fairy, my aforementioned colleague, Keith Curtain, has offered up his backyard granny flat for us, an offer that grows more attractive as the chill of the deep southern autumn begins to set in. We have been blessed with an idyllic week of weather along this stretch, but it can't last forever. Rain and plummeting temperatures are forecast.

It's impossible to know how these offers of hospitality will play out, how comfortable your lodgings might prove to be, how convivial your hosts. Keith and his wife, Fiona, have recently added a baby girl, Kitty, to the family, and I know well how testing the early days of new parenthood can be. Yet they are insistent we are welcome, and it seems too good an offer to refuse. Keith texts me on the road in the afternoon to say that dinner is sorted. The granny flat turns out to be a comfortable two-storey cottage at the bottom of a picturesque fairy garden, complete with en suites and vintage surfboards resting in the corners – Vivi and I are, for once, equally won over by our surroundings.

Port Fairy, despite its less-than-intimidating name, had a heavy reputation when I was a kid just getting into surfing in suburban Melbourne. I was flat-out too scared to even try and surf here, terrified by stories of violent retribution against any visitor foolish enough to even paddle out in its waves. Though the localism has mellowed in recent years, it's still a place to tread carefully and show plenty of respect.

I don't wish to put my host in an awkward situation. So, I am happy to report that the waves in Port Fairy absolutely suck, and you should on no account detour to its surfless, charmless coast.

Port Fairy does provide me with one solution to the question of how one takes their family surfing with them. The answer is the increasingly popular stand-up paddleboard. My host, as well as publishing the definitive surf industry trade magazine, runs a growing surf school business, specialising in the relatively new art. These large gondola-like craft have divided the surfing community between those mature surfers who see it as a way of staying in shape during indifferent surf conditions and those shortboarders who decry them as the latest dangerous curse to clog the waves. But on a sunny day of small waves, with wives and small children to entertain, there is no denying their family-friendly appeal.

Our wives go for a paddle while Keith and I pose as modern men, taking care of the kiddies. Kirst, despite having surfed only a handful of times in her life, takes to it immediately, and she and Fiona spend a pleasant half hour paddling laps of a flat lagoon, chatting, admiring the reef and fish life below, and the sight of their husbands chasing small children about the beach. Soon we swap places and I take the kids out with me. They love it, riding tiny ripples shorewards, hooting and waving their paddles like banshees. Only once we've performed these familial duties do Keith and I take to the boards on our own. Neither of us can help ourselves, however, and soon we have paddled half a kilometre offshore to a nearby reef and have been thoroughly cleaned up by the occasional head-high sets. On my stand-up paddleboard debut (apart from a couple of brief flat-water forays years ago), I fail to ride a wave successfully, but I love the workout and am quickly hooked on the view of the surrounding ocean from the elevated perspective. I vow to buy one as soon as we get home.

The tuna are running offshore, Keith informs me, and the recreational fishermen of the region are having a field day, hauling in huge quantities of the prized fish. I am a sashimi junkie but have been bitterly disappointed by the limited opportunities to procure fresh seafood along this coast. And so I set out in the afternoon determined to provide a fresh fish dinner for our hosts. A failure as a fisherman, I trawl the local fish shops instead, only finding sad, limp, defrosted morsels of salmon and some indistinguishable grey-white fish flesh with unfamiliar names – for forty dollars a kilo. It seems preposterous.

Keith has suggested it may be possible to loiter down at the local boat ramp and approach one of the returning fishermen to purchase some of their catch. I feel awkward and conspicuous as I approach the boats. Lots of cheery fisher blokes hose down their opulent craft, slice up huge chunks of tuna and deposit them in oversized eskies. I hover about, wondering how to make my approach. I finally ask a couple of blokes at the fish-cleaning table if they want to sell any. They regard me suspiciously, as if I am attempting to buy drugs, and grunt their refusal. I am about to slink off, defeated, when I spy one esky positively brimming over with large tuna carcasses.

'You got any spare you want to sell?' I ask a friendly looking bloke.

He looks me up and down. 'You ain't from fisheries are you?'

I nearly laugh, wanting to launch into my abalone escapade, but instead shake my head solemnly. He pulls out a chunk the size of a large phone book.

'How much?' I ask.

He shrugs his shoulders. 'Twenty bucks?'

I pluck one of the orange notes from my wallet before he changes his mind. He bags the rich red meat and we make the exchange. I return triumphant with my chunk of tuna, cut it into thick strips, coat it in oil and Cajun spices and lightly sear it on each side. Kirst does up her now famous pilaf and we dazzle our hosts with our culinary offering. Keith retrieves some of his prized home brew from the fridge and our taste buds are soon rejoicing. I like Port Fairy enormously.

The following evening, Keith introduces me to his home brew buddies: Jock, a lawyer and part-time writer, and Louie, who I only know for his abalone diving prowess. The three of them have combined their street names to come up with a grand title for their home brew syndicate – the William Cox Union. They have exotic names for their various brews like the Witch's Tit, the Flaming Sanchez, the Bert Wrout Stout, the Kauaian Iron (in honour of the late surf champion Andy Irons) and the Liverpool Kiss. They have their own home brew blog and have even won a prize at the Victorian Home Brew titles in nearby Koroit for their Kitty Bitter Wheat Beer (though they later admit they were the only entrant in the division). I spend a delightful evening making these fine men's acquaintance over a few of their brews and shallow-fried abalone caught by their own hands that very day. Again, I have that deliciously warm sensation that we could slide right in here and make a life for ourselves. Their wives and children are all delightful. They live in gorgeous, renovated old stone cottages picked up for a relative song and seem to have thriving careers far from the big smoke. They are good people living what appear to be wonderful lives, from the romantic vantage point of an outsider on a brief visit.

If only they weren't cursed with a complete absence of any kind of vaguely surfable wave, I'd move here tomorrow.

7

LIFE ON THE EDGE

IN 2000, WHILE THE world's media gawked at the spectacle of the Sydney Olympics, South Australia's desert coastline was making news for all the wrong reasons. Two fatal shark attacks in two days ensured that all those assembled international journalists, keen for local-colour stories, were able to confirm the rest of the world's worst fears about Australia's natural predators.

At a rustic desert surf campground in the Great Australian Bight, a New Zealand couple, Cameron and Tina Bayes, were enjoying a working honeymoon holiday around Australia. On the morning of Sunday 24 September, Cameron rose early so he could get a few waves before the crowd hit. By 7.30 he'd already gathered half a dozen good rides before anyone else had paddled out. This is how my colleague DC Green described what happened next in his *Tracks* magazine story, 'Cape Fear':

> At 7.30 am a great white launched itself completely out of the water at the Cactus end section – seemingly the shallowest and least likely place in the entire bay for such an encounter. Clearly hurt after the first strike, Cameron crawled back onto his board. He managed to paddle five metres towards shore before the shark seized him again. It dragged him and his board some fifty metres further out and began thrashing in a circular formation with such ferocity that a whirlpool formed. Cameron was tossed completely out of the water.

All that was ever recovered was the back half of Cameron's board, with an enormous bite through it, the foam blank stained pink.

The next day, as the aftershocks resonated through the South Australian surfing community, in Elliston, on the western side of the Eyre Peninsula, seventeen-year-old Jevan Wright was attacked by a great white pointer as he paddled in from a surf at Blackfellas. The shock turned to outright panic. Some longtime locals simply gave up surfing. There were the usual conflicts between the bloodthirsty, vengeful calls to hunt and kill the beasts responsible, and the lofty, academic urge for calm and understanding.

As long as I can recall, I have always been anxious about surfing in South Australia. And for good reason. The Spencer Gulf, which takes an enormous pie slice out of the coastline, is renowned as a nursery for great whites. The large 'tuna ranching' operations at Port Lincoln – catching enormous schools of tuna in nets far offshore and then dragging them into the coast to be fattened for market – is an activity seemingly designed to woo white pointers. Cage-diving operations, which promise tourists up-close encounters with the fearsome creatures, burly the waters with fish offal to attract them.

It is the one Australian coastline I have never surfed and so, as we cross the border from Victoria to South Australia, via the sleepy coastal hamlet of Nelson, I am gripped by a gnawing anxiety that seems completely at odds with our scenic surrounds. We reach the town of Robe, described to me as Port Fairy with limestone instead of bluestone, around 5 pm. I know nothing about this coast, only that there is surf around and the swell appears to be up. It is predicted to blow onshore for the next few days, though, and I am planning on turning my back on the ocean to get some work done. It's not that simple.

The town is yet another variety of 'quaint' I haven't encountered before – a beautiful, historic fishing village with numerous, well-preserved limestone buildings from its heyday as a trading port well over 150 years ago. Crayfish have brought a new wealth to the area, and the crusty fishing town is offset by evidence of lots of new money – big boats and four-wheel drives, garish modern beachfront palaces, fancy cafés and, in the midst of the industrial area, incongruously enough, a boutique coffee roaster and espresso bar. It is a heady mix of new and old influences, and I have trouble pinning it down.

We go out to a decent Chinese restaurant for dinner, as we're low on supplies, and I sense we're all going to like this place. There is a little bookstore, with a café and playground, and Vivi requests a packed lunch and a blanket so she can spend the day there. There is a skate park for Alex. It's Kirst's birthday and she only wants a massage, a yoga class and the chance to go for a walk on her own. Robe can provide all three.

It is freezing overnight and our lakeside camp site gives off the vague aroma of rotten eggs, much to the children's extravagant sense of disgust – a minor drawback, really. Despite my best intentions to work, I've done a little research online and identified an intriguing local surf spot. When the surf sites I scan in the morning show that it's offshore with plenty of swell, I am almost annoyed. The only thing as emotionally draining as getting skunked for surf wherever you go (like Tassie) is getting surf wherever you go. I have done precious little writing in the last couple of weeks and Kirst has offered to take the kids into town for the morning on bikes so I can work, but I can't resist a cruise of the local beaches first, just to torture myself. I take the kids for an early surf check, and it is indeed dead glassy with what appears to be four to five feet of clean, straight, sou'-west swell. The prime surf beaches are all down winding four-wheel drive tracks, and I don't want to torment the kids with yet more driving, so I take Alex to the skate park for a spin on his scooter before I hand them over to Kirst for the morning. 'I hope you get lots of work done,' she encourages cheerily.

'Ah, I might just go check one other spot,' I offer meekly, stashing my wetsuit in the back of the Rav – just in case. The family sets off into town on bikes, and I skulk off on my guilty mission. I crisscross backstreets, looking for a way to the coast. It's fascinating how a lot of these towns have clustered around safe harbours and sheltered, surfless beaches, turning their backs on the open ocean beach as a kind of badlands, a dangerous forbidden zone of rips, kelp and rocks, shipwrecks and large marine creatures. The remote, windswept back beaches are places where burnt-out cars are dumped, lustful teenagers grapple or sly grog sessions around fires masquerade as fishing trips. It is only in relatively recent times that surfers have colonised these badlands with their trademark off-road tracks and camp spots, which have since become more heavily frequented tourist trails. In many ways, I'd argue, surfers have been pioneers of so much of this coast, pre-dated only by Indigenous Australians, shipwreck survivors and particularly hardy fishermen.

I drive past the cemetery and through the industrial enclave, glimpsing the local tip, looking for signs to the beach. I spot a promising dirt road winding off through the bush and figure this is a likely trail.

Ordinarily, I love this stuff, the thrill of the chase, beating unknown paths to the coast. Today, however, I am feeling wearied by the need to work and the ever-present conflict of taking time away from the family. Yet I know from experience that if I ignore this gnawing surf lust and don't at least have a peek, it will come back to bite me in grumpy moods and bitter regrets. And so I press on, down one dirt road after another, looking for telltale signs, hoping to glimpse another car with boards on the roof, craving some local guidance or even a willing surf partner.

A sign warns that there is soft sand ahead and advises to reduce tyre pressure. I'm acutely aware how easily an ill-judged sand track can ruin your day, so I pull over and walk ahead just to check. It looks fine, so I press on, the smooth, blue ocean horizon drawing me on now as it bobs in and out of view over the peaks and valleys.

I emerge onto a small, rough car park right on the beach, and I'm confronted by a heaving stretch of beach breaks – as smooth as glass with just the gentlest offshore breeze. This is, yet again, a bitter-sweet discovery. Escaping crowds had been the priority back on the teeming beaches of the Gold Coast. The notion that I might struggle to find people to surf with had honestly never occurred to me back home, as if it were some distant, nostalgic condition that no longer existed in the modern world. Yet standing here, on this craggy limestone coast, confronted by the raw power of the Southern Ocean, I again feel puny and ill-prepared.

So this is to be my South Australian debut – in thumping, empty beach breaks in front of gnarled fingers of rock and thick with kelp beds, with no idea what unseen hazards linger beneath the surface. Yet I can't drive away. I have been cowardly enough this trip already, and I am frustrated with my own nervousness. Isn't this what I wanted? The great wilderness surf experience, escaping the rat-race of the modern surf world and the overflowing line-ups of Coolangatta?

I occasionally check the webcams at one of my local point breaks back on the Gold Coast and watch literally hundreds of surfers scratching into brilliant, peeling barrels under sunny skies. A friend has forwarded me an email reporting on the perfect waves that blessed the Alley Classic, an annual surf contest at my home break in Currumbin. I'm dumbstruck by the images while not feeling the slightest bit envious. The numbers of surfers in the water, from this distance, appears surreal.

Australia, I've realised, is not the country I thought it was – it is wilder, more raw, bigger, less populated than I had really grasped from my suburban vantage point. Of course, I knew there were vast, empty spaces – I just didn't appreciate quite how vast and empty they were.

And, so, as I stand on this craggy limestone coast, I realise I am going to have to paddle out – regardless of deadlines, family duties, shark paranoia – or this trip will become a sham. I am likely to be confronted by many more empty surf scenarios in our travels; if I retreat each time I feel daunted, vulnerable, ill-prepared or lonely, I am only going to surf with the kind of crowds I've fled. There are plenty of close-outs in between the perfect A-frames, so I'll just duck out there, sneak into a couple and get the hell back on dry land.

There's a pretty obvious paddle-out spot at least, a clearly defined channel through a keyhole in the rocky foreshore where the water is rushing out between two peaks. I don my damp, frosty wetsuit, rake the wax comb over the rock-hard wax on my 6'4" to improve its traction and trot between the jagged rocks down to the beach. This doesn't feel like fun. It feels like a dare I am forcing myself to honour.

Out in the water, it's even harder to find the good waves. I go left and nearly end up on the rocks before kicking out desperately. I scamper about the line-up nervously, find a couple of quick in and outs, dodging close-out sets, trying to maintain my line-up position in front of the Rav. What appears to be a flapping strand of kelp out beyond the line-up catches my anxious eye. I am caught inside by a smaller set and go to duck-dive without concern. Before I know it, the wave has flipped me on my back and pinned me to the bottom with my board on top, as if I were a spider caught under a saucer. The only way I can get free is to ditch my board and swim to the surface, struggling against the turbulence and gasping for air before I even break the water. If that's what a small four-footer's done, what about a six-footer? It's amazing how quickly nervousness can tip over into panic.

Now I just want to catch one in. As I scan the line-up, something else breaks the surface just beyond the breakers, and this is definitely no strand of kelp. The flash of a fast-moving grey fin sets my heart racing, and I am ready to start paddling for the beach before I have even registered that it is only a seal. Now that I've processed this information, I can't decide if it's good or bad news. Where there are seals, as my paranoid mind and numerous shark attack accounts have concluded, there is likely to be those creatures who dine on seals. And that is something I don't want to dwell on too much in my current emotional state.

Now I definitely want to head in, and I scratch around anxiously until I find a little right, paddle into it, leap to my feet and ride the small close-out towards my paddle-out spot. The keyhole is now running out pretty hard with the outgoing tide, and I have to work hard against the current to get in. Eventually, I make it to the sand and stagger up the beach, breathing hard. Looking back, the ocean now resembles a mass of close-outs with only the odd makeable wave. I wonder what I was thinking.

Still, I'm feeling exhilarated. It's nice to be back on dry land. I towel off and survey the surrounding coast for other waves. Not that I'm going back out in a hurry, mind you, but the potential is staggering. Bombies break way outside. Peaks barrel away in the distance in both directions. Who knows what might lay just up or down this coast? Dirt tracks stretch off through the dunes and I ponder which ones to follow. I start driving down one but I'm soon confronted by an impossibly steep dune and give up. It's time to return to the family. Kirst's overdue for some time off and tomorrow's her birthday, so the kids and I are going shopping for presents while she gets a massage.

Soon, I am immersed in a world of gift shops offering gourmet jams and relishes, shells and whitewashed timber picture frames, beach chic in all its many guises. The kids are determined to find the perfect present, and we trawl through every gift and homeware shop in the main street. I see a bar of soap – cucumber and green tea – for $12.50, a jar of 'body butter' for close to $50. The land appears hardly less perilous than the sea. Alex settles on a little wire bird and Vivi goes for a couple of blocks of nougat. Only I am left empty handed, but I've learnt my lesson from the smelly soaps in Tathra and decide to let Kirst choose her own gift. As it turns out, she's interested in morning tea at a local café after her yoga and massage, and an afternoon excursion to the lovely Cape Jaffa biodynamic winery. I'm working hard to try and restore some semblance of balance to the pursuit of our respective interests, and the winery seems to do the trick. We pick up a cheeky rosé, (back in fashion, apparently) and a rich, hearty cab merlot, snack on local cheese and emu meat while the kids fall in love with the winery pooch.

I'm quite taken with our latest van park, despite the lake's aroma. Little civilising influences, like the piped music in the communal bathrooms, are a nice touch. News of Osama bin Laden's death seems even more surreal from the vantage point of the tidy kitchen area, a gang of senior citizens glued to the screen like it's the moon landing. Accidental exposure to the media is often our only contact with the world at large, and it comes as a jolt, breaking the spell of our dreamy, nomadic life.

In other news, I discover Tasmania has just endured its wettest April in fifteen years, with many of the roads we travelled now under water. Queensland and much of the New South Wales coast are still battling floodwaters. Meanwhile, we're enjoying brilliant sunshine in these supposedly frigid regions. I have a sense of racing across this southern coast with winter and calamity at our tail, and I wonder when it will catch us.

We skirt the Coorong wetlands, alive and full of water from recent rains. We stop for a Coorong mullet burger at a local roadhouse and go for a short bushwalk to take in a small part of this coast's vast inland waterways. Quite unexpectedly, at a turn in the road, we have to catch a small car ferry across the mighty Murray, now flowing wide and high towards the sea.

THE JUMPING PILLOW

The idea of showing our children the country, of inspiring a sense of wonder and appreciation for Austalia's natural bounty, has been a prime motivator for this trip. But after turning up their noses at bushwalks from Booderee to Ben Boyd to Wineglass Bay, the great wonder that stops them in their tracks is the Port Elliot Family Van Park 'jumping pillow'. This wondrous installation is a cross between a jumping castle and a trampoline – a large, inflated 'pillow' of heavy-duty vinyl the size of a tennis court that the kids are happy to jump on to the point of exhaustion. It seems to have a similar effect on every kid in the park, providing a bouncy village square for little people, freeing their parents for the serious business of collapsing in camp chairs and sipping afternoon refreshments. I may get one installed in our backyard.

Port Elliot on the Fleurieu Peninsula (impressively named by the great French explorer Nicolas Baudin, who passed this way in his ship *Le Geographe* in 1802) provides a handy stop-off point en route to Adelaide, and I have no great expectations of the waves. There are placenames I've vaguely heard of, which I can just recall from grainy black-and-white surf photos by local photographer Mark Sutton during my time at *Tracks* twenty-five years ago – Waits, Parsons, Victor Harbour. Then there's the dreaded Middleton, or 'Dribbleton' as it was dubbed at the inglorious Australian Titles back in 1975, when interstate competitors were less than impressed with the feeble beach breaks they had driven vast distances to surf. It was an age when interstate air travel was prohibitively expensive, and the knowledge of shadowy secret spots beckoning on the wild desert coast a relatively short hop to the west must have added to their frustration. Dribbleton had seemingly been chosen for the proximity of a sealed car park and the ease of carting a PA system to the beach rather than wave quality.

The gently sloping seabed here means the southern swells break a long way out and produce a weak, rolling wave that may have been okay for the old longboards of earlier eras but was patently unsuited to the new shortboards ripping at the time.

The only other thing I know about this coast is that it produced perhaps the most obscure and least remembered Australian surfing champion of all time, Bill Sedunary, who only made it to the 1983 Australian Titles at Margaret River as a late call-up, fifth reserve, for the South Australian team – when they could find no other takers. I wonder what he's up to these days, figuring he might make an intriguing 'where are they now?' piece. I try googling him, but I can find only the most scant references in a list of past Aussie champs. I figure he's destined to remain in obscurity, that perhaps it's the way he likes it.

Port Elliot's a delight, the van park nestled behind the dunes of a sheltered beach on the outskirts of a town centre made up of historic stone buildings. The surf looks uninspiring – small, onshore line-ups on a grey, drizzly day. I decide to give up the chase for a while, happily cruising the town's bookstores and op-shops with the family. We find a great little Japanese café run by a friendly local surfer and watch the kids jump on the big vinyl pillow.

I'm taken by surprise when the surf bobs up one afternoon and the wind switches offshore. I go for a reconnaissance drive at dusk and find long, straight lines rolling into miles of beach breaks stretching off to the east. Admittedly, they do break a long way out, and many of the surfers are mature age long-boarders, but it still looks pretty fun. I've left my run a little late, though, and hope for better things in the morning.

Maybe it's because I have such low expectations that the next day at Middleton proves so enjoyable. A little rip-bowl left breaking off what is rather optimistically called Middleton Point is providing fast, bowling rides with a lot more punch than the genteel rollers just up the beach. It's not so much a point as a rocky outcrop that interrupts the long, straight stretch of beach and encourages sandbanks to form either side of it. It's a Saturday morning and there are dozens of surf-ers in the water, but the majority of them sit way out to sea, patiently waiting for the larger sets and subscribing to the old-school approach of riding the biggest wave for the longest possible distance. There's only a handful of us on the little left rip bowl – a good-spirited, uncrowded session in the midst of a weekend crowd. My fellow surfers are a friendly bunch, offering waves to each other, providing animated commen-tary on one another's rides, including an outsider like me in their cheery banter. One fellow in a wetsuit cap is gripped by a delusion that there are tubes to be had out here. He paddles back out after one ride and gives me a wide-eyed, breath-less description of the pitching lip he'd narrowly avoided; he coaches an old longboarder on how he'd missed out on an inviting barrel section behind him. These are visions only he seems able to identify in the shifty beach break peaks, but I love his optimism. In most ways, it's a totally unremarkable session at a busy suburban beach break, but it feels good to surf with a bunch of friendly, inclusive surfers.

⌒

I stumble upon a copy of Nat Young's *Surfing and Sailboard Guide to Australia* in a second-hand bookstore in Port Elliot. The proprietor drives a hard bargain. It is priced at $15. 'I can let you have it for thirteen,' he volunteers when I take it to the counter with no intention of haggling. It's an appropriate purchase, given that I had recently bumped into its co-author, Brad Farmer, at Bells Beach. Brad is also the founder of the Surfrider Foundation in Australia and now the driving force behind the National Surfing Reserves, along with my guru, Prof Andy Short. Brad was in Torquay during the Rip Curl Pro, 'rattling the can', as he puts it, for NSR to the surf industry heavies. He'd heard of my *Surfari Highway*-inspired mission and was excited to inform me that he'd had a similar vision back when he embarked on the surf guide with Nat thirty-odd years ago. He'd planned on purchasing an old convertible, just like the one in the book, and retracing the journey of Rick Miller and Jonnie Grant. But then Nat had approached him with the surf guide project and he'd put his idea to one side and somehow never got back to it. He's the first person I've spoken to who has even heard of the original *Surfari Highway*, let alone read and been inspired by it, and it seems fitting that his alternative project is now guiding my own homage to the *Surfari Highway* dream. Brad had gone as far as glassing the original book cover into the deck of his surfboard and assuming the pseudonym 'Rick Miller'. The coincidence seems uncanny.

PERSONAL SPACE

We've managed to schedule some comfortable pit stops with family and friends at fairly regular intervals. We're cosy and content in the Expanda, but a few nights with friends of Kirst's father in Adelaide is hard to pass up. Peter and Judy are insistent we should take up residence in their bungalow for as long as it suits us. It's hard to know what to expect of a 'bungalow', like Andy Short's 'shed' or Keith and Fiona's 'granny flat', but it turns out to be complete luxury: a large, comfortable, self-contained flat with queen-sized bed, fold-out couch, kitchen, bathroom, TV, heater and pool table. Vivi has been decrying her lack of personal space and is given her own enormous bedroom in the beautiful, historic main house. Winter has arrived and we are relieved to have warm lodgings. Peter and Judy are perfect hosts – they feed us up like their own offspring and spoil our children like grandchildren with kindness and gifts. We go to the wonderful Adelaide Zoo, join our hosts for a large family Mother's Day lunch, get the Rav its 10,000-kilometre service and do several large loads of washing. It's the ideal respite from life on the road and we couldn't feel more grateful. Vivi never wants to leave, is in tears when we finally do, but the desert coast is calling, an invitation not be taken lightly.

As we head out of Adelaide, I'm struck by how the scale of our trip has suddenly been stretched out to new dimensions. We are out of the city before I even realise it and a vast, flat nothingness stretches out in all directions. Towns, roadhouses, geographic features of any kind are all now spaced further apart. Mileage and petrol consumption needs to be closely monitored and calculated. It feels like this is getting to the serious passage of our journey, that we have been merely playing up until now, never far from help, a roadhouse, café or the next town. Our first stop is an auto accessory store on the outskirts of Adelaide, where we purchase two twenty-litre jerry cans, a wire roof basket and some ratchet straps to carry and secure them.

The landscape is broken only by small farms, odd industrial enclaves of an indeterminate nature, a large military facility signposted 'Proof and Experimental Establishment', like something out of *The X-Files*. It's easy to imagine all kinds of stuff goes on out here that we never hear about. It's no wonder why some bright spark thought the interior of South Australia was a good place to test atomic bombs.

We have to skirt around the enormous Spencer Gulf to reach our next destination of Coffin Bay, at the tip of the Eyre Peninsula, 250 kilometres as the crow flies but about 700 kilometres by road. We make the industrial harbour of Port Pirie for lunch, its small-town charm, waterfront position and magnificent backdrop of the Flinders Ranges overshadowed by the looming, giant wheat solos that dominate the foreshore. A general ennui and a washed-out, sun-bleached colour palette now suffuses the country. We find a hidden gem in the Café de Florence, whose thickly accented, olive-skinned proprietor serves up simple, delicious and reasonably priced food with a charismatic smile. How does an immigrant family find themselves in this alien outpost, trying bravely to generate some of the convivial ambience of home to a public more inclined towards hot chips and toasted sandwiches? I feel a surge of warmth for the ladies toiling away in a small, busy kitchen out the back.

It's strange and a touch unsettling to find myself in a place where I seem to have no cultural references – I do not recognise it from any books, films or TV shows. I begin to understand why Australian filmmakers are always wringing their hands about the need for us to tell our own stories, because I certainly haven't heard this one. It feels like a no-man's-land squeezed between the city, the ranges, the famous wine regions and the wave-rich desert coast. These heavy industrial ports dotted around the gulf seem to exist only to ship our exports to other shores.

There are innumerable places I can't recall ever hearing a single thing about. Port Germein has its own tourist sign announcing its lone attraction: 'Port Germein Jetty, Waterfront Activities'. It seems a vague and modest boast, and I hope they are selling themselves short. We've quizzed locals about likely stop-off points along the way but have drawn blank looks. Yet there is a meditative quality driving out here on the perimeter, the Flinders Ranges glowing a rich, verdant green in the afternoon sun, stretching east to west as far as the eye can see, the blue waters of the Spencer Gulf sparkling to our left, a great plain of low shrubs and red dirt laid out in between.

We press on and I'm already daunted by the distances. We've only managed two and half hours driving, have another five or six to reach Coffin Bay, with an as-yet-unknown stopover somewhere en route. Kirst has valiantly tackled a good chunk of the driving to allow me to write on the road. Tapping away on my laptop in the passenger seat – Lloyd Cole on the car stereo, the kids happily buried in their iPods – feels luxurious. All I need is an espresso machine mounted to the dash and I could go on like this for days.

One after another, potential stopovers are crossed off our list – Port Augusta, Whyalla, all hard-core industrial towns. The surrounds are strangely beautiful or quietly menacing depending on your mood. It feels like we are entering the mythical 'outback', and my soft city sensibilities recoil nervously. Is this the turf of the outlaw bikie gangs we hear so much about, madly brewing up amphetamines in their bush clubhouses? In the next moment, I am swept up in plains taking on green, grey and purple hues in the setting sun, the dusk clouds reflecting their brilliance.

Vivi is horrified that we don't have an appointed overnight stop planned, that her parents are prepared to just drive and see where they end up by nightfall.

'What if there are no van parks or motels?' she protests.

Alex wants only for me to make good on the suggestion that we treat ourselves to a motel. With a long day's drive and just a one-night stop before continuing on our journey, it doesn't make sense to go to the trouble of unhitching and setting up the van. Besides, the kids will need to be carefully re-acclimatised to the close confines of the van after Adelaide.

THE BLACK STUMP

The only town I can see that looks like it might make a pleasant stopover is the harbour town of Cowell, 100 kilometres south of Whyalla. However, it quickly becomes apparent our options are limited. The local junior footy team is practising under lights in the drizzle as we swing off the highway. There's a strange motel-cum-jade emporium that looks too close to the highway. An elderly receptionist is flummoxed by the appearance of some potential guests out of the damp, dark evening, and we figure we can do better. There's a park of prefab huts that we stop and check out, but they're full. It's inhabited mainly by single blokes, presumably mine workers enjoying a few days off, playing pool and drinking beer in a central tin shed or sitting out the front with their TVs on way too loud, as if so desperate for company they're inviting someone to tell them to turn it down.

There are a couple of old pubs on the foreshore – one is booked out and the other doesn't look too inviting. The kids' moods are deteriorating fast as they cotton on that Mum and Dad don't have things covered. I try a van park; they have no empty van sites left and only one cabin. It's basically an on-site van with a double bed, a set of miniature bunk beds, bad wood veneer panelling, a sink, fridge, microwave and TV. It's ours for sixty bucks. We take it. Spirits are low. It seems silly to be towing the van around and then paying to stay in someone else's, but we just want to eat and fall into bed, and this is the quickest route to that particular goal. Even the trip to the pub for dinner is aborted as the kids grow teary with exhaustion; we microwave baked beans, feed them and put them to bed.

It's bizarre that on a cold, grey, wet and windy Tuesday night on the verge of winter that both van parks in town are full. Someone tells us Wyalla is full too. I would have thought the Grey Nomads had all headed north for the warmth to soothe their arthritis by now. The lady behind the counter at our park is astounded at the busy trade, has no explanation for it other than that the entire retiree population has hit the road.

In the light of a new day, wandering the quiet main street in search of sustenance, Cowell's main tourist attraction appears to be a large and apparently legendary black stump grandly displayed in the main street. The story goes that some wag left a black stump in between the town's two pubs as a New Year's Eve prank back in 1972, with a sign on either side saying, 'The best pub this side of the black stump'. The original black stump was stolen, but Cowell is so keen to trade on this dubious bit of bush folklore that they have found a facsimile stump to display, mounted on a handsome stone foundation with a grand plaque proclaiming its story. Is this the best they can do? Apparently. A tourist map highlighting Cowell's 'Places of Interest' includes a sewage dump, recycling depot and an industrial area.

COFFIN BAY

After my first hit of the open spaces of the South Australian outback, Port Lincoln comes as a shock. It's similar to Cairns – a big, bustling and obviously wealthy town fattened on the back of the tuna rather than the sheep. And as fish stocks dwindle, their value only escalates. In January 2011, a new record tuna price was set in Japan – $395,000 for one fish, or the equivalent of $1200 per kilo. With bans being applied to fishing the northern bluefin tuna, prices for the southern bluefin are expected to skyrocket, making wealthy men of the ranchers.

There are ostentatious mansions overlooking the water, lots

of big four-wheel drives and boats, and a busy CBD. The place *feels* cashed up, and it springs out of the nothingness of the surrounding coast without warning. We stop for a nice lunch in an Italian café, stock up at Woollies – where we spend the customary $200 on groceries – fill up on petrol and buy a bag of firewood. I duck over to the bottle-o for a six-pack of Coopers Stout, and we are off to our next bush camping ground.

Coffin Bay is a quiet little town famous for its oysters and other, more menacing marine life. If I wasn't already intimidated by this place, the names on the map would have me worried – Avoid Bay, Point Avoid, Sensations Beach, Sudden Jerk Island. As well as great wealth, the tuna farms are said to attract great white sharks. Before we left I'd had this area recommended by a friend as a great place to base oneself while exploring the surrounding coast. Then I read about the abalone diver chomped in half by not one but *two* great whites, while his friend and skipper looked on. I'm almost relieved when the weather forecast predicts a week of onshore winds and I can head a bit further north – away from the tuna farms – before having my first South Australian west coast surf.

I speak to west coast local Jeff Schmucker over the phone to see if I can avail myself of a bit of local knowledge. Jeff's an interesting guy, a big-wave charger and fisherman with a teenage son of a similar ilk, who outraged local sensibilities when he helped organise a junior surfing contest in the area. SA west coast localism is infamous, and the crazies were threatening to burn cars, push cars off cliffs and punch out competitors. One contest judge withdrew from the event after threats. Jeff's letterbox was blown up. One nutter threatened to burly the surf spot for sharks the night before the event. Jeff weathers it all because he reckons the territorialism is fundamentally wrong, that anyone has a right to surf these waters, and years of isolation and strong-arm tactics to deter visitors has bred only negativity and small-mindedness.

I'm not sure what the locals are worried about. This place is so far from anywhere that it's hard to imagine it ever becoming crowded. Nat's surf guide is suitably vague about the waves around here, with lots of references to the sharks and gnarly locals and one prevailing instruction: 'seek and ye shall find'.

After the monotonous emptiness of the eastern side of the Eyre Peninsula, the west coast is at least more heavily wooded, with myriad waterways winding their way into Coffin Bay. The township itself is tiny and soon gives way to the pristine coastal bush and high dunes of the national park.

Our bush campground is divided into two sections – one for caravans and one for tents, but the van area is basically an uninspiring car park, so we sneak into the tent area and squeeze the Expanda in among the cosy bush sites on the banks of an intricate inland waterway. A flock of emu strolls past outside. A kangaroo hops through the campground. There are intermittent rain squalls that prevent us from starting a fire, but it feels good to be back in the bush.

On our second night, we head into the little township to meet up with Stuart Valladares, the son of some friends back home in Currumbin. Stuart's an old Gold Coast surfer who headed down here in search of work and cheap real estate. With his wife, Joanne, and three-year-old daughter, Jade, they've built a smart home close to the beach for less than half what you'd pay on the Gold Coast. Stuart has well-paid work on the tuna boats and a rich coast to explore. Stuart's dad, Eddie, is an elite surf coach who has trained national teams, groomed world champions and introduced school surfing to the esteemed sporting excellence program at Palm Beach Currumbin High School. Eddie is as fit and active a sixty-year-old surfer as you'll find anywhere.

I figure we can't go to Coffin Bay without trying the oysters, and so I call into the little general store to see if I can buy some to take to Stuart's. It doesn't seem the wisest place to try and procure fresh seafood, but the old lady behind the counter is happy to shuck two dozen for me for $23.00. How long will it take to shuck two dozen oysters, I ask? She thinks about it for only a moment. 'About ten minutes.' I go next door to the bottle shop to select the appropriate accompaniment – a fine vintage of Coopers Sparkling Ale – and take it to the counter. The same old lady comes through an adjoining door in dish gloves, holding an oyster knife.

'I'm keeping you busy this afternoon,' I try to joke in apology.

'The husband's away – he did the roster and left us short-staffed,' she explains.

I walk out with my oysters and stack them on the roof of the car as I buckle the children into the back seat.

'Watch out,' wisecracks an old bloke sitting on a bench out the front of the shop. 'If those work, you'll need a bigger car.' His several companions dissolve in fits of laughter.

Stuart and Joanne live behind the pub, so they're easy to find. Jade is ecstatic to have some kiddy visitors, and our kids are inordinately delighted to meet a three-year-old girl, such is their relief to have a new social outlet. Stuart's got a small fire going in the front yard, and Joanne's made pizzas for dinner. They're great hosts and quickly feel like old friends.

Stuart's mate, Paul, drops by, and he's the first local surfer I've met who gives me a bit of a vibe. He seems slightly offhand when we're introduced, then has a few pointed questions for me: 'So, are you still doing your journalism?'

Yes, I reply, explaining that I'm writing a book about the family round-Australia trip.

'A book? What, like Mark Warren's atlas?' he snaps, referring to a comprehensive guide to Australian surf spots that raised the ire of locals the country over when it was published twenty years ago. I hasten to explain that, no, mine isn't an atlas, but a simple travelogue of our journey, a reflection on how we try and keep the surfing dream alive as middle-aged family men, hoping this is a theme he can relate to – but he seems unconvinced.

The locals are uneasy after a string of pro surfers have blown through this coast – Mick Fanning and Joel Parkinson, the Bra Boys, the Shipsterns crew.

'But as the boys always say,' Paul quips, 'we're only one shark attack away from it going quiet again.'

BLACKFELLAS

We continue up the west coast of the Eyre Peninsula, pulling into the break known as Blackfellas. Despite some clean, solid, six-foot sets barrelling down the reef, there is not a soul out. As I watch the empty waves, a picnic table with an elaborate tile mosaic on the tabletop catches my eye. I walk over to examine it and realise it is a memorial to shark attack victim Jevan Wright. Jevan was only two weeks shy of his eighteenth birthday when he was taken. The mosaic depicts a surfer and skateboarder surrounded my images of waves, doves and dolphins. A short inscription reads:

> The search is the driving force . . .
> For any restless souls who dream
> Perfect waves hitting an unchartered reef
> The eerie white silence of an untracked powder bowl
> The thrill of discovery
> The gripping rush
> Pure freedom where nothing else matters
> He joined the search.

Back in the nearest town, I see a gang of young guys about Jevan's age, with sun-bleached hair, riding skateboards to the town bakery. They loiter about outside, scoffing pies and chocolate milk, being as loud and uncouth as you'd expect from teenage boys. What must it be like being a young local in a town like this, growing up with uncrowded, quality waves on your doorstep and the ever-present risk of shark attack, knowing no other reality in your surfing life.

That night, I find the coroner's report into Jevan's death online. It makes for chilling reading. I've tried to reassure myself that I can reduce the risk of shark attack by not surfing at dawn or dusk, but Jevan's attack occurred in the middle of the day. The coroner, Wayne Chivell, gives a matter-of-fact account of the day's events. Jevan had been surfing with Graham Chapman, forty, a fisherman from Port Lincoln, and the father of Jevan's girlfriend. Two other men were in the water: Craig 'Nugget' Pringle and Kym Castley.

'Mr Chapman said there were a number of dolphins and also a particularly friendly seal in the area where they were surfing,' the coroner reports. 'At about 12.45 pm, Mr Chapman, Jevan and Kym Castley all decided to go in. Mr Castley caught the first wave in towards the cliffs, and Mr Chapman saw that the seal followed him in. Jevan caught the next wave, but he disappeared soon afterwards.'

As he scanned the water looking for Jevan, Graham Chapman saw a large shark and Jevan's board floating nearby. The shark's tail was larger than Jevan's 6'2" board. Then he saw Jevan's blue helmet and one arm protruding from the shark's mouth as it took its victim underwater. Chapman turned to his friend Nugget and said, 'It's a shark, and it's got Jevan.'

With remarkable courage, the two men paddled back out but could only retrieve a small piece of Jevan's damaged board before returning to shore to raise the alarm. Jevan's body was never recovered, despite a comprehensive search of the area that afternoon and for the following three days.

The coroner's conclusions, in dispassionate legalese, belie the harsh reality of his words:

In view of the evidence, particularly the evidence of Mr Chapman, I have no doubt that Jevan Wright died as a result of a shark attack. Having regard to his evidence, the shark in question must have been an extremely large one . . . I see little point in making recommendations about how Jevan's death might have been avoided. All experienced surfers, particularly people who surf on the West Coast of South Australia, must be aware of the risk, however remote, of shark attack. I very much doubt that any further warning or other preventative measure will reduce the likelihood that such an event will happen again.

There is no comfort to be found here, and all I can conclude is that it is not wise to google 'South Australian shark attacks' when you are trying to muster the nerve to surf these waters.

MEET THE SCHMUCKERS

I meet up with my local contact, Jeff Schmucker, in nearby Venus Bay, a tiny town with a permanent population of twenty, 'which swells to hundreds in the holiday season' according to a local tourist brochure. It's like something out of a Tim Winton novel: rough fibro fishing shacks, a couple of old stone cottages, a general store and petrol pump, a small van park and a boat ramp. Jeff's just come in from a day's fishing, packing his twenty kilo catch of King George whiting in a foam box with ice, taping it shut. The *Adelaide Advertiser* van will collect it from the verandah of his fishing shack that night and take it to market. Jeff will receive between $14 and $18 a kilo for his catch, which will then sell for $60 a kilo by the time it reaches a fish shop in the city.

Jeff is built like the proverbial brick shithouse – thick, sinewy arms and barrel chest – and can obviously look after himself. He'd need to, because his open and welcoming attitude to visiting surfers is enough to earn the ire of most locals – he's commonly referred to by a word that rhymes with his surname. Strangely, upon our first meeting, he reminds me of another surfer who attracted criticism for opening up sensitive surf spots to visitors, Martin Daly, skipper of the Indies Trader fleet of charter boats in the Mentawai Island, Indonesia. They both have the same piercing eye contact, firm handshake and no-bullshit demeanour, the same sea-worn air of authority. Both don't mind falling out with the pack. Jeff's happy to give me advice and directions to local surf spots, but he's too busy fishing while the whiting are running to join me for a surf.

Jeff's fixing up his own charter boat to take visitors out to fish and surf some of the region's most secret offshore islands and reefs, a business venture that is considered sacrilege by some locals. Jeff reckons most of the aggrieved are 'blow-ins' who've moved here from interstate. His son, Josiah, is an aspiring pro surfer, sponsored by Billabong, and the pair have hosted plenty of visiting pros and photographers, defying a virtual surf media ban that has prevented exposure of the area's waves for decades. Jeff's more than happy to stare down his critics, but how is it for his son in a small town, where everyone knows everyone else and old feuds can easily fester? How do you resolve the pro surfer's mission to gain photos and footage and the locals' pressure to draw no attention to the place?

Given the current climate, I figure I'm going to keep my head pretty low, hopefully score a few waves and move on. We pull into the local van park and nab one of the last remaining sites. The annual Whiting and Lawn Bowls Festival is on, attracting almost the entire Grey Nomad population of the country.

With the family happily installed in yet another coastal town, walking distance to all amenities, I go exploring. And I don't use the word lightly. Only a couple of the better known breaks in this area have been highlighted in the various surf guides. The directions I have to others are vague at best, involving counting cattle grids before turning off down dirt roads. Every second surf spot seems to have some sort of shrine dedicated to a surfer taken by one of the region's great whites. There's lots of driving down bumpy roads, across the flat, dry limestone coast. The mesmerising nothingness of the landscape, alone, listening to vintage Talking Heads, is strangley hypnotic.

I pull into a dirt car park overlooking one of the more well known left reefs that immediately brings to mind Uluwatu in Bali. It looks to be three to four foot with no one out, peeling for a couple hundred metres. Two older guys have just come in and reckon it's pretty fun but getting a bit fat with the high tide. A lone bodyboarder is hurriedly exiting the water.

'I wasn't going to stay out there by myself,' he says. 'I've seen too many big fish round here.'

I'm keen to get wet but not so keen on surfing by myself either. 'Just wait a while and someone else will turn up,' one of the older guys assures me.

I go for a drive and check out some of the surrounding coast while I wait for the tide to drop a bit. Though the wind is wrong for most of the more exposed breaks, the potential is staggering – reefs, points, bombies, all copping the brunt of a solid sou'-west swell. I drive like this for hours, marvelling at the set-ups, wishing I had company and questioning my sound-track. 'You may ask yourself, "How did I get here?"' David Byrne wails.

I eventually turn off to check out a sign-posted lookout. A woman in her forties with long sun-bleached brown hair is coming up the timber walkway from the beach with a board under her arm and a gang of kids straggling behind her. We get chatting, and she has a thick New York accent but hasn't been back to the city since the September 11 terrorist attacks in 2001.

'I was in the Bronx – I could hear it and smell it, but I didn't see it, thank God,' she says.

I ask her how she ended up in Australia. 'I came here and fell in love with the place,' she says simply.

I decide to ask her for directions to the spot I'm looking for. 'I don't know if it's classified information,' I add, trying to be cute.

'I don't mind,' she says, laughing, and gives me some basic instructions that are simple enough to follow. 'Then it gets kind of tricky,' she says seriously. It's about a kilometre walk in from the car park, and then the final instructions are vague and confusing, but I decide to press on. I know the winds aren't right today, but at least I won't waste time tomorrow looking for it in good conditions. I follow the instructions: a left, then a right, then turn off at the second cattle grid. It's a rough dirt track that seems to get narrower and less distinct as I drive on, until it ends in a small clearing. I get out and walk over the dunes along what appears to be a vague track hugging a fence line. I try and make mental notes as I go so I'll find my way back.

Finally, the ocean comes into view and it is a wild-looking coast – big, messy, random peaks exploding on a stretch of shallow reef, a funky left breaking against a sheer cliff headland. It's hard to tell if this is a surf spot at all, but there is a large wooden lookout so I must be in the right place. I can't spot anyone, and there is no way I am going out there. I watch on in awe and can see how the rawness of this coastline would rub off on people – make them harsher, harder, a bit grumpy. There is nowhere to hide from yourself out here, with none of the big-city distractions we use to suppress our deeper feelings. I can understand why crew out here would drink heavily or smoke a bit of homegrown. The environment is so powerful, so untamed – you'd need a little something to take the edge off.

I've been driving around for three hours and still haven't

got wet, so I hightail it back to the first spot, figuring the tide should be okay now. I pull into the rough car park and it looks prime, the long lefts more hollow now, a handful of guys out, a few others getting changed on the rocks below. I get straight into my wetsuit and jog down the stairs to the beach. The vibe seems mellow enough, and I hang back, trying to pick up a few scraps. But somehow I find myself in position for a set that no one else paddles for, so I swing late and go, stumble into a crude and clumsy pig dog, grab rail and hang on. The lip throws over me and smacks me in the back of the head as I side-slip down the face. It's an awkward execution, but I manage to stay on my board. A few more locals paddle out; they clearly all know each other and exchange witty banter about a pair of twin girls in town that are causing some confusion and cases of mistaken identity. I manage a nod and a smile and a few pleasantries with a couple of the guys. The bodyboarder from the morning is out and we get chatting. He asks about the Firewire I'm riding and shows me his purpose-built drop-knee bodyboard.

I manage to get my share of waves, and the crew is polite and friendly, taking it in turns. It's a far cry from the local aggro I've expected and one of the most enjoyable sessions of the trip so far. I surf for a couple of hours until I get caught inside by a rogue set and make my way in.

I quickly discover why the local crew get changed on the rocks below. It's cold, windy and muddy in the car park. 'A rookie mistake,' I quip to another local bloke who notices me struggling out of my wetsuit. When I mention the set-up reminds me of Uluwatu, he says, 'I haven't been there since 1975.' He was in Nias a few years later, just after the Storm Riders crew blew through, and has seen what media exposure did to that place. 'We've managed to keep this pretty quiet,' he says proudly. 'We just shut the fuck up.' I feel a pang of guilt.

Back at the van park, the family is happy. Alex has teamed up with a mate, Jayden, and they've been fishing with his mum,

Julie, and actually caught a couple of flathead. I've barely been missed.

I nod and smile at two other surfers who pull into the van park later in the afternoon. They are probably in their early thirties, one almost Indonesian looking with dark skin and a tangled mop of black hair. The other guy's a smooth hipster in black duffel jacket and goatee. They're obviously living the *Surfari Highway* dream. We exchange surf news of the day and it turns out they are regular visitors. The hipster's been coming here for six years, this time for five weeks. 'You always get barrelled,' he reckons. We discuss prospects for the next day, and they are keen to hit the radical reef I'd checked earlier. 'You've got to get in early before the locals. It'll get crowded and they get a bit grumpy. They don't like you getting set waves, even if they don't want them.'

To have come here for six years for up to five weeks at a time shows a fair deal of commitment, and to have made no inroads in winning over the locals seems harsh. It suddenly occurs to me that this is one place where it is actually an advantage to be the middle-aged family man rather than one of the young bucks. But I can't help thinking the local crew might actually find it's not such a bad thing to have a few more visiting surfers pass through town. It'd be good for local businesses. There might be a few more girls. They might make some friends whose hospitality they could enjoy if they ever travelled. It doesn't have to be such a fearful thing to have a few more surfers in the water.

To live in such a wave-rich paradise and then live in fear of losing it seems a sad fate, perhaps a microcosm of our own national psyche. It reminds me of our attitudes towards refugees, our inherent fear of the 'other' coming in and taking what's rightfully ours – jobs, girls, waves, that affordable block of land close to the beach. Perhaps this fear lingers in our unconscious because we are the heirs to a stolen land, that it is our karma to feel displaced, dispossessed, overwhelmed by a tide of new arrivals, whether we actually are or not.

On Sunday morning, out at a little reef peak on a beautiful stretch of beach, the surf is four to five foot, sunny, offshore – pretty much perfect. There are eight guys in the water when I paddle out, only four of us for the second half of the session; it's pure joy. I bump into a few guys I saw at the long left yesterday, and they are friendly and keen for a chat. The bodyboarder is out and, when I tell him we are heading to the Desert Camp next, he has a dire warning.

'Look out for Billy,' he says.

Billy? Billy who?

'He'll try and chat up your missus,' he says, deadpan.

'Billy' is local muso Billy February, and I've seen his flyer in a few pubs. He cruises the coast playing gigs and has, according to my new friend, scheduled a few days at the Desert Camp, just to play around the camp fires, taking it to the people. 'He likes to try and race off with blokes' missuses,' he warns.

How will I know him? I imagine some dashing Julio Iglesias-style Latin lover. 'You'll know him when you meet him. He's got big, frizzy hair like Crusty the Clown. You'll meet him within five minutes of getting to the place,' he predicts.

I tell my wife, figuring the forewarned is forearmed, so she can steel herself against his seductive charms. It becomes a bit of a running gag: how will our marital vows stand up to the lures of Billy February?

THE TIGHTROPE WALK

I've been keen to meet Jeff Schmucker's son, Josiah, probably the best surfer the area has produced, to see what it's like trying to forge a pro surfing career in this secretive environment. We arrange to meet at the pub for a beer and a chat. It turns out we'd pass each other on the track to the peak I surfed that morning. He's nineteen, a good surfer and a handsome young bloke who charges big waves and can pull all the moves in small beach breaks. Surfwear giant Billabong has seen enough in him to grant him a modest sponsorship, but it can be tough fulfilling his job description of earning surf media coverage in a surfing community that hates publicity. Josiah walks a tightrope between his dad's open and welcoming stance and keeping the peace with his peers, who dislike all the attention. Such is his dilemma that he asks me not to mention the town he's from. It seems an odd kind of quandary.

'A few of my mates are a bit like that – "There's been heaps of photos in the mags, you should chill out a bit",' he says. 'And a few of the other guys, the other locals, have a go at me about it. Usually, when people read a mag and they see my name they know where I'm from, but I try not to say too much about the spots. I want it to stay the same as it is now, as long as we can keep it.'

He does endorse his dad's attitude of welcoming visitors, though. 'For sure, because Dad's pretty well travelled, he's just started bringing his friends here. He's like, "I want to share this place. This is where I grew up. I want people to know how amazing it is." The place has given that much to him – he may as well help it out if he can.'

Read some of the nastier surfing web forums, though, and you'll see the Schmuckers roundly accused of selling out the place to try and bolster Josiah's career. 'There were rumours going around with some of the guys, saying that Dad's pushing me in surfing and blowing the place out, crap like that. But I've always wanted the same thing. I've grown up here – it's amazing and I want to share it with my friends. Just let people see how I live and see how beautiful this part of the world is.'

The localism, he reckons, has definitely mellowed in recent times. 'I've only seen a few blow-ups and no biffs or anything like that, so it's definitely changed in the last five to ten years. I've heard stories of guys getting sent in and their cars getting waxed up and a few guys getting bashed. There were a couple of loose units here, but they've either quit surfing or moved away. They used to dip crew's heads under water, semi-drown them. It was pretty full on.'

Josiah came second in the junior big-wave event his dad helped organise, only fuelling the claims that Jeff was engaged in clearing a path for his son's career. But Josiah reckons it has done nothing to increase crowds in the water, and most of the feedback he's had about the event was positive. 'Because it was huge waves, it's for the select few surfers who want to do it, and it wasn't too bad. I haven't seen another ski rock up to surf the place yet, so it hasn't done anything for it really.'

He remembers it chiefly as an epic day's surfing. 'That was the day of days, for sure. The best day in the best waves I've ever seen anywhere. It was amazing . . . I was just stoked I got to surf all day.'

Josiah's grommethood sounds like something out of Tim Winton's novel *Breath*, about two country kids graduating up the food chain of their local big-wave spots. 'When I started surfing, my mates were just taking me out to the local beach-ies, and they're not too heavy. And then I started getting taken out to the some of the local slabs, and then started surfing the local bombie when I was about fifteen. I'd only been surfing for a year, so I was sort of thrown in the deep end. It's also a bit hectic dealing with the shark factor here. Growing up, you always hear the stories, and you see a few too, with Dad being a fisherman.'

It's one thing passing through the place for a few days, but surfing here day in, day out, year after year, must feel like an ongoing game of Russian roulette. 'I only surf one spot by myself. Unless it's all time, like best day of the year, I won't go out by myself. You end up just psyching yourself out.' That can mean walking away from perfect waves on a regular basis because you have no one to go surfing with.

I ask if he's had any close calls? 'Not really, just surfing by myself and a big grey shadow swims past, and it pops up and it's a dolphin. That scared the shit out of me,' he says with classic country understatement. But then the stories slowly come out. 'I've been paddling in the water when my mate's been out on a jetski and he's seen a ten-, twelve-foot pointer cruising about fifty metres away, coming to check me out. They burnt over and grabbed me out of the water. That was pretty full on that day. You try not to think about it, but it plays on your mind all the time. Everyone else catches a wave to the inside and you're still sitting out the back. You start looking down, pick your feet up. So, I sort of struggle with it a little bit, getting my mind around it . . . I've had surfs where I was going to the beach and had just seen three cars driving back and thought, *What's going on here?* I got out and there was no one there, but I didn't really think about it, paddled straight out, surfed for a couple of hours, came in and got messages from my mates saying everyone just got chased out by a pointer. The other week we were surfing down the coast a bit, and there were two fifteen-, eighteen-foot pointers eating a seal only five k's from where we were surfing. You think about it, it's sort of hectic.'

Given the nature of the waves, the harsh desert environment, the shark factor, it's hard to imagine crowds will ever be a huge issue here. 'I've got a few mates from Adelaide who come over, do a few trips a year. They always come over for a week, and that's all they can really handle. They end up getting this thing called "desert fever", and just get over the driving and the hot weather, surfing every day. They get over it, need to get back to their city life.'

I run the comment by him I heard recently, that it's only ever one shark attack away from going quiet again. 'Yeah, exactly. I think that too. If there's another shark attack this year or next year, no one will rock up. Half the surfers stop surfing here too,' he says. 'It was pretty heavy when that ab diver got taken. I didn't surf for a week. I was too scared and it was pumping. If there was another shark attack, a lot of guys around here have families and it's not worth it. They'll just chuck it in.'

THE DESERT CAMP

It's a short drive on to the desert camp from our latest fishing town van park, but it still seems to take most of the day. It's 10.30 by the time we pack up, refuel and I stumble through the unfamiliar routine of filling the jerry cans and attaching them to our newly purchased wire basket roof racks.

It's an hour and a half to the next major town for lunch. There's an oyster bar on the highway west out of town where we've been told to stock up on the famed local seafood before heading into our remote coastal camp site. It sounds far-fetched, an oyster bar out here in the desert, on the outskirts of a country town, but, sure enough, we're met by a cheery husband and wife team happily shucking oysters on pace with the steady stream of passing travellers. If we had time, we could order a bottle of sauvignon blanc with our oysters and retire to the upstairs deck, with panoramic views of the surrounding landscape. But we're keen to move on, so we order a dozen to go, plus a kilo of fish fillets. The lady talks us out of the whiting, claiming it's over-priced, and recommends the garfish. I'm more than happy to take her at her word.

The turn-off from the highway to the coast is marked on the map as a small town, but that almost seems an overstate-ment when we reach it and find a roadhouse, pub, general store and an old stone building – the former town hall – now con-verted into a surfboard factory. The roadhouse has showers and the general store offers a small laundromat, presumably for sand- and salt-encrusted surfers to wash off their desert experience. I've been congratulating myself for being so well prepared for this leg. With the newly installed jerry cans, we're carting 120 litres of water and 100 litres of fuel. We've been told we can get our gas bottle filled at the general store, but the large man behind the counter informs us their gas hose is broken and they've been waiting five weeks for a replacement. I know our bottle is low, but I'm unsure exactly *how* low. It's touch and go if we'll have enough to run the fridge and cook for our few days at the desert camp, and I curse myself for not filling it back at the last town. It's another harsh lesson: don't take anything for granted out here.

This desert camp has been widely known in surfing circles since the late 60s. There's been a book published about the place – it's practically a household word – but I still prefer to be discrete about naming it. When you consider it found its way into the surf media and the collective surfing consciousness around the same time as Bali, Noosa, Kirra and Margaret River, it's astounding to realise how much all those places have changed and how much this joint hasn't. Partly, that's due to the sensitive management of two successive owners who have resisted the overtures of developers and surf companies wanting to turn it into a high-end surf resort or training facility. Add to that a determined campaign by some of the most gnarly locals around. And lastly, those pesky white pointers continue to conduct their own fear campaign. A memorial plaque on a wooden bench overlooking one surf spot is a grim reminder of the risks here.

I have no idea what to expect as we cruise in through the salt plains, past the peculiar pink lake, approaching those astonishing sand dunes that tower over the otherwise flat, nearly featureless landscape. A soundtrack of *Nirvana Unplugged* only adds to the eerie vibe. There has not been a single sign to indicate the presence of this mystical surf spot, not at the turn-off from the highway or along the road in. The closest you get is a vague 'beach this way' sign, which I briefly suspect is a red herring.

We eventually find our way to the coastal campground, swing open the gate and shut it behind us, and cruise the meandering dirt road through the low shrubs in search of a vacant camp site. Even out of holidays, midweek, it is surprisingly busy. There are old caravans that look like permanent fixtures, smart camper trailers, old-school canvas tents, even a teepee. Here and there, crudely built limestone walls have been constructed to provide a wind shelter around a metal fireplace or a pit toilet. It is simple, basic beach camping, with bore water and a central, open-sided kitchen area. I fall immediately, deeply in love with the place.

I jog up a timber boardwalk to a beach lookout and am stopped dead in my tracks. It is a pristine, golden afternoon, and as I come over the rise of the dunes, I see a brilliant peak at the western end of a rocky bay pitch and reel away in both directions. There are eight guys in the water. Other waves break along the edge of the bay – a running-right in front of me, a left at the eastern end, a small bombie off the end of the point, which heaves and spits as I watch, eyes agog.

I've tried to be pretty restrained about satisfying my surf lust this trip, to meet family commitments before feeding my own selfish urges, but now I am a desperate man. I rush through the heavy lifting of unhitching and setting up the van. I feel bad doing the bolt, but this is one time when I am ready to get down on bended knee and beg for a leave pass. The swell is dropping. The waves are perfect. This is a break that I have longed to surf for years. I have a two-hour window before sunset, and it's not the sort of place you want to surf on dusk. Kirst recognises my condition and benevolently shoos me along.

I bump into a fellow camper, a guy with long dreadlocks and a beard, and ask him the quickest route to the point. He advises me to drive back through the camp and take the next left on the way out. It leads me to a crisscrossing maze of dirt tracks through the coastal heath, and I'm not sure I'm even going in the right direction, but finally I see people and cars in the distance.

I emerge on a dirt plain and a rocky foreshore overlooking the line-up. Old four-wheel drives are lined up in rows. A few good old boys are gathered around a fire on heavy wooden benches, billows of smoke arising from their circle. A modern-day midden of oyster shells forms an enormous pile next to them, testifying to innumerable afternoons of beers and oysters at the point. I bolt for the water, giving a nod and a g'day to the boys and immediately think I am in too much of a hurry, too excited for these laid-back country environs. I need to shed my Gold Coast head and slow down.

It's a precarious tiptoe across a shallow rock ledge covered in thick weed. I expect it to be flat underneath, but it's sharp and uneven, and I nearly stub my toe several times. The last thing I need is to paddle out here trailing blood.

The vibe in the water is mellow. Everyone's taking it in turns and there seem to be plenty of waves to go around. I want to blow off some of my nervous excitement without making a prick of myself, so I catch a few smaller waves that no one else wants, and manage to pick up a few wide sets that catch the pack too deep. The wave is a joy, a long wrapping right that keeps bending back at you, asking to be belted. The sun is setting low in the west, just where the vast stretch of desert coast and the ocean meet the horizon – a vast pie chart of land, sea and sky. The majestic dunes dominate the foreshore. Everything is bathed in the most exquisite golden light. I feel like I am tripping.

I surf for an hour, keen to get back to camp and light a fire before it gets too cold, to ensure the family are happy and content – and prepared to stay here a while – only to return to discover they're all well on their way to falling under the desert's beguiling spell. We cook over open fires, surrounded by a bunch of cool neighbours. There are other kids for ours to play with and they form their own rolling posse.

CHOP WOOD, CARRY WATER

The wizened old camp manager, Ron, drives around in his battered yellow ute on dusk, his little, curly white-haired dog, Cherry, in tow, delivering small piles of wood to each fireplace. He's like a Zen high priest, quietly tending to the needs of his surfing guests, chopping wood and carrying water.

He pulls off a gardening glove, has a rubber glove under it, and excuses himself from shaking hands. He has long grey-white hair, and his slight frame is encased in blue workman's coveralls. He bought this place twenty-five years ago off surf filmmaker Paul Witzig, who established the camp. Ron reckons in that time, in today's prices, he has hauled in around $400,000 worth of mallee roots for firewood. That'd take a while to recoup at the ten dollars he charges per adult per night.

Of everywhere we've visited, this feels like a holy place. The landscape is a patchwork of a thousand shades of green, clusters of small coastal shrubs – saltbush, native cherry, coastal daisy, sea heath and pig face. The place looks remarkably lush and Ron is incredibly protective of the fragile vegetation, telling me they've had good rain the last couple of years. Prior to that, he says, it was bare, the desert sands blowing away in the wind. The only way to rouse Ron's otherwise gentle demeanour is to threaten the well-being of any of these native plants that literally hold his land together with their delicate root structures.

On the outskirts of the camp, there is a small colony of a dozen or so caravans under carport-type structures, some with their own rainwater tanks, presumably permanent fixtures for regular visiting surfers or long-time locals. In their own way, this small-scale development has helped keep this camp afloat, even though Ron still struggles with the sight of it. The shark attack in 2000, apart from costing a man his life and a wife her husband, decimated his business.

'I could have got through the divorce, but then the shark attack nearly finished us,' he says quietly. 'I don't like to put a price on a man's life, but it probably cost us a hundred and fifty thousand dollars in camp bookings. It took us six or seven years to get back to where we were before.' Unable to buy out his ex-wife, Ron was faced with selling.

In his darkest hour, Ron was overwhelmed with a flood of goodwill from long-time visitors and locals who helped him hang on to the place. A dozen or so allotments were leased to these regulars on a ten year tenure, and they happily paid $25,000 in camp fees up front, on a handshake, to reserve their allotments. Some only visit once a year, but they have reserved their own slice of a surfing utopia and helped Ron keep it pristine.

In a sense, Ron thinks the death of the surfer helped preserve the camp. 'As clichéd as it sounds, the loss of his life breathed new life into the place,' he says.

Ron's still on good terms with his ex, understanding better than anyone that the desert can just get too much for some people. 'I spoke to her tonight. She lived here from the time she was nineteen to the time she was forty. I don't blame her. It's a tough environment.' They were married here; their children were born here. When he had a heart attack two years ago, the children came back to help out.

'I told the kids if they ever sell the place I'll come back and haunt them,' says Ron.

'It's special,' I agree.

'The most special,' he says quietly.

'It looks like you're doing a great job.'

'It's a labour of love.'

The kids are entranced by the desert landscape, though Vivi pronounces it 'intimidating'. Alex is simply stoked to charge around the dirt roads on his bike.

'I've never met a kid or a dog who didn't love it here,' says Ron.

We've scored some excellent neighbours. There's Mark, a fifty-something family man from Sydney who's taken a couple of weeks out on his own here to surf, read and enjoy a glass or two of good wine in the evenings. He's generous to a fault, shares his Tim Tams with the kids and his excellent selection of wine with us around a fire in the evenings. Alex adopts Mark enthusiastically as a kind of surrogate uncle and takes to visiting him at every opportunity, and Mark always makes him more than welcome.

Another, younger Mark and his wife, Kate, are twenty-somethings from Lennox Head, heading to Karratha in search of work with their two young kids, Phoenix, three, and Nirvana, twenty months (named after the NSW Central Coast board label rather than the band or the state of eternal bliss). Mark is a plasterer and Brad Pitt look-alike, who's finding it hard to get work at home. Kate is a willowy blonde and former fashion model; she sold her 'ethnic clothing store' in Byron searching for greener pastures. They've heard there is plenty of well-paid work for anyone keen to take it on in the mining boom town.

'I'll give anything a go. I've been a plasterer since I was fifteen,' says Mark. They reckon you can earn eighty dollars an hour cleaning schools or watering gardens. The Chinese economic miracle is having profound impacts on our country, inspiring young families to pack up their lives, leave their homes and communities to join the great gold rush. Their story captures my imagination: travelling vast distances across a land in search of better opportunities, the great driver of human migration since time immemorial.

They have a classic old-school van, loaded down with Mark's enormous box of tools, and they're running to a tight schedule and budget. Kate has smuggled her crystals on board, in defiance of Mark's decree to travel light, and has them arranged in a cross on the ground outside their van to achieve a favourable flow of energy. Despite having three boards strapped to the roof, Mark doesn't manage a surf in their two days here before it is time for them to push on.

They remind me of an Australian version of the John Mellencamp song, 'Jack and Diane' or Tracy Chapman's 'Fast Car'. I feel a little concerned about their desperate dash across the country, but the older Mark is unfailingly positive about their mission as we swap stories around the camp fire, and even I feel reassured by his optimism.

They are worried they may need to backtrack to Ceduna first, over seventy kilometres, for urgent supplies, unsure if they'll be able to obtain them on the road ahead.

'What do you need?' I ask.

'The Pill,' says Mark candidly, his expression betraying just what an urgent priority this is.

I wake on day two and the surf is small, and the wind comes up a little sideshore during the day. I'm glad I got my late arvo session in yesterday or I'd be freaking. As it is, I feel completely at peace with my surroundings. The kids and I go for a coastal walk with young Mark and Kate and their kids, granting Kirst a bit of solo time. In the grey and windy afternoon we put on a DVD for the kids, and I see a window to get another little surf in marginal conditions.

I jump in the car and drive to the point. Though uninspiring from our vantage point in the camp, up close the surf looks more impressive. I see a set reel down the reef and can't believe my luck. There is one other guy suiting up in the car park, and

I am relieved to have company. He paddles out a bit ahead of me and we casually trade waves. He's just having a quick one before he returns to Adelaide: 'Gotta go back and see the missus and earn a few brownie points before I come back down.' When he goes in I sit out there, wondering what to do. A splash out beyond the line-up gives me a start – it's just a flash of a fish's fin, but enough to get my nerves on edge. There follows a prolonged lull, and I hunch my feet up onto the deck in front of me anxiously. But the waves are too good, and I catch a succession of set waves on my little Neal Purchase Jnr 6'0", finding my rhythm in the fast rights. There are a couple of cars in the car park and I will someone else to paddle out, but no one does. Finally, I decide the paranoia is not worth it and make my next wave my last, until I kick out in the shallows and see another fella paddling out, so I extend my session. Soon a chopper appears, flying parallel to the coast, and I wonder nervously what it's about. 'Probably a cop dope chopper, but they're a couple of weeks too late,' my new friend observes.

The next day I take the kids out to nearby Point Le Hunt for a swim, and we are all gobsmacked to discover a large modern jetty here in the middle of nowhere. This was once a bustling port where wood and wheat from nearby farms were loaded onto cargo ships. Holiday-makers and school kids flocked here for carnivals. Photos from the past show a bustling foreshore packed with cars and beach-goers. Plaques record the rich history of the place. Now, it is completely deserted, a ghost jetty. An older guy in the campground has recommended it to me as the most family-friendly beach, but one sign stops me in my tracks as the kids pile out of the car. In 1975, an eleven-year-old boy named Wade Shipard was attacked by a white pointer as he swam out to meet a crayfish trawler to collect a free crayfish for his mother.

'Fishermen from the trawler and bystanders on the beach watched helplessly as this young man was brutally attacked,' reads the plaque. 'The tragedy was a huge shock to the community as the family was well-known and especially popular . . . The distress suffered by all in the district was enormous.' A photo of Wade shows a gorgeous, smiling, cherub-faced boy beaming at the camera.

In response, the local community banded together and built a shark net off the jetty to provide a safe swimming area. Vivi reads the plaque and, strangely, doesn't seem the least bit put off about going in the water. We don wetsuits and carry their soft surfboards into the water, paddle out to a floating pontoon and swim, dive bomb and play pirates. It's a magical afternoon in the shadow of an awful event, but I'm buoyed by the last lines of the plaque: 'Wade's two younger brothers still enjoy Point Sinclair and share its beauty with their families.'

BILLY FEBRUARY UNMASKED!

I've been keen to make the acquaintance of the great Billy February, if only to assess the threat he poses to my marriage. My first surf here, I pulled up at the point and parked next to a white van emblazoned with his name, professionally written in large letters, but there was no sign of the man himself. A couple of days later, I finally meet him out in the surf, and he is thoroughly charming. From that point on I seem to run into him everywhere. Happily, though, he's parked at the other end of the campground.

We get chatting out in the water one day, and he lets slip that he's a former Australian surfing champion, and I notice he surfs with a strong, bullocking style. I'm pretty up on my surfing history, and I'm pretty sure there's no Billy February in the record books.

It turns out Billy February is just a stage name. His real name is . . . Bill Sedunary, the obscure former Aussie champ I'd been vainly googling back in Port Elliot. No wonder the name drew a blank. Bill Sedunary no longer exists. I ask him how he came up with his alias?

'Well, I was taking Chris Isaak surfing . . .' he begins casually.

'Hang on – how did you come to be taking *Chris Isaak* surfing?'

'His people rang my people,' he answers.

It turns out the famed US crooner and keen surfer was on tour in Australia and looking for a surfing buddy. One of his entourage had heard of the former Australian surf champ turned muso and got in touch.

'He's just a regular guy,' Billy insists. 'In fact, he's such a regular guy, Chris Isaak cleaned my windscreen.'

'Really?' I say, thinking it sounds like a good name for a song.

'He got out at Morphett Vale service station and cleaned the windscreen of my old Mazda 808,' Billy elaborates. 'I said to him, "You don't need to do that. Why'd you do that?" And he said, "Because it was dirty." That's how much of a regular guy he is.'

The way Billy tells it, Chris Isaak just started riffing on a stage name as they drove to the surf that day, convinced he needed something catchier. 'Bill Sednuary. Bill Sedunary. How about Billy February?' he eventually suggested.

And so Billy February it is. He now cruises the South Australian coast playing one-night stands at tiny country pubs, occasionally migrating up the east coast to favourite haunts like Angourie.

He's just one of the classic characters we've encountered at the desert camp. I've expected to find the archetypal, feral desert-dwellers here, gnarled *Mad Max* extras, refugees from the modern world bunkered down in their dilapidated caravans. The reality is far more intriguing.

I meet Martin, who looks like a retired rock star with his long hair and Keith Richards complexion. He strolls out of his permanent van and annex to check the surf each morning and discuss the state of the stock market. The ASX finished slightly up yesterday, he informs a fellow surfer as we look out over the Southern Ocean. About twenty-five points up. The Dow is up about fifty points, too. Long-term analysts are predicting another ten years of boom in Australia, he reckons, while the short-term analysts with an eye on Europe are ready to jump off a cliff. 'It all depends who you listen to,' he observes wisely. He's been living at the camp for five years or so, apparently overseeing his investments from this remote outpost.

A constant parade of regulars sit around the fire, overlooking the main break each day. The crew strikes me as a kind of Lost Boys tribe who never grew up, guys in their fifties or beyond who have clung to their surf-at-all-costs lifestyles, still laughing about who drank or smoked what last night, with estranged families and abandoned former lives elsewhere. It is a writer's heaven, an Australian desert coast Cannery Row, and I wish we could stay longer to render it all in sharper focus. I can see how this environment gets in your blood, how Ron and others simply can't leave, how it's become the great romance of their lives, a marriage to a place and a wave and a way of life, forsaking all others.

It strikes me, too, that despite the fearsome reputation and the occasional acts of hostile localism, the old crew are really all about preserving surfing as it once was. The mood and the manners in the water are the best I've ever encountered. Cars are left unlocked. Surfers take it in turns, talk to complete strangers, ask them if they want the next wave and call each other into sets. Yet if anyone stepped out of line, became greedy and disrespectful, I imagine retribution would be swift and harsh.

I hear one classic story about veteran pro surfer Matt Hoy pulling up here with a gang of Quiksilver grommets. Hoyo made the kids sit in the car while he went for a surf, knowing all too well that it would not be acceptable to unleash a gang of hyped-up young pros on the desert crew.

The book that documents the surfing history here is remarkable, full of fascinating tales and rich archival photos. I stumble across it in the homes of several surfers we visit over the course of our trip and eagerly devour it in instalments.

There's the story of the Nullarbor Nymph, a kind of land-dwelling mermaid myth that started among some blokes drinking beer in a nearby pub. Over a few brews, clearly starved of female company, they concocted the fantasy of a beautiful, feral blonde woman who was seen running with the roos, semi-naked, through the desert. The story quickly spread. It was reported prominently in the South Australian newspapers and reported sightings were recorded from one end of the Nullarbor to the other, until it was eventually revealed as a hoax . . . in December 1971.

The first desert surfers clearly did it tough to surf these waves, starved not just of women but of most modern comforts. 'We made a lot of sacrifices to surf those waves. Living on the edge, no money, no social life, little food and even less water,' one of the desert pioneers says. 'Heat, sand, torn wetsuits, broken boards, sea ulcers, etc. Living [here] is extremely hard.'

Ramshackle huts went up in the dunes in the early 70s, made from whatever early surfers could get their hands on – driftwood, limestone, old corrugated iron. A man's shack was a sign of status in the crude desert camp. 'It was hard to keep a girl . . . but if you had a shack you had a chance,' says one surfer. Paul Witzig famously constructed the $3 house, which was its total budget, and it featured in the pages of *Tracks* at the time.

But the desert camp began turning feral, with sanitation and environmental problems coming to a head. Newspapers began running articles about the freeloading surfie bums on the dole and high on drugs living in this lawless shanty town in the desert. In the autumn of 1975, local police moved in and burned down the shacks, ending an era.

Out of the ashes, the present campground was founded, with proper pit toilets, rubbish collection and environmental guidelines. Volunteers have helped replant and regenerate the fragile coastal vegetation. In every way, it seems to me a good news story. We are so accustomed to stories of surf spots exposed, exploited, overcrowded, degraded – it is heartening to discover a place that has been enhanced over time, all its natural allure intact. It seems a place that has found a kind of delicate equilibrium, perfectly poised between eras, suspended in time.

8

ONCE UPON A TIME IN THE SOUTH-WEST

THE NULLARBOR PLAIN LOOMS as our next test, and I have to confess to a deep, subterranean nervousness. I first traversed this notorious desert highway as a chronically carsick five-year-old, stuffed into a tiny Fiat 125 with my two older brothers and whisked across the country in just three days from Melbourne to Perth. Our little Italian jalopy was so ill-designed for such an epic road trip – in the middle of summer, on largely unsealed roads – that I wonder why no one reported my parents to the

Department of Child Services. We three boys sat squeezed together across the narrow bench seat in the back, bickering and elbowing each other the whole way. I began vomiting more or less continuously and was moved to the front passenger seat to be nursed by my poor mother.

Mum had come equipped for this road marathon with a foam cooler of Schweppes lime cordial and a packet of Ovaltine tablets. I still can't stomach the taste of either. On the last of the three days we drove fifteen hours in order to get to Perth in the cool of the evening, rather than endure another stifling day in the scorching desert. We kids slept in the car, my eldest brother across the back and two of us on the reclining front seats. My parents slept on camp beds under the stars. The trip's only comic relief came the night it rained and Mum and Dad demanded to be let in, while we locked the doors and squashed our noses against the glass. We stayed in Perth for two weeks to celebrate Christmas and the New Year with grandparents, aunts and uncles, then turned around and drove back. I'm not sure any of us ever fully recovered.

I tell my own children constantly – the two of them sharing the spacious back seat of the Rav, plugged into their own personal entertainment units as we travel at a leisurely pace – that they should count their lucky stars. Incredibly, rather than brightening their moods, my stirring pep talks seem to have quite the opposite effect.

So, with trepidation in my heart, I steer our rig out from the desert camp into this great, flat expanse of southern Australia. We are slow getting away on our first day on the Nullarbor and pull in at Penong to use the roadhouse showers and wash off the desert, though I'm not entirely sure I want it washed off. It's almost 11 by the time we hit the open road. Initially, all I want to do is get to the other end, goading the family at every roadhouse to hurry up and get back in the car so we can press on. Kirst urges me to slow down, take in the beguiling environment, enjoy the moment.

It's often assumed that Nullarbor is an Aboriginal term, but it's actually a Latin one – *null* for no and *abor* for trees. We're taking our cues from Alison Lester's picture book *Are We There Yet?* along this initial stretch and aim for the Head of Bight to see if we can spot a whale. There are no whales this day, but there are the spectacular Bunda Cliffs, a very smart visitors' centre and icy poles for the kids for three bucks each. The day's already getting away from us and I'm not too keen on driving on dusk. So far our roadkill toll stands at zero, and it's a record I want to keep intact.

We pick out a likely free camp site in our *Camps Guide*, and it turns out to be a beauty, perched on the edge of a towering escarpment with spectacular views up and down the coast. There are small, clean beach breaks peeling away in both directions and some rough dirt tracks crisscrossing the foreshore, but it's late, cold and I have no idea how to get down there.

We've done surprisingly little free camping this trip. Some people we've met have done almost nothing else, making it the mission of their journey to pay camp fees as seldom as possible. We find a nice place to park the rig among half a dozen others to take best advantage of the view, and I wonder why we haven't done more of it. There's a wonderful sense of liberation in just pulling in and setting up camp out here – no infrastructure, no rules, no signs. We leave the van hitched to the car to allow for a quick getaway in the morning, and with our solar and gas we have everything we need.

Kirst whips up a quick gnocchi and pesto for dinner while the kids ride their bikes around and quickly meet a few of our neighbours. One couple have dubbed themselves 'Free Radicals' and, before I know it, Alex is in their van chatting to the lady while Vivi is holding court outside with the husband – a striking, Ernest Hemingway look-a-like. He tells how he first drove across the Nullarbor in an old kombi in 1970. I do the maths and this is the same year I did it in the Fiat, not that he looks familiar.

The next day we stop at the Eucla Roadhouse with the giant kangaroo and the enormous signpost that points to many of the great cities of the world, displaying their distance away – Berlin (16,025 km), New York (15,025 km), Paris (17,204 km), Cape Town (4667 km), Moscow (15,613 km). It's sobering to realise we could drive to any of these international cities (if there were roads that went there) quicker than we could do a lap of our own country.

We cross the South Australia–Western Australia border and undergo a rigorous quarantine check. All of our fresh produce – even honey – is confiscated. Little do I know then that it will be 600 kilometres before we sight a green vegetable again. I imagine some opportunistic business person would have set up a fresh fruit and vegetable stall a short drive over the border, but we have to survive on roadhouse fare for the next day and a half.

Despite some privations, I am slowly falling under the Nullarbor's spell. There are themed trees on the side of the road that travellers have begun hanging dozens of items of clothing on, without explanation. There is an undies tree, a bra tree, a hat tree and a shoe tree. Contrary to its name, there seems to be quite a bit of vegetation out here, courtesy of recent rains.

Not so charmed was the 25-year-old explorer John Eyre, when he made his epic overland journey from Streaky Bay to Albany 160 years ago, describing it as 'a hideous anomaly, a blot on the face of nature. The sort of place one gets in in bad dreams.'

And he didn't have to pay $2 a litre for petrol. We have limited fuel range, carting our heavy load, and so we stop at every roadhouse – Nullarbor West, Eucla, Madura, Caiguna, Balladonia. They are all varieties of a similar species of establishment – witty outback humour stuck on the walls in the form of jokes and whacky newspaper articles, photos of an enormously fat cat, lists of the most commonly asked stupid questions and their answers (Q: Is that the right price on the petrol bowser? A: No, we just did that to trick you.), 'Extreme Hunting' video games and, invariably, next to every clock is a sign that reads, 'Yes, that is the right time.'

Balladonia has the considerable asset of the Skylab space station remnants that fell to Earth in a shower of sparks across the night sky near here on 12 July 1979 and made it briefly famous as a veritable gold rush ensued to souvenir some of the fallen debris. NASA reportedly offered $98,000 for a piece of space junk, and a Hong Kong newspaper offered an ounce of gold (worth $259 at the time) for every ounce of the station it received. This brief moment of international attention has also apparently won them the right to charge $7 for a stubbie of Coopers Pale Ale.

We spend our second night in another free camp site on the side of the highway in a parking bay of red dirt surrounded by peculiar orange or 'salmon' gums. The trees look like they have imbibed the colour of the soil, or else been coated in a liberal layer of fake tan, shimmering like Gold Coast socialites. The next day we pull into the sleepy mining town of Norseman at the end of the 1213-kilometre trans-Nullarbor drive, and I'm almost sorry it's over.

Norseman is an odd place, a dilapidated mining town that looks a few decades past its prime. A thin film of dust has settled over everything. A sleepy main street features a pub, a grocery store, a café, a second-hand bookstore-cum-doll museum and several roadhouses on its outskirts.

Alex has spotted a skate park on the way into town and is busting to ride, but within minutes he's nailed himself, hitting a gap in the cement, flying over the handlebars of his scooter and face planting spectacularly. I carry him back to Kirst; he's howling, bleeding from his upper lip, and the whole town stops to offer their condolences.

Vivi hits the second-hand bookstore then quickly returns

265

to ask for the entrance fee to the doll museum. Only a couple of bucks grants her entry to allegedly the largest doll collection in Western Australia. The proprietor is a jovial woman with an English accent, who tells me she had planned to retire to the scenic coastal town of Esperance before she and her husband lost their super in the GFC – so they settled for Norseman instead. It seems a cruel fate.

We don't linger in Norseman. I'm keen to glimpse the ocean again and this far south-west coast holds the promise of some rich treasures. I think of it as Tim Winton country, the landscapes and themes rendered so evocatively in many of his books abound. I want to surf Barney's, minus the resident white pointer. I'm not so keen on Old Smokey or Nautilus, the hideous offshore reefs Winton describes in *Breath*. These days a few of the modern big-wave crew are charging the very outer reefs that inspired Winton's fictitious death slabs with the aid of jetskis, documenting their heroics in photo and video.

Kirst's keen on the romantically named Cape le Grand National Park. Its magnificent granite coast offers little surf to speak of – the myriad bays and inlets are protected from swell by a string of offshore islands. We settle on Lucky Bay, so-named by Matthew Flinders back in 1802 when he found shelter from a storm and his onboard botanists came ashore and discovered around ninety previously unknown species of native flora and fauna. The weather's wild and the wind's onshore, so I don't mind foregoing surf exploration for a few days. Kirst's desperate to eschew the local van park in Esperance in favour of the bush environs of the national park, even though we need to do laundry and a shop.

I drop her at Woollies while I drive laps of Esperance with the kids, looking for a laundromat. The kids are proving remarkably patient after three days of near constant driving and some 1400 kilometres. I herd them into the laundromat on the outskirts of town, lugging two loads of washing. Alex has just had worms, so all the sheets need washing and we need to find a pharmacy to get some de-worming medicine. This is the unglamorous side of the great family road trip. It's raining and I find laundromats slightly depressing places at the best of times. A succession of down-at-heel characters watch their spin cycles as their kids read women's magazines. It's another sixty kilometres out of Esperance to our camp site, and it's going to be a long day to round out our Nullarbor marathon.

As we drive out to Cape le Grand in the late afternoon, storm clouds gather and the wind whips across the plains of stunted trees. It looks like someone has created a huge, free-range bonsai garden.

Like Flinders 200 years before, we find shelter in the protected cove of Lucky Bay. By now Kirst and I are able to set up the van within minutes. Kirst has dinner on the go, and before we know it she's serving up butter chicken with rice and naan. Even Viv is impressed. 'Gee, you guys are good,' she marvels. A storm's raging outside but we are safe, warm and well fed

It was almost dark by the time we got into Lucky Bay, so dawn reveals its full magnificence – a white sand crescent beach and aqua-blue ocean, spectacular rocky mountains spilling down to the water's edge, an archipelago of offshore islands decorating the horizon. We've met up with Julie and Jayden again from Streaky Bay Van Park, so Kirst and the kids have company. Julie's an inspiring character, a middle-aged mum who's brought up four boys and decided it's time to do something for herself. She's left the three eldest teenagers at home with their dad and taken her youngest with her to fulfil her long-held dream of driving around the country. Her vintage Toyota Cruiser minibus has given her a few mechanical problems along the way and they've nicknamed it 'Frankie,' short for Frankenstein because it's made up of so many borrowed parts. But she's gamely piloted it across the Nullarbor, after a prolonged pit stop in Streaky Bay at the mechanics. I think of my own nervousness about this trip, with a brand-new vehicle and van and my whole family with me, and I'm humbled by her courage.

Typically, I'm comfortable doing the surfless bush camping thing for a couple of days before I start getting edgy. And when the forecast predicts offshore winds and a moderate swell, I figure it's time to go exploring the nearby coast. The family is happy at Lucky Bay, so I set out early with the promise of tag-teaming at lunchtime so the women can go for a bushwalk unencumbered by complaining children.

There are only so many ways of describing a spectacular stretch of coastal road – Victoria's Great Ocean Road. Wollongong's Grand Pacific Drive. In Esperance, they've settled for the wholly unoriginal hybrid of Great Ocean Drive, a modest forty-kilometre loop that takes in the stunning beaches to the west. I know little about this area, but the coastal drive reveals one outrageously scenic strip of beach after another. It's sunny, offshore, and there's clearly a little bit of swell.

There are plenty of decent-looking beach breaks, but disappointingly no surfers, so when I see a van in a car park with boards and wetsuits out I pull in. Jarred and Melena are a friendly, twenty-something couple doing the Big Lap in a tricked-out Toyota HiAce van with their bull terrier, Bella. We get chatting, comparing notes on the coast we've traversed, only to find out they're from Burleigh Heads, approximately ten minutes from where I live. Jarred's just as keen for a surf companion, and there are some reasonable, if slightly fat, beach break peaks going unridden out the front.

He asks what I do for work and, when I admit to my shameful profession, they both laugh: it turns out they've been following our journey on the Coastalwatch website, where I write a weekly column, passing each destination a week or two before us. 'We've been cursing you – "look, he's scoring everywhere we got skunked,"' Jarred marvels. *Really?*

Jarred's a good surfer, riding a fine-looking Simon Anderson 6'0", and I ask him if he likes his board.

'Yeah, I work for him,' he reveals. I've recently finished working on Simon's biography, *Thrust*, documenting the illustrious career of the great surfer–shaper. Jarred is his glasser. It's another example of big country, small world.

We agree to hit it out the front despite the average conditions – four to five foot, wobbly, Bells-like walls. In other circumstances, it would be an entirely forgettable session, but I'm buoyed by the happy chance encounter and having a surf partner.

Off the eastern headland there's a crazy-looking, mini-Teahupo'o-style slab, a favoured booger haunt apparently, heaving and spitting over almost dry reef. Jarred paddles over for a look, rides a couple of shoulders but reckons it's pretty sketchy. We both race a few long walls in the middle of the beach before we're joined by dolphins and dive-bombing seagulls. Are they trying to tell us something? It's only later that I reflect on the name of our chosen surf spot – Salmon Beach – and learn of its popularity with sharks who enjoy such a delicacy. And I thought I was safe when I left South Australian waters . . .

We swap mobile phone numbers and exchange texts in the days and weeks ahead, comparing notes and favourable surf spots, and it now seems like the surf gods are extending their blessings. A huge part of this trip, I've come to understand, is the people you meet along the way. Despite fluctuating surf fortunes, in this regard we've been blessed.

TIM WINTON COUNTRY

From Esperance we head west to the historic harbour town of Albany. I'm surprised by the distance and the emptiness of the landscape, figuring we were back in civilisation after the

Nullarbor. But this far south coast of Western Australia is sparsely populated and full of unknown possibilities. My father and stepmum, Breffni, are coming down from their home in Perth to rendezvous with us, and they've rented a charming old holiday house with panoramic views over the harbour. We had planned to spend a night somewhere en route, but the lure of a cosy, warm beach house is too strong – we motor right through.

I love Albany and our abode immediately – its stone foundations, wraparound timber verandah and old table in the corner of our massive bedroom, where I can see myself writing. I'm having a bit of a Tim Winton moment, and his presence echoes everywhere we go. The next-door neighbour's kitchen was used in the filming of the TV series *Cloudstreet*, based on the Winton novel. I meet a guy at the local beach break who claims *Breath* was based on his family.

'I guess that's what he does – collects stories – but it feels a bit weird,' he reckons.

We visit the old whaling station, the last one closed in Australia, now the Whale World museum, but it seems macabre to pay good money to take the kids to a tourist attraction that celebrates the slaughter of these giants of the sea. We don't make it past the gift shop and head to the beach instead, which proves a much nicer option on a brilliant late autumn afternoon.

Warning signs are everywhere on these beaches and rocky headlands, alerting witless tourists to the very real possibility of injury or death if they take this raw Southern Ocean and its coastline lightly. There is nothing between us and Antarctica but a couple of thousand kilometres of heaving ocean, we are frequently reminded. It's not hard to believe that the landmasses were once joined. The ocean is prone to spontaneous and unexpected displays of awesome power in the form of rogue waves. It's a nervous business leading young children about this bit of coast.

Albany's enormous wind farm provides half of the town's electricity, and the kids gaze up in awe at their massive dimensions as twelve turbines spin almost soundlessly in the moderate off-shore breeze. I understand there are arguments about the health effects of living near wind farms, and I'm sure some have been built too close to residential areas. You wouldn't build a coal-fired power station next to someone's house, after all, but they seem such an elegant contributor to our energy needs. The fact that this huge infrastructure can exist on these coastal cliffs, and we can wander up and walk around their bases without any safety issues, seems remarkable.

Just checking the surf is a mission not to be taken lightly around here. I go looking for a break called Blowholes early one morning, and it's easy enough to follow the signs to the car park, but once there the whereabouts of the actual surf break has me mystified. I go walking down a long bush track, leading to a huge rock headland littered with enormous boulders. The rock falls away steeply to the ocean far below; I start to feel nervous just standing there. A life preserver is hanging on a pole, presumably for the rock fishermen who are washed away on an alarmingly regular basis. The blowhole that gives the spot its name groans and yawns eerily, as if the rock is breathing, before an enormous explosion of spray rockets skywards. Off to the west, some small beach breaks can be seen peeling into a cove, but from this distance they aren't enticing enough to convince me to try finding a way down to the beach, let alone surfing them by myself.

I end up back at a reliable swell magnet that has become my favoured spot during our time here. A clean, orderly swell is rolling into miles of beach breaks, with only a handful of surfers dotted across innumerable peaks. It is a long, steep trek down a huge timber staircase – over 500 steps, in fact. When I get there, I am greeted by the sight of three large salmon heads left gruesomely on the sand. An overweight, elderly fisherman is heaving a bag full of fish carcasses and his rod up the beach, preparing for the massive climb ahead.

'I've only got one lung,' he tells me, as if I might be able to do something about his onerous situation. I can't help wondering why he hadn't thought this through before he descended these 500 steps and hooked a bag of fish.

The salmon heads are a chilling sight before I paddle out, and I never really get over it, as if it has cast some sort of curse on my session. I paddle back and forth nervously between the shifting peaks, jagging a few short rides. At one stage I'm sitting out the back when I see a large grey object under the water, basically round in shape, and I assume it is a rock or a bit of exposed reef. When it starts moving towards me I have second thoughts. Eventually, I figure out it's a large sting ray, and I paddle away quickly, not wishing to have a Steve Irwin moment along with my Tim Winton moment. I come in soon after, thoroughly spooked. When I get to the top of the enormous staircase, a woman with a couple of young kids informs me they've just been watching a shark cruise up and down the beach. 'They're there all the time,' the woman's husband tells me, casually. I wish someone had passed on this information before I'd spent the past four mornings surfing here.

In every other way Albany has been exceptionally good to us – the comfortable old holiday house, doting grandparents keeping the kids entertained, bustling weekend markets to amuse the family while I go looking for surf. Winter has arrived while we've enjoyed these comfortable digs, open fires and warm beds. The return to van life on Western Australia's far south coast in winter is a slightly daunting prospect. We are already anticipating our journey northwards to warmer climes, and I watch the weather reports, eagerly eyeing the mid-twenties temperatures in Carnarvon, Exmouth and Broome with relish. But we have plenty of coast to explore before then.

We move on to a smaller, cold-climate version of Byron Bay thirty years ago, where the alternative lifestyle community has taken root. There are lots of massage therapists, health food stores, a busy environmental centre, an award-winning bakery, and plenty of dreadlocks and baby slings in evidence. We quickly warm to it. This is where our new neighbours, Michael and Michelle, back in Currumbin settled for three years in the middle of their own trip around Australia. It's the sort of place where it would be easy to decide to bow out of the rat-race. The bakery comes highly recommended, with a wall full of ribbons and awards to its credit. (Is there a bakery in country Australia that hasn't won an award?) I sample their Vinda-roo pie – curried kangaroo – and it lives up to the ribbons and hype.

We pitch camp at the River Bend Caravan Park on the banks of Wilson Inlet, bounded on two sides by water. The weather forecast has been bleak for a couple of days, but we seem to be dodging the worst of it, intermittent showers giving way to brilliant sunshine in the afternoon. We're only a bike ride from town, with plenty to keep the family entertained, and I've run into a local surfer who reckons we met in Bali twenty-five years ago. Paul's a born-and-bred local, a bit contemptuous of the sea/tree-change migrants moving into town and pushing up real estate prices. Cabins in the van park sell for $300,000. 'Once you could have bought the town for that much,' he reckons. The shortest stay he's seen from any of the new arrivals is two weeks – city escapees who'd sold up everything, bought the country dream home, moved down and quickly discovered they hated the same remote, small-town isolation they'd once idealised.

Paul's offered to pick me up in the morning for a surf and, after months of blundering around unfamiliar coasts by myself, it feels like an enormous boon. He's been surfing these waters since he was seven. He's a bit wary of my role in the surf media, but I'm sworn to secrecy. Short of blindfolding me, he's remarkably generous in sharing his coast. *Breath* was pretty clearly set in this general area, and Paul reckons he can identify many of the characters, including the old expat American in town who Winton's big-wave guru, Sando, is based on.

Paul often refers to surfing here as the South Coast Fitness Camp, because of all the walking and paddling and duck-diving it requires. It's a phrase that falls from his lips often, when I'm caught inside by a set or trudging up a steep set of steps at the end of a session. He takes me to a local, reliable beach break option that involves a long four-wheel drive up the beach on high tide — not that there's much beach to speak of. The waves are lapping at the tyres, and I'm glad it's his car and not mine. Several other similarly beaten-up four-wheel drives are parked along the water's edge, their owners paddling about a smorgasbord of peaks that appear to be breaking for miles to the east. It's a simple matter to just keep driving up the beach until you get a peak to yourself. We surf here a couple of days in a row, in fun four- to five-foot beach breaks, never with more than six or eight surfers within eyesight. I'm assured it gets crowded here, but I'm from the Gold Coast. These surfers don't know what crowds look like.

On our second day, I'm ready to get back to the family after a couple of hours, but Paul's keen to keep surfing, so he insists I take his old LandCruiser. He'll get a ride back with a mate in the water. It's exemplary country hospitality, but I'm a bit nervous negotiating the beach at high tide. 'If a wave hits you, just stop,' Paul advises. As I make my way up the beach, a couple of drivers coming the other way stop and wave, recognising the vehicle and assuming I'm Paul. They look at me quizzically as we pass, probably wondering if I've pinched their mate's car. We're heading off today, so Paul's asked me to just park the car at the van park and leave the keys with the office.

It's been a joy having a local guide in the area, but I have bigger fish to fry in this neck of the woods. I am stalking a mystical river–mouth–right I've heard whispers about, patrolled by a large great white. Paul has surfed it by himself in perfect conditions, but was chased out of the water by the monstrous resident shark. He shows me a photo and it looks sublime. There is a huge swell coming, originally estimated at eight metres, seven days out, but the forecast is down-graded as the fateful day draws closer. I'm not sure if it will be big enough for the river mouth, but we install ourselves at a local van park just in case. The only access to the break is by water, and you can hire tinnies for $50 a day.

It's another beautiful setting on the edge of a large inlet on the outskirts of a small town. Pelicans waddle about the jetty. Fishermen come and go in their tinnies. On our first night a massive thunderstorm roars through and it feels like we're going to be blown or washed away.

The new day dawns with clear skies and brilliant sunshine, but Paul texts me to say the swell has dropped overnight and the mystical river mouth won't be breaking. Scoring this place would have been a coup, but the prospect of a face-to-face encounter with mortality had kept me tossing and turning all night.

I'm down by the boat ramp at the van park with Alex kicking the footy the next day when two fifty-something surfers pull up on their jetski, boards stashed by their sides. They've clearly been out to the river mouth, and I can't resist asking what it was like. I'm not sure what variety of grumpy localism might prevail, but they are friendly and open. The swell was indeed too small and it hadn't been worth the effort, they say.

It's almost a relief to give up the wave chase for the day. I've been promising Kirst some downtime, a week when the wind blows onshore relentlessly and surfing is not an option, but across the entire southern coast of the country through autumn it just hasn't happened. After Tasmania we've had waves everywhere we've been. I'm not sure if I've just been really lucky or whether autumn is always this good down here. And it looks like there's more to come at our next stop in Margaret River, with yet more swell and offshore winds predicted.

I know I badly need to clock up some family time before I indulge in too much more surfing. Winter is starting to bite and we have the offer of a friend's house to enjoy when we get to Margaret River, while the owner, Perry, joins the great mining boom in the north-west. Perry's the former head judge of professional surfing's world tour, now earning unimagined sums in his original trade as an electrician, fitting out new, hastily erected miner's accommodation, working two weeks on and one week off. After a few frosty nights on the far south coast, the impetus to get to Margarets and a warm house intensifies.

We take the kids to the spectacular Tree Top Walk, a metal walkway suspended high among the canopy of a giant tingle forest. Due to changing climactic conditions, these tingle trees only survive in a tiny area of the south-west and have long been a favourite tourist drawcard. The oldest of them are 400 years old, and it was once an obligatory stop on every family road trip to drive through the largest of the hollowed out trees for a photo opportunity. Despite their massive dimensions, the tingle trees have a remarkably shallow root structure, and all this human traffic caused the unthinkable to happen in 1990 – the most giant of the tingle trees toppled over. This inspired Western Australia's Department of Conservation and Land Management to install boardwalks in the Valley of the Giants and build the suspension walkway to allow visitors to continue to enjoy these forests without damaging them.

Not everyone has been so awestruck by the timeless magnificence of this forest, though. As one early settler enthused in 1927, 'If only you could see the pastures, you would realise with me the pleasure one feels in conquering nature. The self-confidence one gets and the sense of power as a keen axe bites deep into the immense karris to bring them crashing to earth, robbed of their majesty.'

DRY-DOCKED IN MARGARETS

By the time we get to Margaret River I am feeling my age. This is roughly our halfway point, in time if not quite in distance, and all the driving, surfing and writing – and the deepening winter cold – is starting to catch up with me. If I needed a reminder that I am not a carefree youth, my seized-up neck and lower back provide it. I've been promising Kirst that I'll have some time out of the water at some point. Now, finally, my body says enough.

I pull into the car park at Surfers Point late on a Friday afternoon and the booming swell down south has hit here with full force, the winds are a gentle offshore and the point is firing – but the car park and the line-up are also packed. After the empty south coast, it comes as a bit of a shock, like we have rejoined the surfing mainstream. Despite the glorious conditions, with the way I'm feeling, it is not too hard to pass up. I can't afford to put my back out this far from home. We have another 10,000 kilometres or so to negotiate on the return leg north and across the top.

But I also realise an odd thing: I feel satisfied. I have surfed more new and empty waves in the most stunning environments in the past few months than I have in my entire life. I feel no need to hustle in these busy line-ups, on a long weekend no less. And Margaret River offers an embarrassment of riches to the travelling family.

Over a few days, we visit the region's spectacular caves, its glorious wineries, cruise its little towns and stunning forests, my wife and kids delighting in collectables stores and kid-friendly beaches. I start to feel guilty and begin to appreciate just what a sacrifice my surf time means for the family, how much more we could see and do together if I wasn't always dashing off for a wave. I am almost craving the return journey through the surfless Top End to experience a pure family holiday, free of my own pursuits and the constant siren song of the surf. But we'll see how long that novelty lasts.

BEREAVEMENT LEAVE

It's in Margaret River that we receive sad news. Kirst's Auntie Mal is going into palliative care back home in Queensland after a long battle with cancer. Her mum is flying out from her home in Italy to be at her sister's side. Kirst doesn't hesitate and books a flight from Perth to Brisbane to join them. We'll be in Perth for a week and a half at my father's so, as sad as the news is, it's at least fortunate timing. Then early one morning, we get sadder news – Auntie Mal has passed away. It is a strange, unsettling and sobering time. Vivi can't quite comprehend that her mum can just fly home to Queensland like this, whatever the circumstances. Vivi's been battling some serious bouts of homesickness and we've repeatedly counselled her that, well, we can't just *fly* home.

I drive Kirst to Perth airport to catch a 6 am flight to Brisbane, cruising deserted city streets in the pre-dawn darkness. Suddenly, as we approach the domestic airport, a minor traffic jam materialises out of nowhere. As we inch towards the terminal, Kirst's departure time ticking ever closer, taxis are depositing an army of workers in trademark fluoro miner's jackets. This is the fly in/fly out crowd providing the well-paid labour force of the mining boom. There are stories of mining company recruiters installing themselves at the airport and attempting to poach their rivals' workers, so severe is the labour shortage. It's a sad goodbye as Kirst leaves on her mercy mission and I'm left in charge of our nomadic family.

Fortunately, we're in good hands with my dad, stepmum, my brother James and their ageing Scotch terrier, Freckle. In any other setting, Kirst's departure would be a severe trauma for the kids, already out of their comfort zones, but with constant distractions and amusements, a comfortable home away from home, they lap up their extended family's embrace. There's a public library just down the road, where Vivi just about takes up residency. There's the Swan River a short stroll to the east and Cottesloe Beach only a slightly longer walk to the west. The kids have their own rooms, proper beds and city conveniences. We go to SciTech, Perth's fabulous science museum, and satisfy a long-held craving for yum cha. Dad and I take the kids to a game of WAFL, the local Australian Rules football competition that was decimated by the AFL's national expansion but is now a low-key family day out with jumping castles, a farm animal menagerie and a couple thousand spectators. East Perth is playing Subiaco, the team Dad used to play for, at Leederville Oval, one of his old stomping grounds. Three generations of Bakers partaking in the football at a ground rich in family history feels special. You can still run on at quarter- and half-time to have a kick of the Sherrin, and Subiaco rally for an unexpected win to mark the occasion.

I created my own bit of family folklore as a five-year-old at my first game of Aussie Rules with my father and grandfather when I badgered them incessantly for sustenance at every quarter-time break, until I was finally denied a snack at three-quarter time.

'We didn't come here to eat,' my grandfather chided.

'Well, I didn't come here to starve,' I protested.

This petulant childhood refrain has become a family catch-cry, brought out whenever I exhibit my enthusiasm for food, and the kids are keen to re-enact it. I've packed plenty of snacks for the occasion to spare them the dodgy footy ground pies and hot dogs, but we do indulge in a gelato on the way home.

I also have a couple of days of schools visits booked, giving talks and conducting writing workshops, hopefully inspiring a new generation of storyteller – not to mention supplementing our ailing bank balance. It's a busy week and feels slightly surreal going off to work in the midst of the great road trip, after so much time in the wilderness. I shower, shave, floss, trim rogue nose and eyebrow hairs, launder mud-stained clothes and attempt to present myself as the civilised travelling writer the schools have booked.

Finally, after a week, Kirst flies back from her mercy dash, emotionally spent and with a cold, and I'm not sure who's more relieved to see her, me or the kids. We're lucky to have her back at all – the Chilean volcanic ash cloud has thrown airline schedules into chaos. The morning after she flies in at midnight all flights into Perth are cancelled.

The great north-west leg awaits – the mystical desert lefts, my own family ancestral homelands, Ngalooma country and the descendants of the Indigenous Australians my great-grandfather befriended. It looms as perhaps the greatest challenge of the trip – this territory will be entirely new to me. Even the thought of the waves up there are enough to send a shudder through me: ferocious offshore reef breaks roaring down a barren desert coast, far from civilisation. A short hop from the town of Carnarvon, where my great-grandfather spent much of his life, is a surf break known as Tombstones. A fitting name for a place where I hope to get in touch with my ancestry, to understand the harsh pioneering lives of my forebears and stand by my great-grandfather's grave.

9

NORTH BY NORTH-WEST

PERTH SEEMS TO BE straining northwards, desperate to get closer
to the mining boomtowns of the north-west. It's not just the
itinerant mine workers jetting up to Karratha and Port Headland, or the overland migrants driving cross-country to seek
their fortunes – even the suburbs of Perth are stretching north,
as if dragged by the magnetic pull of all that iron ore.

As we head out of the city, the newly opened Indian Ocean
Drive hugs the coastline, revealing one new beachside housing

estate after another. Entire suburbs appear as if they have just fallen out of the sky overnight, complete with brand spanking new schools, shopping centres and service stations, with names like Grasstree Park and Beachridge. Who thinks these things up? Will they be officially recognised suburbs in time, included on maps and electoral rolls? Will there ever be an Australian cricketer, Olympic medallist or Nobel Prize winner from Grasstree Park? Where they haven't yet had time to build houses, they've laid out roads and curbs in endless grids of suburbs-to-be, already celebrated on massive billboards of handsome couples strolling empty beaches on sunset. (The fact that these developments mean no couple, however handsome, will ever get to stroll an empty beach around here has not deterred the marketeers.)

Up north in the mineral-rich Pilbara, developers are spruiking their plans for a 'mini-Dubai' of high-rise apartment buildings to accommodate all those mine workers, sparing them the rort of paying $500 a week for a van park site or a converted freight container with an air-conditioning unit attached. Once, the north-west pioneers decried the spread of bitumen roads, bringing more tourists from the city. Soon, the city might be literally on their doorstep.

We pull in at the once sleepy fishing town of Yanchep to visit our old friends Roscoe and Sarah, who have watched the suburbanisation of their coast at close quarters. Roscoe is a talented artist, a mate from my days as a surf magazine editor when I commissioned him to produce his evocative surfing artwork. These days, he works closely with Aboriginal communities in the Pilbara, helping them develop tourism enterprises and environmental initiatives. I tell Roscoe about my great-grandfather Aubrey Hall and his dictionary of the Ngalooma language. He brings out a book of Aboriginal poetry from the Pilbara, many of them in Ngalooma (or 'Ngaluma', as it is sometimes spelt) and translated into English. The book is called *Taruru – Aboriginal song poems from the Pilbara* by C.G. von Brandenstein and A.P. Thomas, first published in 1974. Interestingly, this is the same C.G. von Brandenstein who was instrumental in publishing Aubrey Halls's vocabulary of the Ngalooma language. He was a noted linguist and spent many years sitting around remote camp fires learning Aboriginal songs and poems. The collection makes for fascinating reading, traditional verse alongside the modern, including this gem about the rapid modernisation of the north-west.

DEVELOPMENT

There he sits bald as an egg
And wants to tell us
That railway tracks will criss-cross the desert, the liar!
They'd even cross the Pilbara, near Warden's Pool.
So he lies, the idiot!
Sand is all he'll find up here
To wipe his arse with,
                    The big shot from Perth.

Though the unnamed author may have underestimated the economic potential of the north-west's mineral deposits, it provides a powerful insight into an Indigenous perspective on the white man's activities in this part of the world. Aubrey himself recognised the mineral wealth of the Pilbara, sending rock samples to the Department of Mines in Perth, only to receive curt advice that 'these deposits would not be an economic proposition'.

Given that the surf spot we are headed to up north is known as Gnaraloo (pronounced *Nar-loo*), surely a derivation of Ngalooma, I am keen to learn more about this slice of my family history and its intersection with both Indigenous culture and surfing.

THE DARKEST HOUR AT THIRSTY POINT

Our first day on the road heading north is a long one. The distances in WA require a whole new collaboration of scale. What appears a small hop on the map turns out to be hundreds of kilometres. Road signs are thoughtfully placed at regular intervals, reminding us to relax. 'Soft shoulders,' they counsel the weary driver soothingly. I take a deep breath and try to follow their advice.

After the pit stop at Roscoe and Sarah's, it's still a long haul to our planned camp site at Greenough Rivermouth, on the outskirts of Geraldton, where I have two days of writing workshops to deliver at John Willcock College. Greenough Rivermouth appears to be the most pleasant camping spot within striking distance of this regional centre. There is also the small matter of some promising beach breaks where the river meets the ocean but, as the afternoon's drive drags on, it becomes apparent we aren't going to make it to camp before nightfall.

We pull in at the Pinnacles, where a friendly attendant informs us that we can unhitch the van and drive through the striking desert landscape of natural stone towers, or we can simply park and explore it on foot. We opt for the latter. As we follow a winding walkway past the visitors' centre and through the scrub, the Pinnacles suddenly come into a view, a vast rock forest of phallic protrusions looming out of the yellow soil. It's an arresting sight in an otherwise flat expanse of nothingness.

The sun is already low by the time we get back on the road. I try to avoid driving on dusk because of the risk of running into roos. There is enough roadkill out here already, twisted corpses often still carrying orphaned joeys.

We start consulting our camps guide for a likely roadside camp site. We wind up at Thirsty Point, the most unremarkable bit of coast we have encountered so far – just a small dirt car park off the highway surrounded by head-high scrub. There's a corrugated iron structure housing his-and-hers pit toilets, a waveless beach piled high with rotting seaweed and an enormous rubbish skip sitting smack bang in the middle of what would have otherwise been its best feature: a serene ocean view. We have just enough time to set up before dark, and a light sprinkle of rain begins to fall. It's a slightly depressing scene, certainly not the most auspicious start to our great north-west adventure, and Vivi is soon reduced to tears.

We've been in Perth long enough for our kids to have grown accustomed to the extended family's affections and comforts. Hitting the road again is a wrench. Vivi has moved from a love–hate relationship with the family road trip to one of outright loathing; she's even lost interest in her blog. She leaves us an angry note: 'I HATE EVERYTHING ABOUT THIS TRIP!!! I don't care how beautiful everything is, I just want to go home . . . I am not pretending. I am really, really homesick and I mean it!! This stupid, idiotic caravan will never be my home!!! P.S. I almost ripped up my journal, and that's saying something.' She ends this scrawled diatribe with a drawing of our car in a circle with a thick diagonal bar through it.

Even Kirst seems wearied by the renewed demands and is already talking about getting home with undisguised longing. Until now, despite whatever tests and trials the road has presented, I have always felt secure in the belief that it will all ultimately prove a bonding experience for our little family. But Vivi is becoming anxious that she will fall behind at school. Kirst wants to know if we can pick up the pace and get home early. Alex is increasingly wilful and defiant, and Kirst's diagnosis is that he needs the civilising influence of school as soon as possible. And I want to have a quiet word with Lenore Skenazy about this whole free-range childhood thing, specifically what she would recommend when a free-range child tips over into feral.

In many ways, Alex seems to be thriving on the nomadic lifestyle, making new friends easily, jumping on his bike and confidently exploring each new camp site and van park. Yet he has become almost completely uncontrollable, defying every parental decree with frightening stubbornness. Kirst and I have exhausted our arsenal of strategies to moderate his behaviour. With two solid days of work ahead of me in Geraldton, while Kirst is on her own with the kids in yet another van park, I genuinely begin to question the wisdom of this whole expedition. The daunting juggle of driving, hitching and unhitching the van, and honouring family duties while trying to fulfil my surf ambitions – and write about them – is starting to feel like too much. I, too, start to miss the simple comfort of our home, our circle of friends, my local surf spots, the ease of cruising down the road to a nearby river mouth or beach break and simply paddling out to familiar faces in the water, knowing every nuance of the line-up.

It's bad timing to get a bout of homesickness. By my calculations we are about as far from home as it is possible to get while still in Australia, with at least another 8000 kilometres of largely unknown and remote outback roads to negotiate before we are back in familiar territory.

If we are counting on the rustic charms of Greenough Rivermouth to ease all this mounting family tension then we are destined for disappointment. We arrive on a Sunday morning just in time for the monthly craft market. A couple dozen trestles, bridge tables and sun shades are arranged around a dirt car park, right out the front of the van park. There's an old country crooner belting out a sentimental rendition of 'I Still Call Australia Home'. Another bloke makes witty timber signs celebrating outback alcoholism, like 'Didjabringabeer' and 'Beer is God's way of showing us he loves us and wants us to be happy'. There's a stall selling fishing tackle, whose elderly proprietor kindly gifts Vivi a handful of sinkers. The kids scored twenty bucks each from their grandpa in Perth, and they are keen to spend it. Alex has his eye on a curious little stuffed gecko, handmade by an adorable old lady sitting at a bridge table, staring out with big, watery eyes from behind rows of toys and jars of jams and chutneys.

The van park is quite unlike any other we've been to. There's a large bird aviary out the front, where the kids quickly fall under the spell of a talking cockatoo. Maybe it's the large permanent population in the park that makes it feel different, like moving into someone else's neighbourhood. There are long rows of vans that clearly aren't going anywhere in a hurry. They've been augmented with annexes, gardens, carports, TV antennas and air-conditioning units. It all makes for an eccentric, colourful shanty town of pot plants, bougainvillea, gnomes and other curious garden sculptures. Do these van park residents, nestled behind the dunes of a pleasant sweep of beach, see themselves as the disadvantaged have-nots or the lucky ones who have seen through the delusion of mortgage servitude and the urban rat-race. Many of them seem to drive expensive four-wheel drives, their cars worth far more than their homes.

The coast, too, is unlike any I've seen, fringed by offshore reefs that block most of the swell from reaching the beach, its whitewater breaking way out to sea. Only the occasional break in the reef delivers surf to the coast. The river mouth provides one such opportunity, but the beach breaks look wild and untamed, and a few surfers gamely paddle around the pounding close-outs without much success.

Feeling like a bit of a van park veteran by now, I reverse the Expanda into place on my first attempt and look around for witnesses, but the kids are off admiring the aviary and Kirst is checking out the quality of the ablutions block. I step out to admire my handiwork as an old bloke with a grey-flecked red beard saunters over.

'That's not how you do it,' he admonishes. I'm momentarily

taken aback, wondering what van park faux pas I've committed now. 'You're supposed to take three or four goes,' he wisecracks. 'The way some blokes go about it you wonder where they got a driver's licence.'

I smile with satisfaction, feeling as if I have finally gained entry to an exclusive club of competent caravanners.

⌇

My two days at John Willcock College pass happily, taking groups of twenty or so Year Eight and Nine students for writing workshops, four sessions back to back each day. It's a multicultural student body. In one session, two large islander boys who look like they could play for the All-Blacks sit up the front, making smart comments.

'Do you know any jokes, mister?' one asks.

Wanting to be a good sport, I come up with, 'What did the fish say when he swam into a wall?'

They stare at me blankly.

'Dam,' I answer, and my clumsy explanation is met with a stony, unimpressed silence.

The library staff is friendly and welcoming, and there are several surfers among the teachers, but surprisingly few among the students. Vivi comes in and joins me on the second day, keen to be among other kids, even if they are a few years older. She happily sets up camp in a corner of the library and charms the librarians with stories of our travels over morning tea and homemade rock cakes.

We celebrate the completion of my teaching duties and the modest boost to the family finances with a slap-up lunch at a brilliant café, Salt Dish, on the Geraldton foreshore. We're all taken with Gerro — its beautiful old stone buildings, bustling CBD and rich cultural life — and I sense a darkness shifting.

THE MOUTH OF THE MURCHISON

Happily, our northern migration is bringing warmer weather, and it's like we've switched seasons almost overnight, from the depths of winter to a gloriously mild spring or early summer, daytime temperatures in the mid-twenties, blue skies and brilliant sunshine. We start stuffing away the heavy jumpers and pulling out the shorts and thongs.

But for me, there is also the realisation that the surfing component of our journey is drawing to a close. I may have as little as a month of surfable coast left before putting the boards away for the two or three months of the homeward leg across the top. In the meantime, I'm determined to make every stop count.

Kalbarri is a unique little fishing village a short drive north of Geraldton. It wasn't even technically a town until 1951, inhabited by a handful of fishermen in rough shacks and known simply as the 'mouth of the Murchison'. My paternal grandfather, Basil Baker, 'Pop' to us, spoke of the mouth of the Murchison as a fisherman's nirvana, where the fish leapt into your boat and crayfish could be picked off the reef at will. Despite its short recent history, no one seems entirely sure where the name Kalbarri came from. Some say it is an Aboriginal word for a local edible seed, others that it was the name of a notable character in the area. Either way, it is a fast-growing enclave of surfers and fishermen on the edge of the desert, its new suburban developments spreading out across the red dirt. There is no real town centre, just a couple of small clusters of shops on the foreshore where the Murchison River meets the ocean, no fewer than three caravan parks, a pub, a small boat harbour for the local fishing fleet and wide, grassy parklands along the riverbanks. The first shop was not opened in Kalbarri until 1954, its first school in 1961. Even today, as increasingly popular as it appears to be, the permanent population stands at just 1500.

The short drive from Geraldton means an early arrival in

Kalbarri, with time for an arvo surf while the family grabs lunch. I've been here once before, twenty years ago, but have only the vaguest recollections. The local point is an abrupt rock ledge that juts out into outrageous barrels. Watching from the beach, it looks like most of the surfers are shoulder-hopping, and you wonder why they are avoiding the first fifty metres of grinding barrel – until you paddle out and look deep into that barrel and see it contorting and sucking square off the reef in a foot of water, with that bare rock ledge waiting to claim the unwary. It is a test of nerve that neatly divides surfers into those prepared to take on the ledge and those who sit a little wider and try to save their skin. I fall into the latter category, even on this relatively small day.

Five or six surfers are happily taking it in turns, and I pick my way out over the rocks, watching a couple of blokes in front of me to find the best place to paddle out. The bloke I've decided to follow is poised on a finger of rock, waiting for a break in the sets to launch himself into the boiling ocean. But he waits too long, gets knocked off his feet by a surge and is swept down the rocks in front of me. If he's my guide then I'm in trouble. I eventually find a safe launching place and wait for a long lull before pad-dling out around the break. I sit wide of the pack, waiting my turn. It's a sunny Wednesday afternoon, the surf's four to five foot with a brisk offshore, and I figure the fishing fleet must be out at sea for the line-up to be so uncrowded. It's a promising start to my north-west surfing leg, and I pick off a few middling set waves, gradually edging a little closer to the peak.

This wild coast has a colourful and bloody history of mutiny, murder and shipwreck. It's just offshore from here, on the bar-ren Abrolhos Islands, that the shipwreck of the *Batavia* in 1629 led to a gruesome chapter of Australia's maritime history. While the ship's captain, Francisco Pelsaert, took a boat and sailed for help, a mutineer, Jeronimus Cornelisz, and his followers terrorised the survivors, eventually murdering 125 of them. Upon Pelsaert's return, he executed Cornelisz and his men. Two of the mutineers, Wouter Loos and Jan Pelgrom, were marooned on the mainland and thus became Australia's first albeit reluctant white settlers near the site of Kalbarri.

In 1712, another Dutch ship, the *Zuytdorp*, was wrecked on reef to the north of the Murchison river mouth, giving its name to the treacherous cliffs that define this coast. In 1839, Lieutenant George Grey, while exploring the North-West Cape, was shipwrecked near the mouth of the Murchison. His harrowing, 500 kilometre overland trek back to Perth made him the first white explorer to traverse the Central West coastal strip by land.

These days, Kalbarri attracts a hardy breed keen to build a life around the ocean. Characters like Rique Smith, an old mate from the Gold Coast who moved first to Margaret River and then up to Kalbarri, finding work on the cray boats and recreation out at the local point, charging these testing desert waves. I arrange to catch up with Rique out at the point one afternoon over a beer. Rique's the son of the great 70s surfer-shaper Col Smith from Newcastle (not to be confused with that other great 70s surfer-shaper Col Smith from Narrabeen). Newcastle Col was an innovator of channel bottom surfboards and rode them with great distinction in the booming waves of Hawaii, winning the Pro Class Trials there in 1977. He died of cancer when Rique was just seven, but Rique honours his father's legacy with a ferocious surfing talent that has seen him win some of the most prestigious and traditional surf contests in the country – the Burleigh Single Fin Classic, the Margaret River Classic and the Mattara contest in Newcastle, often riding his father's old single fins with familiar flair.

After drifting around the Australian coast, Rique seems to have found his natural home in Kalbarri. Apart from working on the cray boats, he's set up a little surfboard factory, producing the kind of sleek channel bottoms that run in his blood. He introduces me to his girlfriend, Katina, and I'm amazed to learn she's the daughter of another salty surfer-fisherman I've met up with on this trip – Jeff Schmucker back in Streaky Bay. I talk to Jeff on the phone a few days later and tell him I ran into his daughter, and he seems pleased with her choice of partner. 'They say you marry your mother or your father. I like to think she's chosen her father,' he says, paying Rique the ultimate compliment.

Another afternoon out at the point, the surf is three to four foot but raked by a strong onshore wind. Regardless, a gang of local teenagers are charging the windblown waves with abandon, blowing their fins out the back on every top turn in a contemporary display of high-performance surfing. I watch a gang of three youngsters attempt to jump off the rock ledge, but one gets washed off and dragged down the length of the point, caught up in the powerful sweep and pounded by sets. He gets washed in, inspects his board for damage, and trots round the point to try again, completely unperturbed. Another lad, maybe sixteen, gets washed in with a broken board and runs up to the car park to grab a new one. It strikes me as a wonderful, well-rounded grommethood these kids are having, far from the surfing mainstream. The rawness of the ocean and the coast can't help but rub off on them, even as they exhibit all the modern skills of aerial trickery.

Remarkably, for a fishing town, I can't find anywhere to buy fresh local fish. Rique gives me a tip that a fishing boat is coming the next morning, so I head down to the wharf early to see if I can purchase some straight from the source. There I meet Bing, a fifty-something surfer-fisherman who moved here from Eden on the New South Wales far South Coast twenty years ago. He's friendly, talkative and keen to hear about our travels, and the waves I scored in his old stomping grounds.

He and a mate have caught 650 kg of fish by hand in one night. I ask him if he has any to sell and he invites me on board his old trawler, opens the lid of the biggest esky I've ever seen, and there, floating in a slurry of ice, are more fish than I've ever set eyes on in one place. He picks out a couple of medium-sized snapper and says they're mine for ten dollars each. The local pub has fresh snapper on the menu – thirty dollars for a small fillet. I wrap ours in foil and cook it whole on the barbie with lemon and ginger, and it feeds the whole family. I fillet the second one and we have it the next night, pan-fried in seasoned flour. That's eight meals of fresh fish for twenty bucks. While I've been frustrated by the lack of fresh seafood on offer in regional towns and fish shops, my record at boat ramps, jetties and fish-cleaning tables is pretty good. I decide I should adopt the nickname 'The Pelican'.

Bing gets me excited about our next surf destination to the north, a desert coastal camp site past Carnarvon. When I tell him we are spending two weeks there, he says, 'You should try six months.' That's how long he used to spend out there as a younger man, surfing, fishing and taking a run into town every few weeks to restock. He tells me the water is unseasonably warm for this time of year, that it reached thirty-two degrees in summer after three consecutive cyclones pushed warm water down the coast from up north. It killed the entire abalone population of this coast overnight – and the lucrative industry along with it. I suspect we're in for many more stories like this in the years ahead. While some seafood stocks are thriving in our changing climate and warming oceans, others are likely to be displaced, out-competed for limited resources by migrating species or completely wiped out, like the abalone.

RESORT WORLD

We've scheduled a couple of days at the unashamedly touristic Dolphin Resort at Monkey Mia, so the kids can engage in the time-honoured novelty of feeding the dolphins. I'm already a bit cynical about the contrived tourist attraction and its slickly marketed resort, but the kids love it. The small van park there is a bit cramped for our liking and our site is right in front of the toilet block, but the proximity to the beach, the clear waters of Shark Bay at our doorstep and a gang of kids next door for ours to play with make it a hit with the whole family.

The ritual feeding of the dolphins on the beach each morning is an odd, surreal affair, reminiscent of the Phillip Island fairy penguins. An MC with a microphone headset directs the crowd to line up at the water's edge as the dolphins swim in on cue and perform obliging laps of the beach in the shallows within touching distance of the crowd, smiling up a little too cutely, as if they have been trained for a photo-op. This whole performance evolved innocently and organically enough, from fishermen feeding the dolphins their scraps as they cleaned the day's catch, but soon became a thriving industry in itself. These days, to avoid the danger of overfeeding and loss of their natural hunting skills, you aren't allowed to touch the dolphins, and they are no longer fed endlessly by whoever wants to toss them a fish.

One mother dolphin is introduced to us, along with the sad news that she has lost six of her last seven babies because she spends too much time here interacting with humans rather than looking after her offspring and teaching them to fend for themselves. It's a tragic tale, but I endure it because the kids lap up the experience and spend endless hours gleefully playing with other kids on the beach. My good humour with the surfless family tourist destination may also have something to do with our next destination, a pure desert surf experience that is likely to throw me all the waves I can handle, and then some.

A DATE WITH TOMBSTONES

We have arrived in the mid-west coastal centre of Carnarvon and set up at the Coral Coast Caravan Park on the outskirts of town. The waves to the north were once closely guarded secrets, but I've been stunned to see large tourist billboards on the highway into town promoting Red Bluff and Gnaraloo with glorious full-colour surf shots.

Our dear friends from home, Chris and Jane Garrett and their daughter, Sally, have arranged to rendezvous with us for two weeks at Three Mile Camp on the desert coast to the north. It's perfect timing for us to see some familiar faces from home and settle down in one spot before the long homeward leg. Their arrival in a little rented camper van after the flight from Brisbane and long drive from Perth provokes unrestrained glee among the Baker clan. I'm hoping our time together will be a morale booster for us all, with plenty of waves, a surfing buddy and writing inspiration for me, and quality company for Kirst and the kids. Within minutes of their arrival, I feel that everything's going to be okay, after all.

Chris is a renowned surfboard shaper whose boards are under the feet of many of the best surfers in the country. These days he's on a bit of a *Morning of the Earth* trip, 'getting back to where it all began'. The Garretts have swapped their prime beachside block in Tugun for thirty acres out the back of Kings-cliff on the New South Wales North Coast. Chris has built a shaping shed at home and another larger shed for the family to live in. Originally, it was only going to be a temporary home while they built a house, but they liked the shed so much they've stayed.

Chris is nothing if not self-reliant. He grows most of their fresh vegies organically, built their own composting toilet and makes his own bio-diesel out of used vegetable oil. He also builds recycled timber boards out of old pallets. He makes no big claims about his eco-credentials, but his reputation is spreading, earning him consultancy gigs in the Solomon Islands, teaching the locals to make bio-diesel, and at a fancy resort in the Maldives, speaking about his timber boards. He's a good man to have on a surf mission. We often joke that when the system collapses we are moving to the Garretts and electing Chris our leader.

The crew of seniors directly over the road from us are into the cans of Emu Bitter at 11 am. We've been engaged in a lively debate about whether the road into Three Mile Camp is passable towing a van, and with our friends in a two-wheel drive rental van. There's been heavy rain overnight, on top of a lot of unseasonably wet weather and the worst summer floods in fifty years. The ground is already sodden, and any additional rain quickly pools on the surface, then degenerates into sometimes intractable bogs. The seventy-five-kilometre dirt road into the camp is officially closed, according to tourist information and the Department of Main Roads. The Gnaraloo station management themselves claim not to know what all the fuss is about – the road is fine, apart from a couple of 'puddles'. Clientele have been arriving all day in regular two-wheel drives without a worry in the world.

The old fella across the road reckons we should give it a crack, while his wife is aghast at this irresponsible advice, prompting a noisy domestic dispute. The bloke tells us he recently drove three young Brazilian surfers into the camp when their own car had broken down and then returned to pick them up two weeks later. That's two 300 kilometre round trips simply to help a bunch of strangers from another country realise their surfing dreams. I can't think of too many other places on Australia's coast where a group of Brazilian surfers would be shown such kindness.

Our party is divided over our next course of action. Chris and Jane are keen to go. They've been here before and are adamant the road will be fine. The van park manager, John, on the other hand describes it as 'touch and go'. I want to wait a day, just to let the recent rains subside, but Chris is a persuasive guy with an infectious sense of enthusiasm.

'Let's just give it a crack,' he urges. 'It'll be fun. If you get stuck, someone will come along and drag you out. They can't leave you there 'cause you'll be blocking the road.'

The camp manager, Paul, gives us an encouraging assessment over the phone in a thick Irish brogue: 'If you've got a four-wheel drive and a two-wheel drive, and a bit of rope, you should be fine.'

In the end, Chris's enthusiasm wins out.

It's all rather more hurried and less organised than I would like: this is our biggest detour off sealed roads and our longest stint having to be almost entirely self-sufficient in a remote campground. The women race around, doing shopping, while Chris does the laundry. My job seems to be holding down the fort back at the van park with the kids. I feel oddly unsettled: after co-skippering our ship for the past five months, I suddenly feel like a bit player, overwhelmed by the group consensus to boldly press on, not wanting to be the overly cautious stick in the mud, but not wanting to be stuck in the mud either. And so we fill the jerry cans, pack and hitch up the van yet again, in defiance of the dire warnings from our van park neighbours and my own gut instincts.

We've also run into Julie and Jayden again from Streaky Bay, and Alex is inconsolable about the too-brief reunion. Jayden is more upbeat, cheering 'may the force be with you' as we lead a sobbing Alex away. Julie informs us that someone she knew had to get pulled out of a bog on a road that had been closed and was given a bill for $18,000 for their trouble. They don't like chump tourists out here ignoring official advice and getting themselves into strife.

But the weather forecast is uncertain and calls for more rain. Chris argues, 'How long are you going to wait?' And so, by the time we have completed our various errands, stopped to fill gas bottles, buy firewood and ice, get petrol and last-minute provisions, it's almost three o'clock in the afternoon. It's normally a ninety-minute drive to the desert camp, but who knows how long it will take in its current condition? It's dark by 6 pm, and I am quietly freaking. Our contingency is to only drive to the end of the sealed road and camp at the Blowholes for the night, then head off fresh the next morning, but those wide-open spaces start to work their magic. The surrounding landscape looks like it has received less rain than in town. The few dirt roads we pass leading off the bitumen look fine.

By the time we reach the Blowholes and the iconic 'King Waves Kill' road sign seventy-five kilometres out of town, I am already entranced with my surroundings. The Blowholes are astounding, the most dramatic I've seen, exploding in a huge shower that erupts vertically for twenty or thirty metres, accompanied by a deep, guttural groan from the coastal rocks. The swell is clearly up. Just watching the Blowholes work seems to clear out my own spiritual carburettor and I feel immediately emboldened. The decision is made to continue on to Three Mile Camp.

At first the going is easy and I wonder what all my worrying has been about. A few puddles, a bit of mud, the odd drift of soft sand, but nothing likely to halt our progress. We are following Chris, Jane and Sally, watching how they negotiate each hazard, when their van rocks and sways over at about forty-five degrees as they cross a large expanse of water at high speed. One side is almost swallowed by a deep trench beneath the muddy water. It happens so suddenly and appears so outlandishly dramatic that I don't know what to think for a moment. Somehow, Chris corrects the van and maintains speed, coming out the other side unscathed. But this has just become serious.

I stop, get out, wade through every square inch of the puddle, searching for any other unseen hazards. There is one deep wheel rut in the middle of the puddle, and we must take a hard right line and stick to two firm tracks through the mud to make it out the other side without incident. I change down to low gear, eye my entry point and charge. We are through before we know it, ecstatic, but have no way of knowing what other hazards lay ahead. It reminds me of surfing a particularly shallow, treacherous reef and having to carefully pick and then hold your line under pressure, or suffer the consequences of indecision or hesitation.

We push on, tackling several more expanses of water in similar fashion – stopping, wading through the puddles and finding the safest line. Mostly, it is firm rock under the water, but every now and again there is another outrageously deep rut waiting to be discovered. This is where previous vehicles have become bogged and scoured out trenches as they attempted to rev their way out of trouble. At one point I'm wading through a puddle, calling out to Chris, 'No worries, it is really shallow . . .' when, with exquisite timing, I sink up to my thighs in water and mud, soaking my shorts through. Many times, it feels like there is only the narrowest tyre's width of firm passage through a particular puddle It is relatively simple to pick the right line for the car but a trickier business trying to make sure the slightly wider van stays out of the ruts.

But I discover an odd thing – I am loving it. Some veneer of caution and worry simply cracks and falls away, and I am like a young boy, giggling deliriously with each little victory. Soon I become aware that we are being tailed by a larger four-wheel drive, and I wonder why he doesn't just blaze past us at our snail's pace. When we stop at the next puddle, he goes forward and drives back and forth through it several times to demonstrate where the safest track is. He hovers ahead of us like this for several kilometers, making sure we negotiate each water trap successfully, ready to tow us out if we strike trouble. He's a friendly fifty-something saint, and I offer him a beer for his trouble, but he declines: 'I'm just returning the favour – someone did it for me once.'

Eventually, he turns around and heads back to town. The sun is getting low and he has given up on his mission to reach a scenic lookout at Red Bluff to shoot some sunset shots. 'It's farther than I realised,' he says.

And so we are on our own. Chris has another near miss, keeling over on his way through another expanse. Showers of muddy water coat the windscreen, as if someone has thrown a large milkshake over it, and the wipers work overtime to maintain visibility. I forget to close my window once and get sprayed myself. The kids are immersed in their iPods, only glancing up as their parents hoot and holler each successful crossing. Just when we think we are through the worst of it, there are three large water traps in a row. It takes careful plotting and altering of our line to make our way through each in succession. 'It's like an obstacle course for cars,' Alex observes from the back seat.

Soon, as the sun begins to dip towards the horizon, the Gnaraloo Station sign comes into view – a heavy timber board mounted over grand stone columns – and we all let out a cheer as we pass under it. Kirst and I high-five. But we are not home free yet. Some of these stations are larger than small countries, and once we pass through the gate the road ahead stretches off into the distance towards an unseen coast. There are a couple of mildly challenging soft sand sections to steer our way through, and then finally the campground itself is revealed.

It's almost dark and we cruise through the winding dirt tracks lined with rocks at walking pace to find our appointed site. The kids fly out of the car to explore their new surrounds. Chris and I make a beeline for the lookout spot to survey the surf. It is glassy and apparently a solid six foot – and not a soul out. I stare out at this astonishing coast, long lefts reeling away endlessly along the edge of the desert, enormous sand dunes rising in the distance. The place is reminiscent of the South Australian desert camp in many ways – small coastal shrubs clinging to the dunes, camp sites dotted throughout, paths defined by rows of limestone rocks, tents and camper trailers, and stone toilet blocks and fire pits.

I've already fetched a beer from the esky. It is a sweet, delicious moment to be here on the western edge of the country, at the farthest outpost of our surfing journey. There's no time for a surf tonight, but my sense of wonder is boundless.

WELCOME TO TOMBSTONES

It's our first morning at Three Mile Camp and Chris is up early, itching to go surfing. It looks big, messy and onshore, but we're both keen to open our account. We walk up to Tombstones along a dirt track, trying to avoid the minefield of rocks. It's nice having an experienced surf buddy showing me the line-up, where to paddle out and the little idiosyncrasies of the reef.

The place immediately reminds me of Grajagan, that other mile-long left reef on the edge of the jungle in south-east Java, in its long paddle over shallow reef at high tide and the three or four successive sections of reef, each growing heavier, more hollow and intense as you surf your way through. Even the names, Grajagan and Gnaraloo, seem to suggest they are sister breaks albeit in sharply contrasting environments – one on the edge of a bamboo forest in an Indonesian National Park, the other on the desert coast of a remote Western Australia sheep station.

Tombstones is so named because of a large, roughly rectangular slab of rock that stands upright near the shoreline. Whether someone has put it there as an ominous portent of what awaits the unwary, or whether it is a natural occurrence, I'm not sure. Either way, it's a telling omen for my first encounter in the water.

We finally reach the line-up and I turn and paddle for a smaller one, keen to find my feet on an easy first wave – it proves a strategic rookie error. I turn around to see the biggest set of the day looming and immediately realise I am in the worst possible position as the set stands up on the boiling reef. I don't know whether to paddle towards the thing or away from it. In the end, I sit and wait for it to break a few metres in front of me, then ditch my board and dive. I manage to get under it and think I'm going to surface reasonably unscathed, but then it grabs hold again and pulls me back down. I'm rolling over and over until I'm out of air and don't know which way's up. I finally emerge, gasping, just in time for the next wave to land on my head. This one washes me halfway to the beach.

It is a slow, thoughtful paddle back out, wondering what the hell I am doing here. Am I really up for this? The little excursion across the reef has left me gun-shy of paddling into the impact zone, and I hover on the shoulder nervously. I'm in position for a bigger set wave, but I'm not keen. I look down the line and it's a mass of boils as the water draws and bubbles over the reef. I feel the sting of regret at an opportunity missed as the wave reels away. I manage a couple of smaller waves but feel like I've blown my first test here.

Still, there are nice signs of camaraderie among the surfers. To scale up the craggy limestone foreshore it is necessary to first place your board precariously on a ledge above you, leaving your hands free to climb. But I find myself in a procession of three surfers who kindly help one another with their boards, passing them up the cliff in a short human chain.

On land, there are fireside chats, guitars, storytelling and a vast dome of stars. The Waifs become our soundtrack for the desert coast, where these folk balladeers often camped out and composed songs as they toured their home state. 'Highway One' seems to have been written about this place, extolling the delights of eating freshly caught fish hot off the coals of a camp fire and sleeping under the stars.

There are little surprises, like the presence of hot showers from bore water in a little wood-chip water heater. The smoke from the heater wafting above the toilet block each afternoon is an eagerly anticipated sign that warm water will soon be available. Remarkably, there is even wi-fi at the little camp shop.

The next day is smaller and more crowded, but clean and offshore – a decent trade-off as far as I'm concerned. Chris and I paddle out at the middle section of the reef, known logically enough as Centres, and it is much friendlier but a long wait between sets. There is an increasingly narrow window of optimum surfing conditions for me as I age – big enough to make it interesting, but not so big that it's life-threatening. I'm in my element today, four foot with some five-, six-foot sets, but it's a waiting game. Still, surfers mainly take it in turns and call each other into waves.

Day three looks smaller in the morning, and Chris and I take our time getting organised. By the time we paddle out it seems like the swell is building and the conditions are flawless – sunny, brisk offshore winds, only a handful of people on the section of reef we're heading towards.

I get a couple of waves and am starting to feel a bit more comfortable – it's amazing what a difference a couple of days surfing a spot can do for one's confidence. Just as I'm starting to get in a groove, I kick out of a close-out but my board gets caught by the lip as I launch skywards. I feel my leg-rope stretch and then that dreaded *ping* as it snaps. I surface to the sight of my board bobbing shorewards in the whitewater and face a long swim. I catch up to my board halfway to the beach and paddle in, with only a dodgy small-wave leggy on my spare board in the car. A friendly surfer on the beach, who I recognise from the campground, offers to loan me one, and I'm back out with a minimum of fuss, buoyed by his kind gesture.

It's a long paddle back out, though, and my arms are burning by the time I make the line-up. Still, I'm in perfect position as a peak looms on the ledge and no one else seems to want it.

I muster the last of my paddling strength and launch into the thing, bottom turn and project down the line towards the next throwing section. As it pitches, I can pull in tight and high or drop and try to bottom-turn around it. In a split-second decision, I grab my rail, duck my head and go for the tunnel. The barrels are pinching shut and I've watched the better surfers riding high to escape the tricky tubes. I try and do the same but it's a difficult move on your backhand, and I cop the lip on the back of my head as it curls over, pushing me to the base of the wave, but somehow I'm miraculously still on my board. It's only a brief cover-up, but I'm buzzing on the adrenalin and my morning has just turned around.

The swell pulses through spurts and lulls, but Chris and I get enough waves to put lasting smiles on our faces as we wile away the afternoon eating, resting, reading, attending to the little domestic duties of camp life. I try and convince myself the swell has dropped and content myself with an afternoon on the beach with the family, along with half a dozen others, variously snorkelling, climbing rocks, making shell murals in the sand and splashing in the shallows. Out to sea, migrating humpback whales spout and breach and slap their tails. Everyone I look at is beaming. None of us, I'd wager, would rather be anywhere but where we are right now. How often in life can you look around at people and confidently say the same?

THE BOOMTOWN SURF RATS

There seems to be a large population of young blokes here with expensive four-wheel drives, brand-new tinnies, generators, enormous quivers of boards and fishing rods, and every conceivable bit of camping equipment. I wonder at the phenomenon for a while before I realise they are the cashed-up young mine workers on their weeks off, the beneficiaries of the great minerals boom in the north-west. I come to think of them as the Boomtown Surf Rats.

There's a lovely bunch of young blokes camping a couple of sites up who appear to be living the mining boom dream, earning unimaginable riches a few years out of high school, four weeks on and one week off up in Karratha. They either drive seven hours down here for a week's surfing and fishing or fly over to Bali, directly from Port Hedland, in just two hours. One young fella, originally from Merimbula on the New South Wales South Coast, tells me he was working in finance in Sydney when he decided to head to the north-west. He's earned his tickets to drive the various heavy, earth-moving machinery, climbing his way up the pecking order for better money and work conditions. He hopes to do it for a few years, salt away enough to buy a modest house back home and enjoy his weeks off in one of his chosen aquatic playgrounds. It strikes me as a great life for a young surfer.

He and his mates are playing happily with our kids; they're polite and friendly to the wives. They call by one lunchtime with a freshly caught and cooked red emperor wrapped in foil. But they are still young men. I spot them packing up a day before their scheduled departure as the swell drops and the wind swings onshore. 'Might go up to Coral Bay for a bit of a sniff around,' he explains. 'We called in there on the way down and there were a few backpackers around.' A man can get lonely in those mining towns.

THE FLAT SPELL

After being caught inside by the rogue eight-foot set on day one, I've been quietly praying it doesn't get too big again, but I seem to have been praying too hard. After three days of glorious conditions, gorging on the exquisite rifling lefts up and down this strip of reef, the swell drops out, the wind picks up and suddenly there is very little to surf.

My romance with Gnaraloo is tested in the absence of surf, the desert's allure now placed under harsher scrutiny. The wind starts blowing a gale, buffeting the tents and camper trailers. This is what makes Gnaraloo a mecca for sailboarders and kite surfers. Chris reckons WA stands for 'Windy Always' or, if it happens not to be windy, 'Wait Awhile and it will be Windy Again'.

We head a short drive north to Gnaraloo Bay, a marine sanctuary with pure white sand beaches, crystalline water and some of the finest southern reaches of the famed Ningaloo Reef, recently granted Word Heritage status. We swim and snorkel over reef teeming with colourful fish and marine life, bury the kids in the sand, build sculptures of sharks and turtles, racing toy cars around them.

Back at camp I bump into Dave Macaulay, ex-pro surfer, once rated number three in the world, now happily shaping surfboards and taking his four kids surfing from their home base in Gracetown, near Margaret River. Gnaraloo is their annual winter holiday destination. Their son, Jack, is fifteen and has been here every year of his life. All their kids learnt to ride bikes without training wheels here, even learnt to drive on the empty dirt roads. They took the whole family on the great round-Australia road trip themselves in 2003.

Dave strikes me as a man who's got it right, combining surfing and family life with an admirable balance. All four kids are keen and accomplished surfers. His three girls – twins Ellie and Laura, nineteen, and Bronte, seventeen – have competed with success at Australian Titles and Pro Juniors. It hasn't always been smooth sailing, though. When the twins were fourteen, Ellie was stricken with appendicitis while they were camped at Gnaraloo and had to be flown to Perth for emergency surgery. Dave's wife, Lorraine, flew down by her side while Dave was left in the camp with their three other children.

'While they were down in Perth,' Dave says, 'we were out at Tombies, Bronte and Laura and I. When it's big it's pretty safe to sit down on that second bubble – you can look in at guys getting pitted off their heads and not get caught inside as long as you keep a bit of a lookout. There are not usually sneaker sets that break way out . . . Bronte was hounding me, going, "Take me to the peak, take me to the peak." She was twelve and Laura was fourteen, and so they both came to the peak, but the surf was starting to pick up a bit – it was about five to seven foot, pretty solid, but getting a bit bigger. We'd been out there a couple of hours, and I was trying to push them into a wave to go in, and next thing this frigging set came and it was every bit of ten foot. One guy made it out, I think, and the rest of us got caught inside, including Bronte and Laura . . . We all got annihilated.

'I was freaking out, going, *My kids are going to drown and it's my fault* . . . I came up after the second one, and I could not even see them because they got dragged about 100 metres underwater. I was paddling in, freaking out. Four boards broke on that set. All these guys got washed in as well, and I finally caught up with Bronte. She was with one of my friends, and then I saw Laura. I got up to Bronte, who doesn't normally swear a lot, but she goes, "Dad, I just got fucking *smashed*." Man, it was kinda funny . . . She was fine. Their boards didn't break or anything. They got a bit of praise in the car park for handling it, so that seemed to make it all right. You can imagine me on the phone – "Oh, Ellie's all right. Well, Bronte and Laura drowned." It was heavy.'

THE QUOBBA COAST

What was known as the Quobba Coast first rose to prominence as a fishing paradise, long before surfers discovered it.

In her book, *The Bluff: A Piece of Surfing History*, Patsy-Anne

Wootton describes how the first incursions by keen fishermen into the region mirrored much of the same angst, media hype and environmental pressures caused by surfers in the years to come.

'Carnarvon locals had been venturing out along the Quobba Coast since the Blowholes were discovered in 1911 during a shooting expedition by fencing contractors Bill and Harry Ladlow,' she writes. 'They described the Blowholes and the large quantities of crayfish on the reefs that they saw to friends in town. After an unsuccessful expedition from Carnarvon by horse and sulky, a group of them decided to go there by boat. Their fishing was successful. They caught seventy dozen crayfish, but noted that "due to undersea disturbances large waves appear without warning" – a forerunner of the famed caution, "King Waves Kill."'

By the late 1960s, the fishing of the Quobba Coast was becoming widely known, written up in fishing magazines in Australia and even internationally. While the environmental stresses of increased visitor numbers was becoming a concern at Red Bluff, Gnaraloo remained almost untouched. 'This was in part due to the staunch refusal of the station management to allow trespassers onto their land,' writes Wootton. 'Gates were locked and parties seriously investigated the legality of public access onto pastoral leases. Confrontations occurred, guns were produced, police were involved. Fishermen and hunters were seen as a nuisance, and surfers who followed later were, to a large extent, viewed in the same light.'

More recently, as pastoralists have struggled to keep their stations viable, tourism has become an important supplement to their incomes. While the first surfers made their way into Gnaraloo in the early 70s, there is debate about who first surfed the wave. Current station manager, Paul Richardson, a non-surfing, non-fishing Irishman, reckons he has met about sixty surfers who claim to be the first to surf Gnaraloo, though it is widely agreed that local surfer-fisherman George Simpson was among the first to surf it on a regular basis.

On a forum on seabreeze.com.au – a surf and weather web-site – a recent thread was started asking who the pioneers of surfing Red Bluff and Gnaraloo were, provoking a flood of reminiscences but no definitive answers. One contribution from a guy called simply 'Thommo' is typical of the early surf-ers' stories:

A couple of mates decided to go exploring in February 1977, which seemed a bit odd to me because Feb is the hottest and flattest month of the year around here. Anyhow, they were lucky enough to end up around Gnaraloo at the same time a cyclone was forming, creating a bit of swell, and got to surf a head-high left that they thought had potential.

Me mate and I went to have a look in May '77 at the start of the swells. After visiting the homestead and getting the go-ahead to look for surf from the station owner, we decided to set up camp at a spot that looked an okay setup. No swell, so went for a dive to get food. Out of my dairy, edited:

'26th May: waves perfect 4'-6', can't believe it. 200+ yard long rides, long sections, unreal tubes, 3 surfs today, could hardly move when we came in. Dolphins still surfing, so much activity in the water it's unbelievable – dolphins, tur-tles, manta rays, sea snakes, mackerel, whales. Swell still picking up. Tide has so much to do with this place. Swell lines are perfect offshore all day. 3 breaks, other two prob 8' and heavy. Right-hander getting bigger, good sign for tomorrow.

'May 27th: Dolphins still surfing, big whales, waves per-fect 6'+. Went out twice, second time was unreal, big long walls, take off in one place, ride through the suck, heavy wipeouts, good tubes, long rides. Came in when I couldn't paddle anymore. Sat on beach and watched unreal spitting out barrels at other lefts, 8'+, super super hollow.'

And on it goes. It's hard to imagine the pure surfing bliss of those pioneer days, the ecstasy of surfing these pristine, virgin waves juxtaposed by the harsh deprivations of life on land when you had to bring all your supplies in with you and any assistance or medical aid was a long way away, down 100 miles of rough dirt road to Carnarvon.

THE YOUNG BOY AND THE SEA

The fishing is still good here, but I worry about the vast quantities of fish being hauled out of the ocean every day by keen amateur fishermen with great arsenals of gear, happily dissecting their catches at the fish-cleaning tables each afternoon. There is no denying the thrill of the catch, though, or the joys of enjoying fresh fish from a coal fire.

The eleven-year-old boy next door, Will, returns triumphant from a fishing trip, carrying a Spanish mackerel almost as big as he is. The sense of excitement in the camp is palpable. It's like a Steinbeck novel – 'The Young Boy and the Sea' – as everyone streams to the beach to bear witness to his feat. He poses for endless photos with his catch as small children swarm around and take turns trying to lift it. His father, Paul, is almost as excited as the boy. 'When we got it on board, it was like a grand final,' he tells me, imitating the roar that went up when they landed their prey. Then the entire family proudly marches back through the camp as Will lugs the huge fish, refusing all help.

'It's like a Mexican wedding party,' Jane observes. The boy chases smaller children, carrying the fish under his arm like a torpedo, and they scream in terror. Later, as we sit around our fire, Will arrives with a bag of fillets as a gift. His mackerel feeds four families for two or three meals. Other, greedier fishermen come here with enormous freezers on the backs of their utes and leave with enough frozen fillets to feed a family for a year. The sustainable fisheries catchcry is 'fish for the future', but I don't think this is what they have in mind.

SURRENDER

As the days pass it gradually dawns on me that there is simply no surf coming. Every day I trudge up to the shop to inspect the seven-day swell forecast posted on the camp noticeboard, and the prognosis is always a stubborn flat line of small seas. But the odd thing is, I don't seem to mind. If this was a hardcore surf mission with a few mates or, worse, a magazine trip with a photographer and a bunch of bored, expectant pro surfers, this would be a disaster. With a family, it is almost a relief. There are luxurious amounts of time to simply be – laze on the beach, snorkel, kick a footy, read a book, hang with the kids while the wives take long walks. There are still small waves to be found along this coast, and Chris and I manage to sneak away and get in the water most days.

School holidays have arrived and the camp is filling up – lots of families, lots of generators droning among the bushes, kids playing everywhere. Alex is free-ranging around the campground, scouting for new playmates. He seems to regard the camp as his personal smorgasbord, inspecting the quality of the catering on offer and quickly learning who is likely to offer him food.

I wake up some nights to take a leak, step outside the van, gaze up at the night sky and the glorious vault of stars, the Milky Way a thick spangled ribbon through the middle of it. My record stands at three shooting stars during one excursion.

And then it starts raining. I feel for the new arrivals, grimly setting up tents and camper trailers in the relentless downpour. Rivulets are soon cascading down the dirt tracks. I see two small dome tents completely surrounded by water, as if they have their own moats. The families in tents, with young kids and outdoor kitchens under sunshades earn most of my sympathy. We are among the lucky few, warm and dry in our van, but just as I'm feeling smug with our mod cons, our solar power runs out and we have no light. We go to ignite the stove burner to boil a kettle and discover we are out of gas. As we get to the end of our two weeks, provisions begin to run low and meals have to be carefully planned.

The sun comes out the next morning and everywhere people are hanging out wet bedding, sleeping bags, mattresses, clothes. Naked kids play with bodyboards in muddy puddles. There is a collective sigh of relief, but the rain is replaced by wind, a vicious northerly that roars through the campground, buffeting tents and mauling the small swell. That night, storm clouds gather and unleash spectacular lightning, thunder and yet more rain. The road out will be further under water, making our departure in two days' time a more dicey proposition.

THE IRISHMAN AND THE SHEEP STATION

I meet Paul the station owner at the camp shop and ask how an Irishman, who doesn't surf or fish and prefers nightclubbing in Ibiza, ended up running a remote Australian sheep station and campground. 'Sheer stupidity,' he replies. I sense there is a story in this and arrange to meet up with Paul for a chat.

It's late in the afternoon when I make the short drive from the camp up to the homestead, but even so it's an odd feeling being out in the middle of all this emptiness alone, following a rough dirt road on dusk. There is more accommodation for travellers available up at the homestead – a dozen small stone cottages, the old shearing shed and shearers' quarters, and what's rather grandly known as 'the fishing lodge'. There are also a few caravans and camper vans parked around the property.

Paul's tale is a twisted and fascinating one. The Gnaraloo pastoral lease had been acquired by Japanese investors with Australian partners in the 80s, but the partnership turned sour and the place had laid idle for years, falling into disrepair. Paul had travelled the Coral Coast as a backpacker in 1991 but hadn't made it to Gnaraloo. He was going through Thailand in 2005 when he had the idea to build a backpacker resort, and he thought he might pick up land cheaply in the remote north-west of Australia, where a steady stream of travellers passed through.

'I thought what I'd do is find a farmer who'd had a bad year and say, "I want an acre in a corner of your property and I'll give you five thousand dollars for it,"' he explains. 'That's when I found out you can't buy an acre of land in WA north of North-ampton, because it's all pastoral leases. So, obviously, we spoke to different stations to find this out. When I spoke to Gnaraloo, the lady said, "Oh, if you're a builder, the Japanese guys are looking for a partner." I thought I could do the work to get my share in the partnership, but he wasn't interested.'

What the Japanese were interested in was off-loading the place cheaply. 'It was just something that happened – a case of, here's an opportunity; if you don't take it, it's never going to appear again.'

Paul snapped up the lease on the 89,000-hectare property and the next day had the unnerving thought, *What have I done?* He'd rather not say what he paid for it, only offering that it was 'more than I wanted to, but hopefully less than I should have'. For comparison's sake, I come across an ad offering Nalbarra station for sale, 350 kilometres west of Geraldton, all 141,716 hectares of it, for two million.

Paul knew nothing about running a sheep station, let alone a hallowed surfing and fishing campground, or the complexities of WA pastoral leases. He has had a crash course in all three in the six years since.

When he removed some semi-derelict caravans from the property used by some of the old-timers for holiday accommodation, he had a drunk surfer chase him around the property with an axe for three hours. A couple of years ago, surfwear label Rip Curl approached him to run one of their pro tour 'Search' events at Gnaraloo. While he was still trying to obtain details of their proposal, the WA minister for tourism put out a press release announcing that next year's Search event would be at Gnaraloo. There was an immediate and massive outcry from WA surfers, fearing an imminent invasion of their mystical surf break. The hastily formed North-West Surfers Alliance set about rallying opposition to the contest, gathering over 3000 signatures, and Paul found himself in the middle of a media storm. Rip Curl senior management received death threats. The event never went ahead, but Paul learnt a valuable lesson in how dearly Gnaraloo is loved by its regulars. He says within three days of putting a small, one-cup coffee machine into the camp store, he received a lambasting on a surfing web forum, declaring that Gnaraloo had now become the preserve of 'latte-sipping yuppies'.

Then there are the myriad government departments to deal with. All WA pastoral leases are set to expire in 2015 and will be assessed on a case-by-case basis. Paul has been told his will be renewed under certain conditions. Ningaloo Reef has recently been World Heritage-listed and the WA government wants to resume all coastal land in a two-kilometre-wide ribbon that adjoins the reef. In reality, government agencies don't have the resources to manage all this coastline, so some kind of co-operative management regime is likely to be put in place. Gnaraloo staff have been trained as honorary Coast and Land Management (CALM) officers. Then there's always the prospect of another change of government and a whole new round of negotiations.

On this constantly shifting playing field, it is almost impossible to make plans for the future of the station. Paul is busily finishing the cabins and renovating the other accommodation at the homestead. Does he have a master plan? 'Get finished,' he laughs. 'Plans? Geez, let's be honest – you could not have a plan with this place. It's just fighting fires everyday. The power went out twice today. You'd have no water. The maintenance . . . Unfortunately, all the new pumps are breaking down. Limestone is calcium carbonate, and when you mix calcium carbonate and water you get caustic soda. Imagine spraying caustic soda everywhere. After a while, it all just disintegrates – Caroma showerheads, nine months and they just fall off. All the electrical gear, the motherboards inside the computers, circuit boards in TVs – they all rust. Starter motors and batteries – we should have bought shares in Exide.'

The list of hurdles and hardships goes on. It occurs to me that the remote north-west is not much easier to tame or develop than it would have been 100 years ago when my great-grandfather was running cattle stations near here.

Yet, like my great-grandfather, Paul seems to have fallen under the spell of this mesmerising interface of sea and desert. How does he envisage Gnaraloo in ten or twenty years' time? 'Exactly the same. Then I'll know we've done a good job, if we've done nothing,' he says. 'Irish management regime – nothing should change.'

FINLESS AT TOMBSTONES?

I receive an email from Richard Tognetti to say they are coming here next year for the second installment of *Musica Surfica*. 'Finless at Gnaraloo? Thoughts?' he writes.

Thoughts? I find the wave terrifying enough on conventional equipment and need every bit of edge I can get to negotiate those hair-raising drops and bottom turns. What Tognetti, Hynd and company might do out here on their finless boards is mind-boggling. Paul is certainly excited at the prospect of having the Australian Chamber Orchestra performing in the old shearing shed. I might have to book my passage back for that one.

Our final night is spent around the camp fire with a few of our neighbours. Wine is brought out. Musical instruments are produced. Chris and I bust out a few of our favourite three- or four-chord guitar jams. Lyall, a friendly family man from site thirty-two on the beachfront, breaks out his alto sax. Rhino, a young bloke from Perth who zips around camp on a tiny mini-bike, lugs his jembay down. Matty B, a rapper from Perth, unleashes a stream of freestyling about the wonders of Gnaraloo, with more rhymes for 'chillin' than I would have thought possible. It's a magical evening that leaves us all buzzing.

But Tombstones has one more trick to play on me yet. We wake up on our last morning and the ocean is as flat and serene as ever, and the conditions are beautiful – sunny, the lightest offshore breeze, a shimmering ocean. As we begin the melancholy task of packing up during the morning, I can't help but direct my eyes towards the ocean every now and again as sets of waves, each slightly larger than the last, begin capping on an offshore reef in front of the camp. The swell is coming up. I can't believe it. After waiting ten days for swell, it shows up just as we are getting ready to leave.

Chris and I confer, wondering how we are going to swing a surf with our vans half-packed and the families ready to hit the road for the long drive out over a boggy dirt road. An older surfer observes our dilemma and offers his time-worn wisdom. 'It's better to ask for forgiveness than permission,' he counsels. Our minds are made up. We return to our wives and present the case for squeezing in a quick surf on our way out, just to let the track dry out a bit more under the now blazing sun. They aren't buying that line, but they agree to an hour's reprieve anyway.

The school holiday crowds have arrived and there's barely room for our rig in the small dirt car park overlooking Tombstones. I park the van and figure I'll deal with extricating it later – time is of the essence. It's a long paddle out over the reef and there are long lulls in between sets. A crew of good old boys is sitting out at Centres, and I throw myself on the mercy of the pack, explaining our predicament of sneaking in one last surf while our families wait in the car park. One of them takes pity and calls me into a set wave. I get a couple, but the wait between waves is excruciating. I drift down to Tombstones, where the waves look better and more consistent, but the crowd is thicker. I want just one more crack at those hypnotic backhand tunnels, but it is slim pickings. I find a couple of decent waves, and then my set appears. I launch into it deep and late but determined not to blow it. Somehow, I make the first section and bottom turn into the second bubble as it pitches, and I pull in high and tight, grabbing my rail and hanging on as the lip hits me in the back of the head. I'm still on my board but I can't see a thing as I'm shunted blindly through the tube. The lip catches me on the back of the head again, this time depositing me reefwards. There's a brief, harmless roll along the bottom and I come up spluttering but happy. I haven't made it out, but it's a nice close encounter with the inner contours of this sublime surfing reef and I'm going to have to be content with that today. The ocean goes flat as our time winds down; I can't buy a wave in. I see Chris catch one shorewards and figure I'm going to have to paddle in. Eventually, I find a little inside groveller and make my way in over the now shallow reef, marvelling at the colours as they race by beneath my board.

I'd hoped to be departing this leg of the journey thoroughly surfed out, saltwater dripping from my nose, to tide me over the great surfless return journey. I may not be surfed out, but at least I've got the nasal drip.

After all the recent rains, the drive out is harrowing. We've barely left camp when we come across our first vehicle hopelessly bogged in a deep rut in the middle of a large puddle and tilted at a crazy angle. It's a four-wheel drive ute towing a small tinny, driven by one of the regular hardcore fishing and surfing crew, Boothy. If Boothy has gotten himself into trouble out here, then how are we going to fair in our Rav towing the Jayco? Not to mention our friends in their two-wheel drive HiAce van. There is no way around the marooned rig, and so we are all stuck. Boothy comes running up from the direction of the camp, more embarrassed than anything, with one of his mates following close behind in a massive LandCruiser. They hitch up a snatch strap and soon have him out, but it is a wakeup call for what lies ahead.

After his inglorious start, Boothy's keen for company for the trip out, and so we travel in convoy – Chris completely fearless at the front, Boothy in the middle and Bakers at the rear. At every large puddle we stop and the three blokes walk through it, our shorts hitched up for the inevitable drop into a deep rut. We confer on the best line to take – right, left, up the middle – or survey the rough bush tracks vehicles have recently created to drive around the worst of the puddles. But some of these detours are tougher going than the puddles, and Chris nearly comes to grief in a soft sand ramp off the road.

What should be an hour-and-half drive takes nearly three and a half. We pass shiny clean cars coming the other way and stop to give them our tips. Among the school holiday influx there are plenty of families in regular two-wheel drive sedans who look like they are new to this sort of thing, and I wonder how they'll fair.

After what seems an eternity, the lighthouse, the Blowholes and the sealed road comes into view and we pull over at the

'King Waves Kill' sign to mark the momentous occasion. When I get out and inspect our rig, I can't find one square inch of clean paint visible on the Rav, but she has done us proud. It's an emotional goodbye to our pals, the Garretts, who are headed back to Perth to return their muddied van before flying home. Boothy presents Chris with a couple fillets of spangled emperor as a reward for his role as leader of our convoy. We all hug goodbye, except Boothy, who we've only just met, after all – not that he seems the hugging type.

And then we are on our own again: our little family, on the side of a narrow coastal road, beside a thoroughly muddied rig. As we pull back onto the tarmac, relishing the smooth ride, we see the Garretts' van slow down and pull over up ahead, some large metallic object blocking the road. *What now?* I think. We pull over and get out, just as Chris is dragging a small tinny off to the side of the road. Some poor bloke is going to get home or stop for petrol and discover that his pride and joy has blown off his boat trailer. Alex climbs into the tinny and stands there like a miniature captain of his little ship, like Max in *Where the Wild Things Are*. I briefly wonder whether we should be strapping the thing on the roof for the return journey.

Finally, safely back in the Coral Coast Van Park in Carnarvon, Kirst has lashed out and booked us an en suite site. I've been a bit contemptuous of this latest concession to soft, pampered caravanners, but it is a revelation. We can step out of our caravan and straight into our own private bathroom, with a gleaming toilet and steaming showers. No more queuing up to perform your daily ablutions, taking in the groans and odours of others. After Gnaraloo, it feels like pure decadence. Kirst has often decried our lack of an en suite at home, wearied by sharing one bathroom with two rapidly growing children. It has taken a trip to Carnarvon and the Coral Coast Van Park for her to finally get one.

Somewhere in me still flickers hope of one more small bite

of the cherry, one last window of surf adventure before our homeward leg across the Top End. My great-grandfather's grave awaits us in the little historic town of Cossack, but before then I have one more opportunity to surf these desert reefs.

10

COMING HOME

It seems ironic that in this quest to know my land, to truly experience the vast Australian surfing coast, I have ended up in a place that was once America.

Exmouth, near the tip of Cape Range and close to the western-most point of the Australian mainland, used to be the site of the North West Cape US military base, rented by the US government from the Australian people for the proverbial peppercorn. Exmouth only began its life as a town in 1967 as a support centre for the military base. There existed what was for all practical purposes a small US town within Australia. You had to show your passport to enter its borders. Once inside, you drove on the right-hand side of the road and used greenbacks. There was a US-style bowling alley and a bar and grill to make the military personnel feel at home. Locals still tell stories of the US military flying in Diana Ross to entertain the troops. It is all still there in the backblocks of Exmouth today, an abandoned American ghost town overgrown with weeds, the buildings falling apart with concrete cancer.

Rows of empty, neglected buildings are labelled 'Bachelor Officers Quarters' or 'Bachelor Enlisted Quarters'. The military hospital enjoyed a brief second life in recent times as the local art gallery before being declared unsafe. All that's missing to complete the picture are tumbleweeds blowing down the deserted streets.

North West Cape was central to the US military presence in the region from the 60s right through to its hurried closure in the 90s, when it was no longer deemed necessary by the US administration. There were vocal protests in the 70s over allowing a US base within Australia that restricted the Australian government's access to its inner workings. World War Three could have been launched from Australian soil without our government's knowledge. A shared US–Australia naval communications station still exists here, with its towering radio transmitters, but the US military base is long gone.

Today, Exmouth is better known as the gateway to the World Heritage listed Ningaloo Reef, Australia's largest fringing reef that stretches for 290 kilometres from Gnaraloo Bay in the south to North West Cape. For me, it represents my last chance to surf for the next 7000 kilometres and two months. That's probably the longest I've gone without a wave in my adult life. I'm not the only one feeling a little nervous about how my mood will hold up for eight waveless weeks, with only the stunning gorges, national parks, wide-open spaces and croco-dile parks of the Top End to sustain me. We will be returning to the Gold Coast in September at the start of the dreaded, generally flat northerly season, when the nor'-east devil wind can blow for months on end. Who knows how long it might be before I see quality waves again?

At the same time, I am almost looking forward to forgetting about surfing for a while. It removes one complex layer of vari-ables from the family road trip. Trying to find surf time while on the road has proved a tricky business and, though my wife and kids have been extraordinarily understanding, it feels like time to pack the boards away for a while and have a pure family holiday.

I've come to regard surfing like one of those old friends who never really grew up, never married or had kids, and doesn't understand the myriad demands and responsibilities of family life. You love him dearly, and it's always fun and exciting when he turns up, but he doesn't necessarily take into account your changed circumstances. He's the mate who'll arrive at 5 am unannounced and wonder why you can't just jump out of bed and head down the coast for the day, or expresses disbelief that you won't commit to two weeks in the Mentawais when he's scored you a cheap spot on a charter boat. He can't fathom why you no longer stay up all night drinking before charging off on a surf mission at dawn with no sleep, or why you can't afford to order a new stick a couple of times a year.

I've taken to referring to surfing as 'Dupree', after Owen Wilson's character in the 2006 comedy *You, Me and Dupree*, the perpetual adolescent who gets kicked out of his apartment by his latest ex and moves in with his now happily married best friend and causes chaos. At his best, Dupree can inject some welcome enthusiasm and freedom into your busy life, charming the wife and kids to buy you a bit more personal time and help-ing you stay fit, happy and young at heart. At his worst, he can be a divisive wedge between you and your loved ones.

Recently, I have begun to feel like Dupree is messing with me. I schedule two weeks of quality time with him at Gnaraloo and he goes walkabout, abandoning me in the WA desert just when I have companions and playmates for the wife and kids, a keen surf buddy and plenty of time on my hands. Then he turns up as we're packing up to leave and wants me to come out and play while the family sit and wait in the car park.

Now, I have two days booked at the completely luxurious Sal Salis resort in Cape Range National Park, featuring five-star safari tents nestled in the dunes a literal stone's throw from the edge of Ningaloo Reef. Out of our entire journey, this is forty-eight hours I have quarantined as uninterrupted family time, snorkelling the reef together, enjoying gourmet cuisine, fine wines and beers in the resort lodge, and retiring under high-thread-count sheets. Then we have four more days in Cape Range, where an old mate from the Goldy, Ray, now works for the Department of Environment and Conservation. More importantly, he has a boat, a necessity for a surfer in this part of the world. The waves of Exmouth and Cape Range are fickle animals. Breaking on the edge of reefs a long way offshore, they're incredibly sensitive to the winds and tides and mostly unable to hold large swells. They require a delicate combination of conditions to produce the goods. It's a bit of a long shot to count on as your last surf fix for two months.

When I originally booked the couple of days at Sal Salis, splashing out about two weeks of our travel budget for two nights in luxury, it was meant to be a bit of a sweetener for the family after enduring two weeks in the rustic desert surf camp while I made a wave pig of myself. As it turned out, of course, I was embarking on the homeward leg rather less topped up with surf stoke that I had hoped.

The plan now is to enjoy a couple of days in luxury, earning me untold brownie points, which I shall then redeem by chasing waves to my heart's content during our final days on the cape.

Like most plans, several problems quickly reveal themselves in the execution. Ray has been summoned to Perth for a series of high-level meetings on bushfire management in national parks, something he can't miss. So I am left without a surf partner and, worse, without access to a boat to get out to the reefs.

Secondly, and predictably, Dupree isn't too impressed with my plans. In my wayward twenties, my favoured method of bringing up the surf was to embark on a spectacular bender. The next day's hangover would almost inevitably coincide with perfect surf. In my forties, I've discovered, the way to conjure up waves is to book in dedicated family time in a luxury resort.

We arrive at this amazing location only to discover that the surfing conditions are absolutely perfect. I am beginning to feel like Dupree is demanding some kind of showdown between mateship and family. And he is beginning to get on my nerves. He knows surf missions here are all-day affairs, and I feel an odd, stubborn resistance to him intruding on this special window of family time. Even with a generous 'media discount', I have still thrown down a substantial sum on our forty-eight hours in paradise. I'm intent on snorkelling the turquoise waters and teeming reefs of Ningaloo with Kirst and the kids, determined to enjoy this break from the world of caravanning to the full.

Sal Salis starts winning me over as soon as we arrive. We cruise into Cape Range late in the afternoon after a long drive from Carnarvon, just as the setting sun shimmers off the ocean and illuminates the mountains in an orange glow. We pull into the specified beachside car park as directed by our email from the resort's management and park the rig. Before us is a white sand beach and sparkling ocean, whitewater breaking on the outside edge of the reef, 500 metres out to sea.

'It doesn't look like there's a resort around here,' Vivi puzzles as we scan the empty dunes around us. It all feels like a clandestine rendezvous with undercover operatives. Shortly, two friendly young men in Sal Salis uniforms arrive in a solar-powered golf buggy to welcome us. They pile our luggage into the back and give the kids a ride into the resort, while Kirst and I opt to walk. It's a gentle 800-metre stroll along a winding dirt track before we arrive at a series of safari tents nestled among the dunes, a snaking network of timber boardwalks linking them to a central lodge.

This is ecotourism at its most sophisticated. The whole thing exists here within a national park under a rigorous lease agreement that requires the strictest environmental conditions are met and regularly audited. If the resort fails in any of these undertakings, it has to be removed and the whole site returned to its natural state. The entire resort is solar-powered, with a small backup generator. Guests are allowed only twenty litres of water a day for personal use, brought in from Exmouth. Toilets are composting. All rubbish is removed from the site. The senior guide, Greg, is a qualified and passionate marine scientist who educates guests on every aspect of the reef and how to enjoy it without doing it harm.

As we enter the lodge and are met with cool drinks and chilled handtowels, a pod of humpback whales begin spouting and breaching out at sea, as if on cue. We are shown to our tent and feel like Arabian royalty. It is large and beautifully appointed, with a king-size bed for Kirst and me, and deluxe roll-out swags for the kids in a front annex. It even has its own en suite, rather more opulent than the one we've recently enjoyed in Carnarvon. Kirst is in danger of getting used to this, and I'm not sure how any of us are going to deal with a public ablutions block ever again. The kids are beside themselves, as if they have stepped through the looking glass. I'm impressed by the resort's taste in beers. Kirst is fetched a glass of Moët. I am a hero.

I take a moment to myself down on the beach as the sun sets. A little black-tipped reef shark cruises by in the shallows as the sea and sky turn infinite shades of orange through to pink. There are perfectly smooth pink rocks arranged in pretty patterns on the beach, having washed down from the cape's spectacular river gorges. A brilliant double rainbow, as God is my witness, arcs over the mountain range behind the resort.

I've never been especially motivated by material wealth, but if this is how it feels to be rich, I'm trading in surf writing for merchant banking or gun running. High on the moment, I engage in another bout of video blogging, and it makes a striking counterpoint to my most desperate days in north-west Tasmania earlier in the trip. I appear almost drunk, but boyish, grinning stupidly, eyes sparkling. A full moon rises over our little cluster of tents as a series of stunning canapés are served before a gourmet three-course dinner. My family members are all gazing at me adoringly. I want this to never end.

We are awakened early the next morning by our boy bursting to descend on the camp kitchen to see what delights breakfast holds. I take him for a walk on the beach as the sun rises, while the girls have a sleep in. I don't even want to look, but there is obviously swell and the ocean is sheet glass, with barely a breath of wind. I feel like my old mate Dupree has turned up on my dream date, burping and farting and wanting me to swill tequila. From this distance, the long, zippering close-outs look too fast and too shallow to surf, but I've heard whispers of other locations where passes in the reef create the most exquisite waves. I've been warned that hiring a tinny or boat charter in Exmouth this time of year is almost impossible as every seaworthy vessel in town is earning top dollar ferrying tourists out to view whale sharks, migrating humpback whales or chase fish. I again ponder my options: leave my family here while I drive up and down the coast searching for some kindly soul to ferry me out to the reefs in their boat, or, simply, surrender.

Surprisingly, I don't even need to think for too long. I look about me and realise, this time, I'm not going anywhere. The last long-range forecast I've seen has predicted a small bump of swell today, with more serious swell arriving later in the week. I decide to roll the dice on foregoing these waves and hopefully still getting my surf -time when we step back through the looking glass.

After fruit, muesli, coffee, juice, croissants, eggs and sausages – and the requisite rest to digest it all – we head to the beach to see what all this World Heritage hullabaloo is about. Before our first snorkel, Greg, our expert instructor, delivers a stirring talk on the significance of the reef and the need to care for it. We find out that Ningaloo is home to 700 species of fish, 300 species of coral and 650 species of mollusk. Whale sharks and migrating humpback whales are among its most famous inhabitants. An estimated 10,000 turtle nests are deposited along its coast annually.

All this teeming biodiversity is made possible by the meeting of two currents – the warm Leeuwin Current from the north and the cooler Ningaloo Current from the south. It also represents an overlap of temperate and tropical species, and the region is actually the interface of four distinct types of environments: arid, marine, temperate and tropical. Cape Range itself, the rugged, rocky mountain range that forms a stunning backdrop to the reef, was an island many millions of years ago, creating a rich concentration of endemic species found nowhere else on Earth.

Greg informs us not to expect a fringing reef, close to shore, to resemble the technicolour wonderland of a barrier reef a long way off. This is an altogether different beast, he explains, although still impressive. The reef has been damaged by recent cyclones and coral bleaching events, but it is constantly regenerating, the electric-blue tips of finger coral revealing brilliant new growth. The fish life is as abundant and diverse as ever.

We walk up the beach, don flippers, masks and snorkels, and allow ourselves to drift back down with the current. Almost as soon as I wade in and stick my head under water I am overwhelmed. Brightly coloured fish swarm about us, and at one point I find myself surrounded by a school of hundreds of what I later learn are convict surgeonfish, bright yellow with black stripes. Into their midst darts a smaller school of tiny neon-damsel fish, electric blue and positively gleaming in the dancing sunlight. I feel like someone's put something in my drink. In the distance I see a small black- tipped reef shark cruise by completely disinterested in us. I look about and my whole family is flapping and swimming about, gazing and pointing in wonder. We've been taught a series of hand signals to communicate under water, and Vivi gives me the 'okay' signal to let me know that she's fine. I'm not sure what the signal is for utter euphoria, but I hope the stupid smile on my face communicates it.

Between snorkelling sessions we live like kings. The accommodating chef, Andy, even tolerates our children invading his kitchen like *Junior MasterChef* contestants. Andy introduces each dish at dinner with a little explanation of what it is and where it came from, and Vivi's triumphant moment comes when he announces the arrival of the seafood chowder that she has made. There are only four other guests in the resort: a well-to-do English family with two boys proudly sporting brand-new Akubras, who happily befriend our kids, teaching Alex chess and swapping stories of their Australian travels. I'm glad there are no cosy couples expecting an intimate, romantic getaway, with our kids free-ranging like crazy.

It's over too soon. Walking back out along that winding dirt track through the dunes, I feel the spell is broken. Once the staff delivers our bags to the car park on their golf buggy, we are on our own again, having to fend for ourselves, prepare our own meals and make our own beds. There is no bottomless esky of boutique beer and Moët in the Expanda.

But things aren't so bad. It's a short drive along the snaking coastal road to our new digs. Ray has set us up in what is affectionately known as 'the Bothy' – a simple, rammed-earth, one-bedroom cottage usually reserved for visiting marine scientists carrying out important research on this biodiversity hot spot.

The Bothy doesn't have an en suite, but it does have an impressive indoor composting toilet that remarkably doesn't seem to smell at all. A scoop of sawdust is tipped down the hole after each ablution and seems to eliminate any odour. There is an enormous bank of solar panels outside and a hybrid solar, wind and generator system that powers this and the other staff residences, workshop and the large visitors' centre nearby. It's an impressive set-up that gives me hope that humans can occupy a place as special as this without degrading it.

In Ray's absence, one of his mates in marine parks has stuck up his hand to take me for a surf while I'm in town. His name's Matt Smith and I begin tracking him down as soon as I arrive at the Bothy, desperate to tee up a surf and avail myself of some local knowledge. He's an elusive character, busy patrolling these waters during school holidays. One day on the beach with the kids I spot the marine parks boat coming into shore and being loaded up with fuel. I walk over and find Matt aboard. He says he'd love to stay and chat, but he has a stranded baby humpback whale down near Ningaloo Station to rescue. He might have the next day off, he says, except he has a feeling this whole whale situation could get complicated.

I'm left standing on the beach with the kids as he roars off on his heroic mission, pondering how much better *Ningaloo Rescue* would be as a reality TV show than *Bondi Rescue* – or *Bondi Vet*, for that matter.

That afternoon I hear from another ranger that Matt's whale rescue has become a whale euthanasia – a stranded calf separated from its mother stands no chance of survival in the wild. Matt's day off has evaporated, along with my hopes for a surf guide. But the swell has predictably dissipated anyway.

And, just to twist the blade, swell is predicted to arrive the day after we are scheduled to leave on our journey northwards. This is too much. I can't believe Dupree is being so petty and churlish. Though I hate to pander to his childishness, I consult Kirst and gravely explain the necessity for a stirring surfing climax to my carefully crafted narrative arc. She is as understanding as ever, and graciously agrees to a day's extension. The Bothy, however, is booked out, perhaps this time in the name of science, and so we find ourselves back on the beachfront in the rather less exclusive but hardly less delightful Tulki Beach Campground. Camp sites in Cape Range are highly sought after – there are only 100 or so spread across six or seven campgrounds – and they're allocated on a first-come, first-served basis. Campers begin queuing up at the gates as early as 3 am to try and score one of the few sites made vacant each day. We consider ourselves lucky.

Without a boat, I have my eye on a well-known break at the northern tip of Cape Range known as the Lighthouse Bombie. My little pocket surf guide has this to say about the wave: 'Monster, hollow, classic left reef break . . . Free-fall take-off followed by an intense barrel section. Awesome power. Forget the paddle, boat it! Big rips and currents and sharks. Crazies only.'

That hardly sounds encouraging, but it should at least provide the dramatic climax I'm after. The swell is predicted to come up overnight, and I am hoping to score the bombie on the drive out the next morning while the family enjoy brunch in Exmouth. It's a daring plan with little room for error. We spend another enjoyable day on the beach at our campground, my gaze involuntarily darting towards the reef for any sign of swell. By dusk it is starting to show on the outside edge of the reef in long, fast close-outs, and my hopes are high.

The tide is low early and the bombie needs a bit of water over the reef, so I'm in no great hurry to get away the next day.

We pack up, farewell some of the friendly Nomads who've been indulging the kids and hit the road. It's a thirty-minute drive to the lighthouse, and I coax the rig to the top of the hill to get a panoramic vista over the reefs. The swell's up but so is the wind, and if there's one thing the bombie doesn't like it's wind. There's a fun-looking right breaking closer to shore to the south that keeps drawing my attention. The bombie is the superior wave, but it looks lonely and windblown out there. The right looks gentler but it's an easy paddle from the beach. If it was my home break I'd be out there in a flash, but the right isn't likely to produce the dramatic surfing climax I've been after. Time is of the essence, though, so I uncouple the van and let the family drive into town unhindered while I suit up.

Now, in the surf porn version of this trip, I would heroically paddle out solo at the windy bombie regardless and grit my way into a blind freefall take-off, grab rail and score an outrageous backhand pit that seals this whole surfing road trip on an emphatic high note, all while menacing dorsal fins circle the line-up. That doesn't happen. If Ray Slattery was writing this, I would paddle out and run into the fuming boyfriend of the comely barmaid I had seduced last night at the rough-and-ready local pub and promptly have my lights punched out. That doesn't happen either.

In the real-life version, I bump into a local surfer coming out of the water who warns me that the bombie is virtually unsurfable in this wind and recommends the friendly right that peels for a couple of hundred metres in front of the car park. I take his advice and paddle out to join a couple of sixty-something blokes, one on a longboard and one on a Firewire funboard. There are long lulls, a bit of wind and chop on the face, but also some racy overhead walls and a few nice cut-back sections. I am paddling back after my first wave, thinking to myself, *Well, this is a fairly unremarkable end*, when I spot the old bloke on the Firewire paddling my way, grinning manically.

'How was that ride?' he beams, apparently referring to my rather pedestrian first wave. 'Gee, you had a long paddle back out after that one.' His enthusiasm in the average conditions is impressive. He's clearly keen for a chat. 'I gave up surfing at seventeen, but then I came up here last year and I said to my wife, "Geez, those are the best waves I've ever seen. I've got to get back out there." And so I started surfing again.' He then launches into a long, detailed and emotional description of his reborn surfing life, how he could swim a couple of miles but the first time he got back on a board he could only paddle twenty-five metres before he was exhausted. How his wife is a bit dirty on him now because it's all he wants to do. 'I love just sitting out here,' he bellows.

I look about us, floating here off the coast of North West Cape, the enormous forest of communications towers looming over us onshore, the beautiful mountains of Cape Range stretching off in the distance to the south, the old lighthouse standing sentinel on the headland, and the northern tip of Ningaloo Reef lying beneath us, providing the delightful bathymetry that produces these thoroughly pleasant waves. I have to agree with my new friend. After nearly six months, around 18,000 kilometres and more roadhouse bacon and egg rolls than I care to admit, there are certainly worse places to finish a transnational surfari.

In the end, after plenty of waves, there's just me and one other guy out and the sets seem to be getting less consistent. The family is due back soon and I just want a wave in. A set looms. Most of the larger sets have been breaking wide and catching us inside, and so I scratch for the shoulder to try and get onto it, but this one peaks deep on the reef. I paddle too wide and miss it and have to watch it peel away the length of the reef, all the way to shore. That was my wave in.

The other guy is in the same boat. 'That was the last set of the swell,' he jokes as we watch it roll away. 'It's going to go flat.' And it very nearly does. In the end, knowing my time is up, I paddle inside to get a smaller one to the beach and, just like that, without fanfare or heroics, my surfing journey is over.

I get to the car park and the family is there waiting for me, again. I reckon I've asked just about enough of them over the past six months. I go through the familiar ritual of peeling off my wetsuit, getting dry and dressed, and strapping the board on the roof. I announce grandly to the family, 'I would like to declare the surfing leg of Surfari Highway over.' I had imagined cheers of relief, but I suspect they may be just as nervous about this surfless homeward leg as I am.

I'm feeling an odd, seesawing mix of emotions as we pull out of Exmouth after the obligatory stock-up at the local IGA. The thought of no longer monitoring swell charts and weather maps, researching new strips of coast and driving around unfamiliar beaches in search of waves feels like a weight has lifted. By my reckoning, I've surfed around thirty spots, most of them for the first time, the vast majority with only a handful of other surfers, spanning around half of the Australian coastline. Surely, that should be enough to get me through a couple of months touring the natural wonders of the Top End.

But I've also realised that this is a thirst that is never entirely quenched, that there is only fleeting satiation to be had before the gnawing sets in anew. I'm genuinely curious to see how I fair, prepared to stare down my surf addiction and explore other worlds.

McLEOD'S DAUGHTERS

It's a long, thoughtful drive heading due east, directly inland, for the first time. Huge termite mounds litter the otherwise flat featureless landscape, like some prehistoric mega-fauna has deposited enormous, petrified poos out here.

We've booked a night at Bullara, a real working cattle

station, as the beginning of our outback adventure. Like many stations, they've added a bush campground and some rustic accommodation to supplement the diminishing returns from livestock.

I've been exchanging emails with the lady of the homestead, Edwina, and I picture her as a matronly, tough-as-nails old woman of the north-west. When we turn up I'm a bit surprised to discover she is a young, attractive, articulate and obviously well-educated mum of three small girls. 'McLeod's Daughters' she calls them.

We are only booked in for one night before we move on to Karijini National Park and then my ancestral homeland of Cossack, near Karratha. But within minutes our kids have discovered a pen of baby emus and a joey in the shearing shed. They're smitten. One of McLeod's Daughters, Mimi, is turning three tomorrow and our kids are soon invited to the party. We've planned on an early start to make the long drive into Karijini but don't need too much convincing to push our plans back a day.

Bullara is actually hosting two birthday parties on the one day. The quaint on-site cabins have been booked out for a surprise fiftieth birthday party. We watch as an ultralight plane carrying the birthday girl in from Exmouth sweeps low over the station, towards Bullara's own airstrip. A few minutes later we hear the roar of fifty of her closest friends and family as she arrives at the campground. Meanwhile, our kids are swept up at their own birthday party, with cake, a puppet theatrette and boundless country hospitality. Kirst is in the kitchen chatting to Edwina when her husband, Tim, walks in with a freshly slaughtered and skinned sheep over his shoulder, ready to be skewered on a spit roast for the fiftieth celebrations. It's a warm and intimate view into another world.

AUSTRALIA IS VERY LARGE

I have used the word 'vast' a lot in this book, but Australia keeps throwing up new levels of vastness that are difficult to describe in any other terms. There are moments when we set off on the latest leg of our journey, come over a rise in the road and a new patch of Australia is stretched out before us, and I feel faint rumblings of nervousness. *I'm driving my family into this?* Some people apparently thrive on this vast emptiness, this empty vastness, but I'm not there yet. I'm awestruck, humbled and re-educated each time about the true nature of my country, but also slightly unsettled.

The scenery out here is both more beautiful and more varied than I had imagined – rolling hills; great rocky outcrops of oversized boulders, a mini Uluru; shimmering fields of bush grass, silver in the morning light. Roadhouses come as an inordinate relief, and I sense I'm not alone. Great clusters of Grey Nomads gather over sandwiches and trade information on road conditions, campgrounds and petrol prices.

Karijini National Park is the furthest inland we've ventured yet, and only because so many people have told us it can't be missed. It's a long day's drive east from Bullara, and by the time we reach the little mining town of Tom Price it is late in the afternoon and we still have sixty kilometres of exceptionally rough dirt road to travel to our campground. This is a fairly lengthy detour for a couple of days to check out the gorges and waterways of Karijini, a sacred place to the Yindjibarndi people.

We are booked into a camp site at what is rather grandly titled the Karijini Eco-Resort. It's a stunning location, straight out of an Albert Namatjira painting – twisted white gums against the vivid red earth and low bush grass, rolling mountains stretching off for impossible distances, all set against a cloudless blue sky. I've read that this campground and national park is managed by the local Indigenous community, and I've been looking forward to this close encounter with Aboriginal culture. So I am initially a little disappointed when we are served by an Irish backpacker. I've come here wanting to learn from those who know more about my country than I do, not less.

The sun is setting and the magnificence of the dusk is only marred by the now familiar drone of the accursed generators. It nearly sours my mood until I take a walk to the far end of the campground, out of earshot of the wretched things, and begin to feel the landscape and its profound stillness. But when I return to the van, have dinner and put the kids to bed, the maddening drone continues on until I can stand it no more.

I step outside to gaze at the stars and send deathly stares across at the evil electricity addicts. The kids are trying to sleep and the noise isn't helping. I march over and, as calmly and politely as I can manage, inquire what time they plan on running their generator until. The old bloke at the site puffs up his chest and tells me the camp rules: they can run it until 8 pm. He's immediately defensive, knowing he's doing the wrong thing, and his self-righteous quoting of the camp rules sets me off. I tell him we didn't come all the way to this beautiful place to listen to his generator. They have meat they need to keep refrigerated, he argues. We have an esky with a block of ice in it, I reply, and march off in a huff. Soon after, to their credit, they turn the generator off and the next morning they move on – a small moral victory.

OUR JOURNEY IN MICROCOSM

We head on to Weano Gorge, unsure what parts of the various gorge walks our young kids might manage. There are high cliffs, unstable and slippery rocks, and innumerable hazards. Lots of the oldies have warned us gravely to watch the kids like hawks at the gorges. Kirst suggests a gentle warm-up on one of the easier walks around the top of the gorge. Alex is hell-bent on tackling what he's dubbed the 'obstacle course' – the steep ladder, precarious rock climb and waist-deep wade through the icy gorge water to reach a swimming hole called Kermit's Pool. Some of the other camp kids have talked it up and Alex doesn't want to know about the soft, scenic bushwalk. I try to tell him that he can't do the hard walk unless he shows me he can do the easy walk without a fuss. Kirst and Vivi go ahead while Alex and I butt heads until I give up and return to the car with him in tears. Having a small boy out here who refuses to follow instructions is a nerve-racking business.

Kirst and Vivi return, buoyed by their brisk stroll, while Alex and I continue our war. We have something to eat and drink in the shade and agree to tackle the gorge walk if Alex promises to listen and do what we say. He solemnly agrees and we set off.

What follows begins to feel like a metaphor, or a microcosm, of our entire journey so far. There is the anxious and uncertain planning, the nervous beginnings, the initial challenge and transition of getting used to new and demanding terrain. There is the icy chill of the gorge water itself, which quickly makes your legs ache – Vivi is close to tears and ready to give up. We urge her on. There are tricky climbs along narrow rock ledges, and then a brief rest at what is called the Amphitheatre – a grand natural opening in the gorge where the rock shelves look like tiered seating overlooking a small pool. We press on down what is ominously dubbed the Spider Walk, squeezing down a narrow chute in the gorge, holding on to both gorge walls with our hands while our feet struggle to find traction on the slippery rocks beneath the water. It requires plenty of teamwork and careful plotting to find the best path forward, and we stop and consult each other on the safest line to take over the most difficult terrain.

I've heard it said that humankind requires a great, universal challenge to overcome its petty differences, and that climate change or an alien invasion might provide just that. The same principle seems to apply to our family and Weano Gorge. Faced with a collective challenge that requires careful cooperation, all squabbling and infighting is silenced. We work as a smooth, harmonious, well-oiled unit.

Finally, after we have squeezed through the narrowest section of the gorge, we emerge at a large pool. This is the point at which visitors are forbidden to go further. Before us is a deep, jade-green swimming hole, sunlight sparkling down through the gorge and dancing on the pool's surface, making patterns on the brilliant red rock etched with black spirals on the floor. Further on, the gorge drops away steeply into a series of pools linked by small waterfalls that are impossible to access without a guide and serious climbing equipment. We can only stand and stare at the gorgeous view before us. Vivi thinks it looks like the gates to heaven. Alex is in an emotional state I've never quite seen him in before – squeezing his knees together as if he needs to pee, almost doubled over but smiling crazily and making incoherent noises of delight. 'It's amazing,' he finally manages.

At last, the children have been overwhelmed by a grand natural setting. There is a family huddle, lots of high-fives and photos. We have made it this far together. It is a wonderful, euphoric moment of family bonding. I take off my T-shirt and jump in the bracing water in my boardshorts, and immediately leap out again, hooting with the cold. We sit and quietly soak in the surroundings until some other gorge walkers arrive and take a photo of the whole family together for us.

I cannot wish for more than this.

THE RAILWAY ROAD

After two intoxicating days, we leave Karijini bound for Cossack and a date with my ancestors. But first we must head into

Tom Price to get our permit for the Railway Road, a private road owned by mining giant Rio Tinto. Railway Road is so named because it runs alongside the largest privately owned railway line in the world, which is used to cart all that iron ore up to Karratha's bustling port to ship to China. The Railway Road takes the most direct line north towards Cossack, about 300 kilometres over largely unsealed road, but it saves about 200 kilometres backtracking to reach Cossack via the main sealed road. It seems like a reasonable scheme. But first I have to go to the Tom Price visitors' centre to watch a twenty-minute safety video to receive my permit.

The friendly Indigenous lady behind the counter tries to talk me out of the Railway Road, pointing out that there is another unsealed but public road that is only seventy kilometres longer and won't be busy with mining vehicles. I um and ah, wondering whether we would be better off sticking to the bitumen. Eventually, I figure the railway road will be an experience, a chance to see the great north-west mining boom up close.

The safety video is an alarming piece of work, full of dire warnings about the awful fates one can meet out on this lonely and dangerous road, lots of scenes of overturned vehicles and an earnest narrator warning of the hypnotic effects of staring at those endless iron ore trains for too long or the madness of trying to overtake a mining truck on a dusty road. It almost psyches me out, but I figure they are being alarmist and we should still give it a crack. Kirst has been doing a quick stock-up at Coles over the road, and by the time we finally pull out of Tom Price it is nearly 12.30 pm.

The road is excellent at first and, just like Gnaraloo, I start to wonder what all the fuss is about. After all, I figure, Rio Tinto can probably afford to keep their roads in better nick than the Australian government. We pass a few trucks going the other way, throwing up huge clouds of dust, and pull alongside a few massive trains running parallel to us, just metres away from the road. Some of these trains are so long that we never glimpse their front or end before they disappear behind a hill or bend. The kids excitedly try to count the carriages, eventually reaching 230 on one train.

We are just congratulating ourselves on our courage and daring – the words 'I'm so glad we took this road' have just left Kirst's lips – when there is a loud bang and our back windscreen shatters. A rock thrown up by our tyres has bounced off the front of the caravan and shattered the glass. So, that's why all those caravans have large flaps affixed to the front of their A-frames. I pull over, break away the remainder of the windscreen and drape a towel across the inside of the back door before closing it, to keep out the dust and any other stray rocks. The kids are a bit spooked and, to tell the truth, so are Kirst and I, and I wonder if we should stick the kids' bike helmets on them. To add to my disquiet, one of the safety chains on the van has come off – the D-shackle that connects the safety chain to the tow bar must have been shaken loose by the bumpy road and is now dragging on the ground. A 'safety chain' sounds like an important bit of gear to me, and I'm not sure what to do. I manage to wrap the loose chain around the end of the A-frame so it doesn't drag and clamp it in place with the van's handbreak, and hope it holds.

When we press on, it suddenly feels like a much grimmer, fraught experience. Our hermetically sealed world where we have at least the illusion of order and control, where we can flick a switch and press a button to regulate the temperature or select our desired soundtrack, has been shattered along with the windscreen. The noise of the road is amplified with the back windscreen gone, and the unsealed road seems to go on forever. The afternoon wears on and I'm feeling drained and cranky. Driving unsealed roads requires a whole lot more concentration and energy than the bitumen. There are sudden dips, large rocks, loose gravel and sand drifts. When a car or truck comes the other way we are suddenly enveloped in a thick red fog of dust and can't see a thing for a few seconds, slowing down until the dust settles. An extra 200 kilometres on sealed road suddenly seems like a good option.

But the landscape is amazing – mountains of red rubble, the silver-grey of bush grass and twisted tree branches, sudden splashes of purple or red wildflowers, the spiky pompoms of spinifex grass dotting the rolling hills as far as the eye can see, dramatic mountain ranges that rise abruptly from their surrounds, their flanks scarred by rocky ledges, as if the mountains have been thrust upwards so suddenly and with such force that they have shattered. You can see the metal in the earth and rock, thick veins of steel-grey iron ore stretching through whole mountainsides. Maybe I'm a bit slow on the uptake, but one thing I hadn't realised is that the red dirt of the Pilbara is actually all that iron ore literally rusting away beneath our feet. No wonder they are in such a hurry to ship it off to China while it's still worth something.

By the time we pull onto the North West Highway, nearly four hours after we left Tom Price, I'm exhausted and our needle is on empty. The nearest petrol station is in Karratha, ten kilometres off the highway, and we pull into the mining town to fill up, see if we can have our windscreen replaced and find a D-shackle for the safety chain.

It's bizarre suddenly being back in a town centre that could be almost anywhere in Australia. I'm surrounded by the ubiquitous department stores, supermarkets and generic chain stores, the only point of difference being all the mining company LandCruisers and men in high-vis jackets. I walk into the local Kmart and find my D-shackle for $2.50, and it strikes me as remarkable – and implausible – that this little horseshoe of metal with a bolt through it is all that stands between us and losing our van if the coupling fails. Kirst is ringing windscreen places and they are all saying the same thing: getting our make and model shipped up from Perth could take a week. We are planning on being in nearby Cossack for two days. We figure we'll order one, have it sent to Broome and tape up the window until then.

It's nearly 5 pm and we are all tired and grumpy when we set off for Cossack and the little hostel we have booked fifty kilometres further on. When I rang their office from Tom Price, they told me I could pick up the keys until 6 pm. I laughed and assured them we'd be there well before then, but now it's looking close.

We take the turn-off to Roebourne as the sun is getting low and eventually find the little road across the salt pans out to Cossack, which was literally a ghost town for decades after its heyday in the late 1800s. It was only turned into a historic tourist site in the 1990s, when many of the public buildings like the courthouse and police station, were meticulously restored. Purely by chance, our visit coincides with the Cossack Art Awards, sponsored by Rio Tinto and judged by none other than Janet Holmes à Court, the generous patron of our old mate Jon Frank's collaboration with the Australian Chamber Orchestra. Janet obviously gets around. It's the largest regional art award in Australia, with prize money totalling $109,000. This is the mining industry trying to give back to its host communities, and the host communities trying to inject some art, culture and soul into a boomtown. That it has landed here in my ancestral homeland seems extraordinary.

We find the little hostel housed in what was once the police station and meet the caretaker, Russ. 'My wife and I are the total population of Cossack now,' he tells us.

I hadn't realised that Cossack was right on the water, where the Harding River meets the sea, with a beautiful old stone harbour. A few Indigenous families are fishing on dusk. The kids tear down to check it out and I follow. Vivi has spotted a seagull flapping out on the estuary, tangled in fishing line and unable to fly. She begs me to do something. I'm no great fan of the rats with wings, but I can't bear to see my girl in distress, so I grab the family longboard, don a wetsuit, and paddle out to its rescue. The last thing I'd expected of Cossack was to get my surfboard out as soon as we arrived. I can just imagine the local Indigenous folk talking about the crazy whitey they saw paddling out to save a seagull. I reach the bird and the fishing line is badly tangled around its legs and wings, and wrapped around its beak. I manage to get a hold of it and try to untangle it while it pecks at me viciously. I get most of the line off, including the hook, which mercifully isn't in its beak, and paddle it to shore.

A young Aboriginal guy who's fishing offers me a Stanley knife to cut the rest of the line free. The gull won't let me get at the line around its beak, so we let it go, hoping it will survive. I get talking to the local and ask him if he speaks Ngarluma. He says that he does and starts speaking in the language, as if I might understand. I don't, obviously, but tell him a bit of my story and he seems interested.

I've remembered the word *mara-junu*, a greeting or welcome, and he acts impressed. One of his mates asks me where I'm from and I tell him Queensland, but that my great-grandfather and great-great-grandfather are buried in the cemetery here. They nod thoughtfully, and I introduce myself and ask their names. I realise I am so desperate to have some meaningful connection with Indigenous Australia that I am blurting out my family history to any dark-skinned character who'll listen. I hope I'm not being pushy or condescending. Maybe they get this all the time, well-meaning whiteys blowing through town, wanting to soothe their troubled consciences by have an authentic Indigenous encounter.

It's been a long, draining day and I'm ready to retire to the hostel, eat, shower and sleep. I open the van and everything is covered in a light dusting of red dirt. Inside the hostel we meet Peter Moir, artist-in-residence for the Art Awards. He is a great character, equally fond of nudes and landscapes, and keeps the whole family entertained while we get the kids fed and ready for bed. It feels amazing being here, walking the streets my ancestors walked, glimpsing shadows and hearing echoes of the lives they led. I cannot imagine their reality any more than they could have foreseen one of their descendants travelling through here on the great Australian road trip under the far-fetched guise of a surf writer. Our kids know their great-grandfather on Kirst's father's side, the indefatigable and sharp-as-a-tack Max, still spritely at ninety-six. I'd always thought of Aubrey Hall as a distant, shadowy, historical figure when my grandmother spoke of him, but suddenly four generations doesn't seem like such a great gap after all.

The next day I wander down to the cemetery and find the grave of Harold Aubrey Hall, together with his brother, Ernest Hall, and their father, William Shakespeare Hall. There is a vague suggestion in the family lineage of a tenuous connection with the Bard himself – one of his daughters apparently married a Hall back in the day, and it's clearly a branch of the family tree the Halls were keen to promote.

I walk to Settler's Beach and read a sign explaining the story of the Dig Down Rock, an early postbox arrangement where passing ships left mail for the inhabitants of Cossack buried under a rock with a large arrow pointing down carved into it. This was easier than trying to navigate the narrow, shallow river mouth. Conversely, the residents of Cossack would leave mail for Perth to be collected by the next passing ship. I've grown up with stories of the Dig Down Rock told by my grandmother, so it's poignant to see official recognition of it as a historical site.

I pick some wildflowers on the way back to town and put them on the grave of my ancestors. Back at Cossack, we go to the William Shakespeare Hall Museum in the old courthouse. It's hard to believe that this little town was the birthplace of the WA pearling industry, that eighty pearl ships operated from this harbour, attracting an Asian population of nearly 1500, giving rise to Cossack's own Chinatown and Chinese market garden. In the late 1800s there were three hotels, a butcher, a baker, a tailor and a horsedrawn tram that connected Cossack to nearby Roebourne. William Shakespeare Hall built a house here that was to become home to three generations of Halls, with large wooden shutters instead of windows, and metal cables strung over the roof and fastened to concrete blocks to withstand the regular cyclones. They kept this home even as various family members orbited about this focal point, running cattle stations and other enterprises.

But Cossack enjoyed only a brief golden age. The town fell into decline in the early 1900s when the hub of the pearling industry moved to Broome, and nearby Point Samson built a jetty that became the area's main port. Cossack was officially dissolved as a town in 1910 and a leprosarium was established on the opposite banks of the river in 1913. Even so, Aubrey Hall found work as the lighthouse keeper on tiny Jarman Island, just offshore, when the previous German lighthouse keeper was interned during World War I.

My great-aunt Connie was once interviewed for a book about the history of the Pilbara and had this to say about their time on Jarman Island: 'As far as we were concerned, this was an absolute paradise. Jarman Island wasn't very big at all. You could walk around it I think in half an hour . . . Mum and Dad had a dear little boat there, which they would take across to Cossack to do their shopping, and Mother said that very often they were followed and escorted by the most enormous turtle. Another thing that was there was a lovely lot of oysters and the fishing was very good.'

My grandmother was always saddened by Cossack's decline. When I was a boy I remember her speaking in rapturous tones about the place, but back then I wasn't interested, couldn't understand why she wanted to impress upon her grandchildren the magic of this place. Now I think I understand. It must have been an amazing childhood here. In the foreword to Aubrey's Ngalooma language book, my grandmother wrote of her father: 'He swam, dived, fished, boated and played with his elder brother and their young Aboriginal companions. This early and long exposure to the language and culture of the local Ngalooma tribe finally led to his compilation of the following vocabulary.'

Despite its largely surfless coastline, perhaps a love of the ocean was encoded into my DNA here. To see Cossack today, full of life, a centre of art and culture in the midst of the great north-west mining boom, seems miraculous.

But I feel like I want something more from this visit, that this is almost all too easy, too pleasant. Visitors flock through the town all day, enjoying the art show, sitting on the lawn outside the café in the old goods store, enjoying sandwiches and coffee. We drive out to Point Samson for lunch at the tavern and it's an unexpected gem – an unpretentious beachfront pub that serves up fresh seafood and ice-cold beer with an ocean view. Tiny waves, not more than six inches high, peel along a shallow sandbar against a rock wall at the harbour entrance. In a cyclone swell it might even offer a rideable wave.

But my eyes keep drifting out to Jarman Island, wondering if it is close enough to paddle a surfboard to. Back at the hostel I ask the lady of the house, Sue, if there is any way of getting out to the island, but she says not. I could try offering to pay one of the fishermen at Point Samson to take me out there, she suggests. Then I notice a kayak around the back of their garage and ask if I could hire it. She says I'm welcome to borrow it but warns me to plan my trip around the tides – to go out with the outgoing tide and come in with the incoming tide – or I may be stuck out there. The tides here are enormous. As it turns out, low tide is 2.30 that afternoon, only an hour away.

I hurriedly pack a small backpack with water, sunscreen and a camera wrapped in a plastic bag. I carry the kayak down to the water's edge, launch from the boat ramp and clamber aboard my own modern-day *pooja*, or paddling log. There is a stiff sea breeze blowing and I am paddling directly into it, and the small wind chop makes it tough going.

It looks an easy paddle but it turns out to be hard work, and halfway there I almost feel like giving up. I make it to the end of a narrow sandspit protruding from the northern bank of the river mouth and drag the kayak behind me in the shallows. Endless mangrove mudflats stretch off to the north. From the end of the sandspit, it is a reasonably short crossing to the island, but it must be close to the turning of the tide by now. The only way I am going to get there is through my own determined efforts. I swig some water and steel myself, put my head down and paddle in long strokes. My shoulders and lower back burn. I watch the island slowly grow larger as I approach. I know I am getting close when suddenly I am aware of the sound of hundreds of sea birds as they squawk and fly laps of the island. It is a tiny taste of the glee sailors must have felt when making landfall after long sea voyages.

I drag the kayak ashore and stare up at the lighthouse keeper's stone cottage and the lighthouse itself, recently restored and resplendent in its gleaming red-and-white paint job. I walk up to the cottage and it is in surprisingly good condition, despite the complete absence of a roof. The stone walls look structurally sound, and it doesn't seem like it would take too much to restore it like the rest of Cossack. I wander from room to room, hoping to discover some small sign of family life here, some broken crockery, the remnants of a child's toy or work tool, but it is starkly empty apart from fallen timber beams and the odd bird skeleton. There are five rooms, large fireplaces and a small outhouse.

My great-aunt Connie also recalled being caught in a cyclone out here as a child: 'I've a very clear recollection of Mother, Father and whoever else was on the island at the time, winching the boat quickly up out of the water so that it shouldn't be torn away. And the howling wind, and the dark, and the hurricane lamps. It was thoroughly impressed on my mind. That was when I was four years old, in 1916.'

Then I wander up to the lighthouse itself and walk around its base. Karratha is clearly visible to the south, with its busy wharf, cargo ships being loaded with iron ore bound for China, the dull thud of heavy machinery clearly audible. A pile driver is ramming in more pylons to extend the jetty, so that we might ship off our mineral wealth more quickly. It seems surreal to be standing here attempting to get in touch with my own family history, to come to know my country, right at the point where our country is being shipped overseas by the freighter load.

And so my personal journey comes to its conclusion here, on a little offshore island where my forebears shone a light out into the ocean to make the navigation of this remote coast less treacherous, in the shadow of the stupefying minerals boom that props up our country in the midst of global economic meltdown.

I'm not sure what I hoped for out here. Perspective, maybe. A sense of belonging. A right to be here. That my quest has brought me to this place, where billionaires battle Indigenous communities over the spoils of mining this land, seems telling. Few waves might break on these shores, but great forces are still at work, sculpting the land more quickly and dramatically than any ocean.

Paddling back, I pause and take a last look back at the island, the lighthouse and stone cottage. Fish jump and seagulls wheel around, squawking overhead. It is an easier return trip with the incoming tide and sea breeze now at my back. As I enter the mouth of the river, two dark figures on the riverbank are walking through the mangroves, one holding a spear. It's a timeless image.

If I'm after a sense of homecoming, I'm not sure I'll find

it in Cossack. Three generations of my family lived varying slices of their lives here about 100 years ago. I was born in Melbourne. My original immediate family was from Perth. Today I live on the Gold Coast with a family of my own. Where do I claim to be from? How might it feel to have thirty, forty, even 60,000 years of history, spanning hundreds of generations, in one place? And to have that place taken from you?

I have begun to know my country, but I am still literally only scratching the surface, surveying the thinnest strip of its coast, and even then bypassing large parts of it. There are some interesting symmetries to this huge island nation. We have perfect rights clustered down our most easterly coast, in subtropical and densely populated south-east Queensland and northern New South Wales. We have perfect lefts rifling away down the remote, mostly empty desert coast of our most westerly point. It is the fantasy surf island we all doodled as kids writ large, blown out to outrageous proportions. Two of the world's largest reef systems neatly bookend the east and west coasts. Most of our population is concentrated into the cool, green, temperate south-east corner of the country that takes in our two largest cities, our centres of commerce and culture. The north-west desert is our most wild, remote and sparsely populated, yet it generates an inordinate portion of our wealth. There is the wave-rich and shark-infested Bight of the South Australian desert coast, and the moist, tropical protrusion of the Northern Territory's waveless but crocodile-infested coast. But for the incursion of Bass Strait, the frigid southern state of Tasmania is a near mirror image of the warm, tropical Cape York to the north. It strikes me as an exceedingly well-designed piece of geography, even elegant. The fact that there is an enormous red rock smack bang in the middle of its vast desert heart is the proverbial cherry on the pie.

My home might still be 7000 kilometres and two months away. But from this distance, I think I've at last recognised my

Shangri-la. It was T. S. Eliot who said, 'We shall not cease from exploration, and the end of all our exploring will be to arrive where we started and know the place for the first time.' This Shangri-la – quality waves for me; a gentle, kid-friendly beach for the family; like-minded souls for us all to share this beautiful natural environment with – already exists at home.

I do, however, wonder how we will settle back into our conventional, suburban, middle-class existence of school, work and chores. I'm pinning my hopes on Joseph Campbell and his concept of the 'hero's journey', enunciated in his seminal work *The Hero with a Thousand Faces*. Campbell identified the common structure and stages of many of our most enduring stories and myths – the 'call to adventure', leaving our ordinary life and entering an extraordinary world, where we face all sorts of tests and challenges on our quest, our 'road of trials'. Having attained the goal, we then return home with some new insight or understanding that helps us better deal with that ordinary existence. I don't wish to suggest that there's anything even vaguely heroic about our journey, but I do sense Campbell's template fitting the narrative arc of our little jaunt – I just hope he's right about the insight and understanding bit. I hope it doesn't breed restlessness and discontent instead.

As we finally carve a long, slow arc across the Top End, through the Kimberley and Kakadu, we'll turn our rig to the south-east, skirting the Great Barrier Reef as we head for home. I like to think we won't have completed a circle so much as set one in motion, sending out ripples that will touch our lives in ways still unknown.

AFTERWORD

SO, WHAT HAVE WE LEARNT FROM ALL THIS?

AT THE END OF our travels I had hoped to have some grand, profound conclusions to justify this indulgent trip, on the grounds that I was divining wisdom for the collective good. I'm not sure how grand or profound they are, but here goes:

1 (a). Driving around Australia with your family as a cure for teeth-grinding is about as effective as wearing hessian underpants to relieve chafing.

1 (b). Driving around Australia with your family to increase your surf time makes about as much sense as doing it to cure teeth-grinding.

If these two factors were my 'key performance indicators' for the trip, it was an abject failure. The idea that I would have long, uninterrupted, carefree days surfing to my heart's content and quelling my middle-age angst now seems ludicrous in hindsight.

I am looking forward to getting home to increase my surf time. Mad, right? Perhaps this is part of the insanity of surfing, this incessant gnawing, this yearning to reach a Promised Land where the surf is always perfect and all impediments to gorging on it are banished. It doesn't exist. Perhaps this desire to resolve the tension between familial commitments and surf time is fundamentally misguided. This push and pull is the stuff of life. We all oscillate between order and chaos, between craving and satisfaction. Waves themselves are simple, energetic, alternating peaks and troughs. The philosopher Alan Watts said it best: no one's ever seen a peak without a trough, a coin with a head but no tail, or a person with a back but no front. It's the duality of life, and we have to learn to enjoy the dance, ride it, use it to propel us on – not try vainly to somehow change or diffuse it.

2. Having said all that, booking quality family time, or even couple time, in a luxury resort definitely does bring the surf up.

When we reached Broome on our supposedly surfless homeward journey, my father-in-law, Ken, and his wife, Jude, flew in to meet us for a week. This presented an opportunity too good to pass up for Kirst and me to leave the kids with their grandparents and sneak off for a night at the swanky Cable Beach Resort. Lo and behold, the next day Cable Beach, which normally resembles an azure lake outside of cyclone season, was throwing up small waves. That scoundrel Dupree was determined to crash my party again. Margaret River was reportedly fifteen feet down south, which translated to around two feet at Cable Beach. But it was still novel to surf its warm, turquoise waters. The kids loved it and surfed more than they had all trip. Here, at least, Dupree managed to conform to family life.

3. I needn't have worried about missing the surf during our homeward leg across the Top End.

Our return journey, originally little more than a practical necessity to deliver us from the desert surf of the north-west to our home on the Gold Coast, has offered more heady highlights than I expected.

The stunning gorges of the Kimberely; the ancient art sites and wetlands of Kakadu; the mesmerising landscapes, waterholes and waterfalls; the rich, intimate encounters with Indigenous culture, have all moved me more than I could have imagined. Wandering the beehive domes of the Bungle Bungles, experiencing the majesty of Cathedral Gorge, flying over this surreal landscape in a helicopter, like viewing some ancient lost city, was a peak experience up there with any surf session.

It would take a miserable sod indeed to experience all this and still spend their time pining after surf. Gorges, in particular, have proven excellent substitutes and have a great natural energy all their own. There are the popular household names overrun by the masses, and then there are the remote mysto gorges prized by an intrepid handful who have searched them out. And they are all about the irresistible force of water in motion.

4. There is far more to this land, and life, than surfing.

This is an unexpected conclusion for me to reach. If I am really honest, I think I embarked on this whole scheme to somehow make me *more* of a surfer, to make up for my relatively late start and the large chunks of my life I've spent indoors at a desk in front of a computer writing about surfing rather than actually riding waves. It's a kind of surf writer's immersive PhD project. But what I've come away with is a sense of what a narrow interaction with the coast, ocean and natural world surfing can be – it precludes so much else, demands such specific conditions and can render all other experiences anticlimactic when nature doesn't come to the party.

While surfing has provided many blissful, intoxicating highlights on this trip, it has also led me to bypass many other wonders that may have been just as awe-inspiring. It has complicated and sometimes strained the already complex business of the great Australian family road trip, moving me to irrational road marathons and moodiness.

I set out on this trip after a grand, indulgent, wave-riding binge. If anything, it has taught me to put surfing in its place, and it has come as something of a shock to eventually concede that its place – for me at least – is not in the centre, but rather as a passionate adjunct to a well-rounded and well-lived life. It is a potent fuel we can use to drive us on, but it is not the vehicle.

My centre will always be reserved for family and the endless joy and challenge of maintaining a happy ship as we navigate life's pitching seas together. (I still cannot resist an ocean metaphor, though.)

5. As a people, we seem to have become incredibly soft in the space of just three or four generations.

Everywhere you look in this country, cast back a hundred years or even less and there are stories of the most excruciating suffering, hardship, misery and brutality: the inhuman toil of timber-getters and whalers, workers on Tasmania's hydro-electric scheme or Victoria's Great Ocean Road, the wretched fates of shipwreck survivors and convicts, the brave pioneering deeds of early settlers in some of the most remote, harsh country imaginable and the atrocities they sometimes meted out on the Indigenous population. Our current era of relative peace, wealth and abundance is a mere bubble in time that might be well spent not whining about the price of petrol or cigarettes – or even real estate.

6. Lots of people are driving around Australia, and this is both a good and a bad thing.

Good, because hopefully more of us will form a lasting connection to our land and thus care more deeply for it and feel more empathy for the First Australians who have cultivated such a connection with it over millennia. Bad, because there are so many of us doing it that we place more pressure on often fragile environments.

Two hundred and thirty thousand caravans and campervans were manufactured in Australia in the past seventeen years, according to the Recreational Vehicles Manufacturing Association of Australia. Annual production hit a new peak of 20,000 in 2010, a figure that has quadrupled in fifteen years.

The Grey Nomads, or Mad Gnomes as our friend Jane has dubbed them, are literally everywhere. And good luck to them. Many have worked hard their entire lives and are now enjoying well-deserved retirements in fine style. Others are more like economic refugees, selling up the family home and embarking on an extended road trip from which there is no return, rather than eking out their days in unaffordable retirement homes or subsisting on the old age pension.

But there are more and more families doing it too, taking long service leave, pulling the kids out of school and giving them an unparalleled life education on the road. We kept bumping into the same families over and over again in our travels, like some sort of strange cross-country folkloric dance where you fall into sync with one partner after another. 'Oh, hello, it's you again.' Almost without exception, we have found friendship, kindness and camaraderie in these many chance encounters, and our trip was enriched immeasurably.

7. I have been unable to confirm or deny the existence of the Grey Nomad Swingers' Circuit.

Although I have not tried too hard.

8. Australia is a very big country with relatively few people.

If there's one thing we don't need to fear here it's too many people or a lack of space. And that applies to most of our more remote surfing coasts outside the main population centres. I was stunned how often I was forced to surf alone, how often I craved company, yet how fearful many surfers seemed of more surfers turning up to share their waves. There is no shortage of waves in this country, just an imbalance in the distribution of surfers.

While I experienced great generosity of spirit from most of the local surfers I encountered, I also sensed a certain meanness of spirit among many others. It's a fear of the 'outsider', a sense that what we have is going to be taken away from us by some threatening external force. The New South Wales North Coast surfers despise those bastards from the Goldy coming and surfing their waves. South Coast surfers resent those city pricks from Sydney doing the same. The far South Coast crew hate people from the less-far South Coast, or those interlopers from Lake's Entrance. The Phillip Island crew doesn't like the Peninsula crew or the Melbourne crew invading their turf. The Torquay crew resent the new arrivals from Melbourne or beyond taking up spots in the line-up and the well-paid surf industry jobs. The Victorian West Coast guys, the notorious Port Campbell Loose Cunts, really hate the Torquay crew. The South Australia West Coast crew hate just about everyone, especially if they have stickers on their boards. The far South Coast WA crew don't like the Margarets crew coming down and taking their waves, and the Margarets crew hate the Perth crew and all the inter-state blow-ins. And on and on. Perhaps if we all swapped places regularly, introduced a systematic, seasonal rotation about the country, we could see how pointless and petty it all is.

9. Our coastline is under greater threat than ever before.

From the suburbanisation of the coast by new housing develop-ments and coastal migration, to desalination plants, breakwalls, boat harbours and sewage outfalls, our great sea change is putting the coast under pressure like never before. Add in the largely unknown effects of climate change and rising sea levels and our coastline might be almost unrecognisable within our lifetime.

If you are looking for threats to free and open access to our beaches, it's hard to go past the hideous monument to wasteful, ill-conceived, environmental vandalism that is the desalination plant. These unsustainable eyesores are springing up all over the country, locking up prime sections of coast at vast expense, sending water bills skyrocketing while generating many more tonnes of greenhouse gases and exacerbating the climate changes that made them necessary in the first place. It would be difficult to purposely design a public work that is as damaging on so many levels.

In this way, the Australian coastline runs the risk of death by a thousand cuts. It and we all deserve better, but the price of that better is constant vigilance.

10. Australia is an incredibly beautiful place.

I have often been scolded for writing about my surfing experiences during the course of this trip and throughout what passes for a career in surf writing. I sometimes think it is not so much a career as the absence of a career, but I have come too far to turn back now. *Why don't you just shut up?*, I am challenged by a few angry internet posts. *Why not pay for your own car, caravan and internet and not say a word about your travels?* They are chastening comments.

I hope there is some point, some substance to this grand folly. Nothing I have read prepared me for the sheer, overwhelming beauty of the Australian coastline in all its grandeur, endless variety and sheer vastness. No one had captured for me the awe and reverence I've felt as I've encountered one magnificent stretch of coast after another. The most majestic of these locations have felt like alternate realities, my first encounters with them as powerful as a hallucinogenic trip. I have watched video of myself arriving at certain stops, and I see myself being transformed, grinning wildly, all pretenses stripped away, entirely overcome by my new and wondrous surroundings. I've attempted through my writing to pass on a miniscule, homeopathic trace of these experiences, to inoculate the reader with a desire to get out and explore, get to know, fully feel and become a true custodian of this astounding land.

We are, I believe, the luckiest people, living in the luckiest country in the luckiest period in human history.

ACKNOWLEDGEMENTS

WE HAVE MET SO many great people on our travels, it is difficult to name and acknowledge them all. Please forgive any omissions, but a heartfelt thanks to the following for their companionship and kindness: Claude and Lydia and their family at Croajingolong; all the crew at Lucy's Café in Mallacoota; Reg and Amanda, Arkie and Joey for the fun times in Tathra; Prof Andy Short, his wife, Julia, and daughter, Pip; Tom and Claire, and Tom and Mary in Sydney; Karl for solving the great driveway conundrum in Tugun; Ken and Jude for the extended hospitality; Mup for the beachfront digs on Phillip Island; Mum, Rick, Maree and the girls for the extended family pit stop in Melbourne; Ryan for showing us around South Bruny; Juz, Aleks and family and friends for the top-notch wedding in Tassie; Jeremy 'Wire' Curtain, Sally Marsden, the Boomerang by the Sea and everyone on King Island for a great weekend and the fabulous Long Table Luncheon; Keith, Fiona and Kitty, Jock Serong and Lilly and family, and all their friends in Port Fairy; Judy and Peter Watson for the warm welcome in Adelaide; Jeff and Josiah Schmucker in SA; Mark for the good-quality company and wine round the camp fire in the SA desert; Julie and Jayden for the companionship either side of the Nullarbor marathon; Paul

SURFARI

for guidance in southern WA; Perry Hatchett for the generous open house in Margaret River; Dad, Breff, James and Freckle for looking after us in Perth; Mark, Olivia and the kids at Monkey Mia; Chris, Jane and Sally, and all our fellow campers, at Gnaraloo for the great camaraderie, especially Paul and Maree, Will and Jack, Matty B, Lyall and Rhino for a great night of music, Gene and Sunny and Drew and Alison and families; students and staff of Vincentia Public School (Jervis Bay), Trinity College and Ashfield Primary School (Perth) and John Willcock College (Geraldton) for the warm welcome and attentive audiences; Tanya and everyone at the Booked Out agency for lining up schools gigs; David at the Currumbin post office for forwarding mail; Jim and Anna and the kids for looking after our house for us; Tim and Edwina and their family at Bullara for the great country hospitality; Rosco and Sarah in Yanchep; Ray de Jong and everyone at Cape Range National Park; Chris and Gill and the girls in Windjana, El Questro and Kakadu; Glen and Nat and the kids in Broome, Kununurra and Kakadu; Bonnie and her family in the Bungle Bungles for the rich, spontaneous cultural experience.

Back in the real world, I'm indebted as always to my agent, Jane Burridge, for her undying faith and support; my esteemed publisher, Alison Urquhart; my editor Brandon VanOver ('editor' doesn't even begin to cover it); everyone at Random House Australia; and cover designer Adam Yazxhi at MAXCO. You are my dream team.

Thanks to Kim Sundell, Doug Lees, Ben Ey and everyone at Coastalwatch; Vaughan Blakey, Matty G and everyone at *Surfing World* for always making my work look good. Your support and faith made this trip possible.

A huge thank you to Nic Lloyd, Lisa Sutherland and everyone at Toyota for the loan of the mighty Rav4. Thanks, too, to Claire Keppel, Andrew Ryan and everyone at Jayco for lending us the Expanda. I have not the slightest hesitation in

362

commending both these companies and their products. I have, quite literally, entrusted my family's lives with them, and they were never found wanting.

Thanks also to Telstra Gold Coast for mobile broadband, the best mobile internet coverage in the country; Tourism Tasmania for supporting our King Island jaunt; Coral Coast Tourism for helping us plan our WA leg; and the Sal Salis eco-resort for a memorable stay in paradise. Special thanks to Rob and Bel Bare, Bree Davies and everyone else at R&B for social media and online consultancy. Who says you can't teach an old dog new tricks?

Thanks to Firewire for the loan of the Dominator; Neal Purchase Jnr and Al Byrne for the quality custom equipment.

Greg and Guil at Climate Wave organised effective and credible carbon offsets for our travel and are expert and passionate at what they do. Thanks, guys.

And, of course, finally and most importantly, a huge loving, heartfelt thanks to Kirst, Vivi and Alex, for coming along for the ride, supporting my dream, enduring my moods, allowing me to work on the road and making it all so memorable. Apart from being my family, you are the best travel companions and greatest mates a man could wish for. Sorry to have aired our sometimes dirty laundry to the world. Please know how much I love you all and forgive my expositions of family life. Let's never forget the wonder and magic of our shared adventures.

ABOUT THE AUTHOR

Tim Baker is the bestselling author of *Occy, High Surf, Bustin'
Down the Door* and *Surf for Your Life*. He is a former editor of
Tracks and *Surfing Life* magazines and currently a contributing
editor to *Surfing World* and Coastalwatch.

You can find blogs, photos and clips from this trip at:
www.bytimbaker.com/blog